Artisans and Craftsmen of Northern India

Reconstructing Indian History & Culture
(ISSN 0971-3824)

1. Society in Ancient India; by Sures Chandra Banerji (ISBN 81-246-0000-7)
2. Political Thought in Ancient India; by G.P. Singh (ISBN 81-246-0001-5)
3. Early Indian Historical Tradition and Archaeology; by G.P. Singh (ISBN 81-246-0005-8)
4. Vasantotsava: The Spring Festivals of India; by Leona M. Anderson (ISBN 81-246-0011-2)
5. Ecological Readings in the Veda; by M. Vannucci (ISBN 81-246-0009-0)
6. Vṛndāvana in Vaiṣṇava Literature; by Maura Corcoran (ISBN 81-246-0024-4)
7. Social History of the Tamils (1707-1947); by P. Subramanian (ISBN 81-246-0045-7)
8. Ancient Indian Coinage; by Rekha Jain (ISBN 81-246-0051-1)
9. Buddhism and Socio-Economic Life of Eastern India; by Bimal Chandra Mohapatra (ISBN 81-246-0055-4)
10. Chandragupta Maurya; by P.L. Bhargava (ISBN 81-246-0056-2)
11. Mṛtyu: Concept of Death in Indian Traditions; by Gian Giuseppe Filippi (ISBN 81-246-0072-4)
12. Yama: The Glorious Lord of the Other World; by Kusum P. Merh (ISBN 81-246-0066-X)
13. Sacred Complex of Ujjain; by D.K. Samanta (ISBN 81-246-0078-3)
14. Vedic View of the Earth; by S.R.N. Murthy (ISBN 81-246-0091-0)
15. Society in the Atharvaveda; by B.S. Kharade (ISBN 81-246-0093-7)
16. Orissan History, Culture and Archaeology; by S. Pradhan (ISBN 81-246-0117-8)
17. Education in Ancient India; by Mitali Chatterjee (ISBN 81-246-0113-5)
18. Surā: The Liquor and the Vedic Sacrifice; by M.B. Kolhatkar (ISBN 81-246-0114-3)
19. Human Ecology in the Vedas; by Marta Vannucci (ISBN 81-246-0115-1)
20. Governance in Ancient India; by Anupa Chandra Pandey (ISBN 81-246-0135-6)
21. The Cultural Glory of Ancient India: A Literary Overview; by Sures Chandra Banerji (ISBN 81-246-0137-2)
22. Kauṭilya's Arthaśāstra in the light of Modern Science & Technology; by Sunil Sen Śarma (ISBN 81-246-0187-9)
23. History of Jainism — With Special Reference to Mathurā; by V.K. Sharma (ISBN 81-246-0195-X)
24. Cultural Tourism in India: Museums, Monuments & Arts — Theory and Practice; by S.P. Gupta; Krishna Lal; Mahua Bhattacharya (ISBN 81-246-0215-8)
25. Ancient Indian Historiography — Sources and Interpretations; by G.P. Singh (81-246-0228-X)
26. Republics, Kingdoms, Towns and Cities in Ancient India; by G.P. Singh (ISBN 81-246-0237-9)
27. Facets of Ancient Indian History and Culture — New Perception; by G.P. Singh (81-246-0238-7)
28. Kamakhya — A Socio-cultural Study; by Nihar Ranjan Mishra (ISBN 81-246-0251-4)
29. History and Culture of Tamil Nadu as Gleaned from the Sanskrit Inscriptions Vol. 1 (up to c. AD 1310); by Chithra Madhavan (ISBN 81-246-0308-1).
30. Life Style of the Vedic People; by Pranati Ghosal (ISBN 81-246-0344-8)
31. History and Culture of Tamil Nadu as Gleaned from the Sanskrit Inscriptions Vol. 2 (up to c. AD 1310 - *c.* 1885 AD); by Chithra Madhavan (ISBN 81-246-0380-4).
32. Matrimonial Alliances and Ancient Indian Polity (*c.* 600 BCE to *c.* 650); by Preeti Prabhat (ISBN: 81-246-0399-5).
33. Artisans and Craftsmen of Northern India by Kuldeep Singh Thind (ISBN: 81-246-0523-8).

Reconstructing Indian History & Culture, no. 33

Artisans and Craftsmen of Northern India

Kuldeep Singh Thind

D.K. Printworld (P) Ltd.
New Delhi

Cataloging in Publication Data — DK

Courtsey: D.K. Agencies (P) Ltd. <docinfo@dkagencies.com>

Thind, Kuldeep Singh, 1964-

Artisans and craftsmen of northern India / Kuldeep Singh Thind.

p. cm. — (Reconstructing Indian history & culture; no. 33)

Originally presented as the author's thesis (Ph. D.) — Kurukshetra University.

Includes bibliographical references (p.).

ISBN 13: 9788124605233

ISBN 10: 8124605238

1. Handicraft industries — India — History. 2. Artisans — India — Economic conditions. 3. Artisans — India — Social conditions. 4. India — Economic conditions — To 1000. 5. India — Antiquities. I. Title. II. Series: Reconstructing Indian history & culture; no. 33.

DDC 338.4774550954 22

ISBN 13: 978-81-246-0523-3
ISBN 10: 81-246-0523-8
First published in India in 2009

Published and printed by:
D.K. Printworld (P) Ltd.
Regd. Office: 'Srikunj', F-52, Bali Nagar
Ramesh Nagar Metro Station
New Delhi-110 015
Phones: (011) 2545 3975; 2546 6019; *Fax*: (011) 2546 5926
E-mail: dkprintworld@vsnl.net
Website: www.dkprintworld.com

Dedicated to

all the artisans

whose silent but important and indelible contribution
to the human civilization
has enabled us to enter
the arena of Space Age

Preface

ARTISANS and craftsmen of northern India played a pivotal role in the socio-economic life of the period between *circa* seventh century to twelfth century CE. Various categories of artisans and craftsmen, located in both rural and urban regions, not only fulfilled the needs of people in daily life, but also achieved mastery in their arts and crafts, and merited fame far and wide. Of course, simultaneously, they also earned their livelihood and satisfied their natural urge for novelty and creation.

Being always active partners in the socio-economic and cultural life of the aforementioned period, and forming an integral component and sizeable section of the society, the class of artisans and craftsmen deserves an exhaustive and critical evaluation in its proper perspective. This is what the present study aims at, also, for another reason that the artisans and craftsmen of the early medieval period have so far received scanty research attention. An endeavour has, therefore, been made here to analyse the professional life of the artisans and craftsmen against the background of the entire milieu of the early medieval period.

The present book, based on the literary, epigraphical and archaeological sources, is divided into two parts. Part One deals with the different categories of artisans and craftsmen individually, and Part Two is devoted to assessing their socio-economic conditions collectively. Chapter 1 presents a brief introduction to the subject. Chapter 2 gives a detailed account of the stone workers, including in its purview the architects, the sculptors and the engravers. Chapter 3 gives information about the goldsmiths and the metal workers of the period under study. Chapter 4 is devoted exclusively to the important class of weavers. Chapter 5 is a miscellaneous account of some other classes of the artisans and craftsmen, viz. the potters, workers in leather and ivory, and makers of mirrors, musical instruments and umbrellas. It also deals with perfume and cosmetics-makers, oil-makers, salt-makers, and some other kinds of artisans and craftsmen of lower category, such as barbers, basket-makers, shield-makers, rope-makers, conch-shell workers, and makers of fans, mats, brooms, etc.

In Part Two of the present book, chapter 6 is devoted to discussing the training of artisans and craftsmen. It deals with the conditions of the training afforded by parents, guilds, individual masters and educational institutions. Chapter 7 gives an account of the guilds of different categories with respect to their nature, organization and functions. The social status and the economic conditions of various categories of artisans and craftsmen are analysed in chapters 8 and 9.

It is my pleasant duty to express profound sense of gratitude to my revered teacher and supervisor, Dr Brajesh Krishna, Professor (retd.) of Department of Ancient Indian History, Culture and Archaeology, Kurukshetra University, for his meticulous guidance, without which it would hardly have been possible for me to complete the research work. My sincere thanks are due to the different libraries, museums and officials working therein for making available the requisite material.

I am grateful to the American Institute of Indian Studies, Gurgaon, for providing me some photographs for inclusion in this book. The visuals, included here, describe the self-skilled workmanship of the artisan class of that time and provide the glimpses and legacy of the rich cultural heritage of pride India.

I am indebted to Dr S.S. Phulia, Principal, Government PG College, Ambala Cantonment, for motivation, and credit goes to him for providing a very congenial and academic atmosphere in the College Campus.

I must particularly express gratitude to my revered parents, family members, dear brother Sh Fauja Singh Thind, and my relatives, who always remain my source of affection and inspiration to whom my debt is unending. My heartfelt thanks are also due to my wife Kavita Swaraj Kaur and my children Malhar and Sarvar, whose devotion helped my full time engrossment in this project. My thanks are also due to my father-in-law Sardar Didar Singh Nalvi, member SGPC, Kurukshetra, who encouraged me to pen down my research-work in the form of a book.

July 7, 2009
Guru Purnima, VS 2066

Kuldeep Singh Thind
<kulsingh66@rediffmail.com>

Contents

PART TWO

Abbreviations

ABORI	: *Annals of the Bhandarkar Oriental Research Institute,* Poona
AbCin	: *Abhidhānacintāmaṇi*
AbRatna	: *Abhidhānaratnamālā*
Ādi	: *Adi-Purāṇa*
AI	: *Ancient India*
Amara	: *Amarakośa*
Āmk	: *Ākhyānakamaṇikośa*
Ārya	: *Āryasaptaśati*
ASI, *AR*	: Archaeological Survey of India, *Annual Report*
ASK	: *Avantisundarīkathā*
ASKS	: *Avantisundarīkathāsāra*
ASR	: Archaeological Survey Reports
ASS	: Ānandāśrama Sanskrit Series, Poona
AV	: *Atharavaveda*
BI	: *Bibliotheca Indica,* Edition, Calcutta
Bj	: *Bṛhajātaka*
BS	: *Bṛhatsaṁhitā*
BY	: *Bṛhadyātrā*
CII	: *Corpus Inscriptionum Indicarum*
CMI	: *Coins of Medieval India*
DKC	: *Daśakumāracarita*
EI	: *Epigraphia Indica*
Hcar	: *Harṣacarita*

HDS	:	*History of Dharmaśāstra*, by P.V. Kane
HIED	:	*History of India as Told by its own Historians* by Elliot and Dowson
Gṛhastha	:	*Gṛhastharatnākara*
IA	:	*Indian Antiquary*
IB	:	*Inscriptions of Bengal*
IHQ	:	*Indian Historical Quarterly*
JASB	:	*Journal of the Asiatic Society of Bengal*
JABBRAS	:	*Journal of the Bombay Branch of the Royal Asiatic Society*
JBORS	:	*Journal of the Bihar and Orissa Research Society*
JIH	:	*Journal of Indian History*
JISOA	:	*Journal of the Indian Society of Oriental Art*
JOI	:	*Journal of the Oriental Institute* Baroda
JORM	:	*Journal of Oriental Research*, Madras
JPASB	:	*Journal and Proceedings of the Asiatic Society of Bengal*
JRAS	:	*Journal of the Royal Asiatic Society of Great Britain and Ireland*
JRASB	:	*Journal of the Royal Asiatic Society of Bengal*
JUPHS	:	*Journal of the United Provinces Historical Society*
Kād	:	*Kādambrī*
Karpūr	:	*Karpūramañjarī*
Kāv	:	*Kāvyāmīmāṁsā*
Kp	:	*Kṛṣiparāśara*
Kss	:	*Kathāsaritsāgara*
Kum	:	*Kumārasaṁbhava*
Ky	:	*Kāvyādarśa*
Manu	:	*Manusmṛti*
MaitSaṁ.	:	*Maitrāyaṇī Saṁhitā*
MASI	:	*Memoirs of Archaeological Survey of India*
Maya	:	*Mayamata*
Mbh	:	*Mahābhārata*

Megh	:	*Meghadūta*
MP	:	*Matsya Purāṇa*
NPP	:	*Nāgarī Pracāriṇī Patrikā*
Naiṣadha	:	*Naiṣadhīyacarita*
PASB	:	Proceedings of the Asiatic Society of Bengal (Calcutta)
Pb.chin	:	*Prabandhacintāmaṇi*
PIHC	:	*Proceedings of the Indian History Congress*
Prm	:	*Paryāyaratnamālā*
Ragh	:	*Raghuvaṁśa*
Ṛtu	:	*Ṛtusaṁhāra*
RT	:	*Rājataraṅgiṇī*
ṚV	:	*Ṛgveda*
Sad	:	*Saduktikarṇāmṛta*
Śāk	:	*Abhijñānaśākuntalam*
SBE	:	Sacred Books of the East
SI	:	*Select Inscriptions*, by D.C. Sircar
SII	:	*South Indian Inscriptions*
Śukra	:	*Śukranītisāra*
Suśruta	:	*Suśruta Saṁhitā*
VājSaṁ	:	*Vājasneyī Saṁhitā*
Viddh	:	*Viddhaśālabhañjikā*
VDP	:	*Viṣṇudharmottara Purāṇa*
VP	:	*Vāman Purāṇa*
Yājñ	:	*Yājñavalkyasmṛti*
YV	:	*Yajurveda*
YY	:	*Yogayātrā*

Transliteration Chart

VOWELS

अ *a*	आ *ā*	इ *i*	ई *ī*	उ *u*	ऊ *ū*	ऋ *ṛ*	ॠ *ṝ*[1]
(Roman)	(palm)	(it)	(police)	(put)	(rule)	(rig)	
ऌ *ḷ*	ॡ *ḹ*[1]	ए *e*	ऐ *ai*	ओ *o*	औ *au*		
(able)		(there)	(aisle)	(no)	(loud)		

CONSONANTS

Guttural	क *ka* (skate)	ख *kha*[2] (blockhead)	ग *ga* (gate)	घ *gha*[2] (ghost)	ङ *ṅa* (sing)
Palatal	च *ca* (chunk)	छ *cha*[2] (catch him)	ज *ja* (john)	झ *jha*[2] (hedgehog)	ञ *ña* (bunch)
Cerebral	ट *ṭa* (start)	ठ *ṭha*[2] (anthill)	ड *ḍa* (dart)	ढ *ḍha*[2] (godhead)	ण *ṇa* (under)
Dental	त *ta* (path)	थ *tha*[2] (thunder)	द *da* (that)	ध *dha*[2] (this)	न *na* (numb)
Labial	प *pa* (spin)	फ *pha*[2] (philosophy)	ब *ba* (bin)	भ *bha*[2] (abhor)	म *ma* (much)
Semi-vowels	य *ya* (young)	र *ra* (drama)	ल *la*[3] (luck)	व *va*[4] (vile)	
Sibilants	श *śa*[5] (shove)	ष *ṣa*[5] (bushel)	स *sa* (so)	ह *ha* (hum)	
Others	क्ष *kṣa* (*kṣatriya*)	त्र *tra* (*triśūla*)	ज्ञ *jña* (*jñānī*)		

अं (ं) *ṁ anusvāra* is a nasal off-glide that immediately follows the pronunciation of a vowel as in *saṁskṛti.*

अः *visarga* = *ḥ* consists in abrupt release of breath after a vowel as in *prātaḥ.*

ऽ *Avagraha* shows non-pronunciation, that is, deletion of "a" after "e" or "o" as in *ime 'vasthitāḥ*. In Vedic Sanskrit, it can also show word division.

HINDI LETTERS (extras)

ँ= m̐	ं= ṅ	ड़ = *ṛa* ढ़ = *ṛha*
(*candrabindu*)	(*anusvāra*)	

1 Longer form of the preceding vowel.

2 Aspirated forms of the preceding consonants. The compound words given as examples should be pronounced without a syllabic break at the underlined places. "tha" and "pha" should not be pronounced as fricatives.

3 retroflexed and written as "L *la*" in certain phonetic contexts.

4 Pronounced like "w," without aspiration.

5 "śa" is palatal; "ṣa" cerebral or retroflex.

List of Illustrations

Part One

1

Introduction

WITH the beginning of agriculture and settled life, the human society required new types of tools and implements. This need gave impetus to the emergence of different specialized occupations which resulted in the formation of the social groups of artisans and craftsmen, and they played an important role in the economic growth of human society.

Archaeological excavations reveal the existence of various categories of artisans and craftsmen during the Indus Valley Civilization, such as potters, copper and bronze workers, stone workers, masons, brick-makers, seal-cutters, bead-makers, weavers, carpenters and workers of steatite, faience, bone, shell, ivory, etc. Crafts like spinning and weaving became widespread in this period. Copper and bronze were the main metals used to make tools, vessels, weapons and other articles. Techniques of smelting, casting and forging were used in this period. Likewise many implements and ornaments were fashioned from stone and other materials. Artisans and craftsmen were evidently engaged in productive activity in both the rural and the urban centres in the proto-historic period.

Artisans and Craftsmen are clearly referred to in the *Ṛgveda*. *Takṣaṇa* (a carpenter) did all kinds of work in wood, including making of chariots (*ratha*s), wagons (*anasa*s) and boats (*nāva*s). *Karmāra* (a smith) smelted ore in the furnace using birds' feathers as bellows. Another outstanding artisan of the Ṛgvedic period was *hiraṇyakāra* (a goldsmith), who made ornaments of various kinds. Among other crafts of the early Vedic period may be mentioned those of *carmaṇa* (the tanner) and *vaptri* (the barber). Women's occupations were sewing, plaiting of mats from grass and reeds, and weaving of cloth. What is particularly noteworthy in this connection is that in the period of the *Ṛgveda* those who practised these crafts were not in any way regarded as inferior members of their community.

The later Vedic period witnessed many new occupations. *Vājasaneyī Saṁhitā* provides a comprehensive list of artisans and craftsmen, including *rathakāra* (chariot maker), *kaulāla* (potter), *maṇikāra* (jeweller), *iṣukāra* (arrow-maker), *dhanuṣakāra* (bowmaker), *kaṇṭakakārī* (female worker in thorns), *vidalakārī* (female basket-maker), *peśakārī* (female embroiderer), *rajayitrī* (female dyer), and *surākāra* (maker of wine).

The material perspective changed considerably during the post-Vedic times, and this had its impact on the development of artisans and craftsmen, their rating in various religious texts and their actual position. The period saw growth of cities, development of trade and commerce, and commodity production by professional artisans and craftsmen on an unprecedented scale. Most of the urban artisans were organized into guilds, which took care of their interests. They were economically much better off than their counterparts scattered in villages and catering locally to the needs of a predominantly agrarian economy.

A distinguishing feature of the Mauryan period was the state control of economy. *Arthaśāstra* furnishes ample evidence of increased division of labour and specialization in crafts and other productive occupations, and prescribes specific areas within the fort walls for residential accommodation of different categories of workers. A number of important towns flourished in this period and became centres of craftsmanship and trade. Crafts flourished extensively in this period, particularly weaving, metal work and jewellery-making The most prized fabrics were the cottons woven in Vārāṇasī, Mathurā and Ujjayinī. Gandhāra was famous for its woollen materials. Artisans and craftsmen had their guilds with their own charters. The state exercised control over the activities of the guilds by way of enforcing their registration with the government and forbidding their transfer from one region of the country to another without official notification.

The contemporary scriptural and epigraphical evidences give a fair idea of the social stature of artisans and craftsmen and of their development in the Kuṣāṇa and Gupta periods. The Jātakas refer to professions of garland-weavers, goldsmiths, jewellers, carpenters, potters, tailors, weavers, blacksmiths, barbers, etc. The list supplied by the Jātakas includes both the productive and non-productive occupations and crafts. The Buddhist text *Milandapañho* mentions nearly 75 occupations, most of which were concerned with various crafts. A more or less similar view of crafts appears in *Lalitavistara*, another contemporary Buddhist work. The *Mahāvastu, Divyāvadāna* and *Avadāna Śataka*, believed to have been compiled in the first four centuries of the Christian era, throw further light on the subject. Whereas Jātakas mention only eighteen kinds of professional guilds, *Mahāvastu* refers to double the number. The *Kāmasūtra* of Vātsyāyana and *Mṛcchakaṭikam* of Śūdraka, assignable to the Gupta period, also give details of the contemporary crafts. *Kāmasūtra* refers to 64 arts in which a *nāgaraka* was to make himself adept. Although Vātsyayāna recommends proficiency in these arts in general for a *nāgaraka*, it is evident from the findings of the period that people frequently adopted them as their means of livelihood. *Mṛcchakaṭikam* gives an idea of the artisans and craftsmen who inhabited the city of Ujjayinī and produced luxury goods.

The period between *circa* seventh to twelfth century CE in north India has its own importance for its political and socio-economic development, which was marked by feudal tendencies. After the fall of the Gupta Empire political unity was shattered, which resulted in the emergence of new royal dynasties, and a conscious regional outlook throughout India. The tripartite struggle for supremacy among the Rāṣṭrakūṭas, the Pālas and the Pratihāras certainly resulted in political fragmentation, which vastly affected the socio-economic life of the north-Indian people. The material milieu of the period had a comprehensive effect on its social structure. The new economic features, such as decline of trade and commerce in urban life, the growing agrarian character of society, and the emergence of a closed local economy significantly influenced the society of the period in the direction of segregation and social exclusiveness.

The unique importance of the period under study consists in the fact that it links the ancient and the medieval India. This period represents first the culmination and then the degeneration of the classical tradition of the ancient Indian culture. The artisans and craftsmen of the period played a very important role in the socio-economic and cultural life of north India. It is fascinating to study the position of the artisans and craftsmen of northern India under the above-mentioned political, social and economic conditions. The vast literature and the numerous epigraphs of the period throw light on this aspect, which has, however, yet not been fully explored.

The literary, epigraphical and archaeological sources of the period under review contain a whole mine of information about the conditions of the artisans and craftsmen. There are available a number of references to artisans and craftsmen — stone, wood, metal, and glass workers, weavers, workers in ivory, craftsmen connected with clay, toy- and brick-makers, leather workers, makers of perfumes and cosmetics, and numerous others.

In early medieval India diverse were the forms and multiple the objects that were produced by artisans and craftsmen for the use of the people in cities and villages and primitive people living in the tribal society. The root of the creative process was, as it has always been, the artisan tradition. Surcharged with ideological concepts — rich in symbol and myth, elegant and sophisticated — the classical stream was responsible for the creation not only of great sculpture and architecture, but also of objects of daily use in the early medieval period. The knowledge and skill in crafts was communicated from father to son, and from master to disciple.

No distinction was made between fine arts and crafts in the period under review. It is also not easy to distinguish between "artisans" and "craftsmen" — both being basically "skilled workmen."[1] As noticed by R.N. Misra, in the ancient period different categories of artisans were clubbed together in one general group called *śilpin*. Likewise, the term *śilpa*[2] was of a wide connotation, and it included within its ambit various crafts, skills and occupations.

It will not be out of context to mention that in the time of Pāṇini, the great grammarian of fifth century BCE, the term *śilpin* was in vogue, and denoted "artisans in general."[3] Pāṇini refers to village artisans as *grāmaśilpin*,[4] and those who had mastered their craft as *rājaśilpin*.[5] Patañjali follows the line of Pāṇini. Both of them use the term *śilpa* commonly for fine arts and crafts. They treat the *śilpa* of dancing and that of the barber and the potter on the same footing.[6] Pāṇini[7] provides us with a long list of industries and crafts connected with wood, dyes, garments both woollen and cotton, gems, and metals like gold, silver, iron and tin.[8]

Yājñavalkya speaks of *śilpa* as one of the ten sources of livelihood, which may be resorted to during the period of distress.[9] Apparently in the period under

1. *Oxford Advanced Learners Dictionary of Current English*, 3rd edn.
2. The term is found in the Saṁhitās and the Brāhmaṇas. For details, see M. Monier-Williams, *A Sanskrit–English Dictionary*, pp. 1073-74.
3. For detailed discussion of the terms *śilpin* and *śilpī*, see R.N. Misra, *Ancient Artists and Art Activity*, pp. 1ff.
4. Pāṇini, VI, 2, 62.
5. Ibid., VI, 2, 63.
6. Ibid., III, 2, 55; III, 1, 145; Patañjali, IV, 4, 55.
7. Ibid., VI, 2, 62; Patañjali, IV, 4, 55.
8. V.S. Agarawal, *India as Known to Pāṇini*, pp. 229-35.
9. *Yājñavalkya Smṛti*, III. 42.

review the term *śilpa* had a wide connotation. *Śilpa* was the main source of earning (*jīvikā*) artisans and craftsmen.[10] Thus the term *śilpin* of the ancient Indian literature refers to artisans, craftsmen, artists and artificers, etc. alike.[11] Similarly, the terms *kāru* and *karmāra* were used in literature alike for artisans and craftsmen.[12] *Arthaśāstra* uses the term *kāru* to designate different classes of artisans.[13] In the present book the terms "artisan" and "craftsman" have been used to represent all the groups of skilled workmen.

According to the Indian canons, the highest expression of form in art takes place through sculpture. In ancient India, *citra* was the term for sculpture, while carving in relief was styled as *ardhacitra*; *citrābhāsa* (painting) was taken to bear resemblance to sculpture, the third dimension or depth being expressed in it by the technique of light and shade (*vartana*). Perfection of form was associated with observance of certain rules of measurement of length and breadth. These rules of measurement were applicable not only to architecture and sculpture but also to functional objects like textiles, gold ornaments, weapons, etc. What made an art object were *rūpa* (shape), *pramāṇa* (proportion) and *varṇa* (colour), and what brought the object to life was its filling, its permeation with *rasa*. The craftsman who deeply understood this knowledge and practised it was the *rasika* or *rasadhārī*, the holder of the essence, and by virtue of that, one who was fully capable of vision and technique. The artisans and craftsmen of the early medieval period seem to have achieved this kind of mastery in arts and crafts.

The basic aim of the work is to expose the major contributions of artisans and craftsmen in portraying the society in different perspectives. These artisans and craftsmen were drawn mostly from the śudras — the lower caste, suppressed and have-not section of the society, but were highly talented. The work is also designed to create interest among the readers and scholars alike, to understand the society of the period under reference through the immortal art of these creative people. The artisans such as potters, weavers, carpenters, architects, sculptors, brick-makers, metallurgy and metal workers, leather workers, painters, and the workers engaged in the profession of ivory, glass and mirror, perfume and

10. M. Monier-Williams, op. cit., p. 1073.
11. Ibid., p. 1074.
12. R.N. Misra, op. cit., p. 2.
13. Ibid., p. 9.

cosmetics, musical instruments, oil, salt and liquor makers, etc. are the heroes of the book, who not only met the day-to-day requirement of the then society, but also portrayed different aspects of their life, in its true color, through their workmanship. It was the architect who designed and constructed houses to live in, as well as water tank, well and channel, royal building, *stūpa*, temple and fort, bridge, pillar and rock-edict etc. which met the need of the society. Carpenter being always the most sought-after person of the society made wheel, cart and chariot, plough, spade, sickle, and agricultural implements, cot and bed, mortar and pestle, household and royal furniture, boat and ship, wooden house and temple, musical instruments, oil-presser and sugar-presser and numerous other articles, which were used in daily life. Similarly, it was the metal worker who was much advanced in metallurgy and engineering, made chisel and hammer, plough-share and harrow, rahat and various other agricultural tools, utensil, sculpture, weapon and armoury, coin, copper-plate and seal, saw, umbrella, jewellery and ornament etc. for daily use by the people.

It appears that the roots of the present socio-economic stratification can be seen in the facets of early medieval period of history. The traditional specialization of work-based craftsmanship, which has continued unabated from generation to generation, has culminated in the present day system of castes, i.e. *kuṁbhakāra/kumahāra* (potter), butcher (meat-seller), *carmakāra/camāra* (tanner), *dhivara* (fisherman), *ḍom/ḍūma* (who plays musical instruments to live), *lohakāra/lohāra* (black-smith), *mocī* (shoe-maker), *nāpita/nāī* (barber), *suvarṇakāra/sunāra* (goldsmith), *tailika/telī* (oil-miller), *takṣaṇa/tarkhān* (carpenter), *vanzārā/banzārā* (trader), etc. which have now been put under "the category of reserved class" by the state governments, central government and are recognized by the Constitution of India in the form of Backward or Scheduled Castes of Indian society. The history reveals that the economic structure of the society is always lean against the productive activity of the artisans and craftsmen in changing the world milieu.

Apparently, this talented workmanship class fulfilled the basic and major needs of the society throughout the human civilization, but socially, economically and politically they are neglected and suppressed by the 'system' as per the social justice stratification in Indian history. In the present book an endeavour has been made to analyse and assess their activity and major contribution during the period under review.

2

Stone Workers

In the sources of the period under review we find mention of different kinds of stone workers needed for erection of monuments, buildings, temples and forts, etc. The stone workers worked together with a sense of co-operation and co-ordination because in the absence of their co-ordination it was not possible to complete the work. These stone workers worked in groups of different categories and formed their guilds. Probably these categories were controlled by the main architects of the project. The different categories of the stone workers are discussed here under the following heads:

I Architects

II Sculptors

III Engravers

Architects

An architect is a person who creates buildings of various kinds as required by the time, occasion, and demand. In the early medieval India, there was needed co-ordination between the work of the architect and the sculptor, and sometimes they worked together in the building activity. Architects were generally put in the larger class of *śilpīs*, though they formed a distinct professional group in the society.

Architecture is an index of the state of development of a society. The economic climate and the social needs generate the architecture and the towns of an age. Thus, so much depends on the expertise and creativity of the architect. Excavations from the Haṛappan sites vividly indicate the specialization of the architects of the time in constructing buildings. The architects of the time were the real builders and planners of towns. There was standardization of the size of the bricks — both burnt and sun-dried — used by them.[1] However, a stunning blow was received by the Haṛappan architecture because of the decline of the culture of the period. Economic stagnation was another factor responsible for the decline[2] of the Haṛappan cities and the extinction of all urbanism. We hardly come across any city or elaborate architectural work in the Vedic period. The Vedic Aryans were probably the destroyers, and not the builders, of the cities.[3] However, the Vedic architects constructed dwellings for tha Aryans, though these cannot be regarded as towns in the Haṛappan sense.[4] Technical words like *sthapati* and *sūtradhāra* for the architect occur in the *Rāmāyaṇa.* We also find a mention of storeyed buildings, such as *anekabhauma,*[5] and *saptabhauma.*[6]

The emergence of second urbanization in northern India in the sixth century established a new pattern of towns and cities. Simultaneously, the number of arts and crafts increased, and the hereditary transmission of architectural skill again started playing a significant role in the building activity. The capital cities of the *mahājanapada*s became the main centres of royal authority, arts and crafts, trade and industry, education and religion. The artisans and craftsmen formed guilds for safe- guarding their social and economic interests. Some of the architects were patronized by the rulers, and this lent them a respectable social status in the society.

The Mauryan period witnessed economic development and urban growth. Architects, stone-cutters and sculptors attained advanced knowledge in their crafts, and worked for the kings jointly. During this period burnt bricks were

1. Bridget Allchin and Raymond Allchin, *The Rise of Civilization in India and Pakistan,* p. 175.
2. R.S. Sharma, *Light on Early Indian Society and Economy,* p. 54; Fairservis, *The Roots of Ancient India,* p. 304.
3. God Indra is credited with destroying many existing cities. He is said to have wiped out Varaśikhās at Hariyūpīya (Haṛappā) and Narmin. In one of the Ṛgvedic hymns Indra is requested thus, "Strike down, O Maghavan (Indra), the host of sorceresses in the ruined city of Vailāsthānaka, in the ruined city of Mahāvailastha"; Bridget Allchin and Raymond Allchin, p. 155; Kameshwar Prasad, *Cities, Crafts and Commerce under the Kuṣāṇas,* p. 2.
4. R.S. Sharma, op. cit., p. 55.
5. *Rāmāyaṇa,* IV, 33.
6. Ibid., IV, 2, 49.

used in north India and both bricks and timber were used in making houses. Megasthenes speaks of wooden structures in the Maurya capital Pāṭaliputra. The archaeological excavations at Bulandī-bāgh and Kumrahār bear out the high skill of the architects of the period. The Lauriya-Nandangarh (Bihar) pillar and best-known pillar capital found at Sarnath (Uttar Pradesh) are the appropriate examples of skillness of the artisans,[7] around two thousand years back. The high technical craftsmanship of the stone-cutters is proved by the caves and pillars of the Aśokan times and later times.[8]

Archaeological excavations and literary sources of the Kuṣāṇa period have brought to light remarkable architectural structures.[9] It appears that architectural activities like house-making, pillar-making, fortification-building, etc. constituted an important form of artisanal occupation. The use of bricks, timber, lime, and tiles by the architects, and provision for hall, kitchen, bathroom, sewerage, well, etc. suggests a high standard of living and a sophisticated taste of the citizens in the matter of construction of houses. The Kuṣāṇas introduced a certain type of shaft, which must have involved a number of masons in its installation.[10]

During the Gupta period the architects, masons and stone-cutters built exquisite, pillars, columns, flights of steps, irrigation works and statues. Some architects seem to have been very highly paid. The Chinese pilgrim Fa-hsien was very much charmed with the architectural beauty of the Buddhist monasteries.[11] Kālidāsa also frequently refers to the art of building and sculpture.[12] The general prosperity of the land and the growing devotional piety of the kings and commoners alike led to erection of numerous temples. Throughout the northern India architects erected these temples under the control of the kings. These temples were not built just by one architect. Every temple had its own master-builder.

ARCHITECT IN THE EARLY MEDIEVAL PERIOD

The literary works of the period under review mention various terms for the

7. Frederich M. Asher, *Art of India*, pp. 29-31.
8. Cunningham, *The Stūpa of Bharhut*, Pl. XXXVIII.
9. Kameshwar Prasad, op. cit., Chap. III, cf, Fredrich M. Asher, *Art of India*, pp. 36-45.
10. N.P. Joshi, *Life in Uttarāpatha*, Chap. II.
11. J.A. Legge, *Record of Buddhist Kingdoms (Being an Account of the Chinese Monk Fa-hsien's Travels)*, pp. 55-57, 77.
12. S.K. Maity, *Economic Life in Northern India*, p. 46.

architect and his profession. A number of different terms, such as *śilpī, śilpin, sthapati, sthāpaka, sūtradhāra, sūtragrāhin, sūtrakāra, vardhakī* and *sūtrabhṛt* have been used for the architect; *śilpī* and *śilpin* are the terms generally used for the maker of buildings in lexicons and inscriptions. The canons sometimes refer to the *sthāpaka,*[13] the actual worker and principal assistant to the *sthapati*. The hierarchical system helped to elevate the roles of actual workers, and that is how in the *Śilpaśāstra* the *sthapati* has a prominent position.

Mānasāra[14] speaks of the origin of the "divine architects." It says that Viśvakarmā, Maya, Tvaṣṭṛ and Manu were born from the four faces of Brahmā. The text further tells us that the sons of these architects were respectively called *sthapati, sūtragrāhin, vardhakī* and *takṣaka.*[15] As regards the areas of their activity, proficiency in painting was regarded essential for *vardhakī,* in draughtsmanship for *sūtragrāhin,* and in carpentry for *sūtradhāra.*[16] The same text accords to *sthapati* the rank of the director-general and consulting architect and to *sūtragrāhin,* the status of the supervisor over the *vardhakī* and the *takṣaka.*

Samarāṅgaṇasūtradhāra of King Bhoja is an important work on *vāstu-vidyā,* which deals with the principles of Indian architecture, and lays down instructions for architects. It is curious to note here that in the first 48 of its 83 chapters, it treats three principal subjects. In the first seven chapters together with the 44th and then 45th, introductory subjects like the need, origin, schools, scope and subject matter of architecture and the qualifications of an architect are dealt with. Next follow, the regional planning, surveying of the land, examination of the soil conditions (*bhūparīkṣā* 8) and the system of measurements (*hasta-lakṣaṇa* 9), and detailed canons of town-planning (*puraniveśa* 10) together with site-plans (Chapters 11 to 14 and 38), different categories of the *vāstū-pada*s fit to be employed in towns, temples, residential houses and palaces of kings. Finally, in the subsequent 30 chapters it deals with house-architecture.[17] Obviously, the skill of architects and craftsmen had by this time reached its fullest development. In

13. P.K. Acharya, *An Encyclopaedia of Hindu Architecture,* VII, s.v. *Sthāpaka.*
14. II, 11-12, 17-20.
15. P.K. Acharya, op. cit., VII. s.v. *sthapati.*
16. Ibid.
17. D.N. Shukla, *Vāstu-Śāstra,* I, pp. 28-29.

building large temples (*prāsāda*s), where hundreds of craftsmen and labourers had to work in complete harmony, however, the traditional fourfold division of the architectural artists in *sthapati, sūtragrāhin, vardhakī* and *takṣaka*, lost its importance. But we cannot ignore the distinction of the highly-skilled architects of huge temples. *Samarāṅgaṇasūtradhāra* acquaints us with two broad classifications of these servants of God and humanity at large (i) the *sthapati*, (the master-architect), and (ii) the *sthāpaka* (the architect-priest), the *guru* (the *ācārya* or teacher). This latter personality had importance only in the planning and setting up of religious structures, that in the *prāsāda*s, the temples; otherwise the *sthapati* was the sole authority in any building activity, civil or royal.[18]

The *sthapati*'s pre-eminent position amongst the artisans has also been stressed in *Śilpaśāstra*.[19] *Matsya Purāṇa* describes a *sthapati* as one who is conversant with the architectural design of a building and foresees (everything), and is a skilful and industrious champion in architectural matters.[20] The *sthapati* is defined by Medhātithi[21] as a *vāstu-vidyājīvin* (one who lives by the science of architecture), such as an architect-mason and so forth. As regards the *sthapati*'s important status,[22] it (the text) records an earlier tradition which may have become non-existent when it was actually committed to writing.[23]

It is worth noting that inscriptions rarely mention the term *sthapati*. The pre-eminent status of the *sthapati*s notwithstanding, the inscriptions relating to raising of edifices usually refer to *sūtradhāra*s, *śilpī*s and *rūpakāra*s, and seem to ignore *sthapati*s in that context. However, there is a mention of the *sthapati-samrāṭ* and royal officials like *bhogika* and *uparika* in the Karitaḷai copper plate of the Uchthakalpa king Jayanāha.[24]

---

18. Ibid., p. 44.
19. P.K. Acharya, *Indian Architecture*, pp. 137-38. *Mayamatam*, IV, 13-14; *Vāstu-Vidyā*, ed. Ganpati Sastri, I, 12-15.
20. P.K. Acharya, op. cit., s.v. *sthapati*, p. 580.
21. *Medhātithi*, III, 153, p. 278.
22. *Samarāṅganasūtradhāra*, Ch. 44.
23. M.K. Dhavalikar, "Sūtradhāra," *Annals of Bhandarkar Oriental Research Institute*, III, i-iv, 1972, p. 218.
24. *CII*, III, p. 118.

The *sūtradhāras* had their requisite qualifications and the theory of their craft prescribed for them. It is laid down in *Mānasāra* that the *sūtradhāra* must be well-versed in the Vedas and the Śāstras. In addition to this, he should also possess an expert knowledge of carpentry. In *Śilpa-dīpikā* the following qualifications are prescribed for a *sūtradhāra*:

> One who is of good behaviour, clever, skilful, learned, free from lust (excessive desire of gain), and who can forgive (rivals), and belongs to the twice-born class.[25]

The inscriptions generally record only the work of engraving for which *sūtradhāras* were commissioned. However in some cases the architect who designed a building or edifice is given credit to that effect.[26] Sometimes the *sūtradhāra,* who was supposed to be the designer and executor of edifices, finds mention merely as the engraver of the record.[27] Probably in such cases his role in the building activity was implicitly accepted. There are, however, certain, records by *sūtradhāras* which define their role properly and in which the *śilpīs* are specifically mentioned as the designers and executors of the monuments,[28] as well as the engravers of the inscriptions.

The inscriptions of early medieval period, in fact, reveal the emergence of a new class of artisan, *sūtradhāra,* who played a significant role in the building activity. The earliest references to a *sūtradhāra*[29] are found in the Ajantā caves and in the inscription of the Pāṇḍuvaṁsī kings of South Kosala. The variants of the appellation are *sūtrabhṛt, sūtradhātṛ* and *sūtradhārin.* There also appear the term *sūtradhāra-pitāmaha,* (the very best amongst the artisans) and *gajadhāra* (the same as *sūtradhāra*).[30] It would be worthwhile to enquire into the circumstances which led to the emergence of the *sūtradhāra* in the realm of building activity. The available evidence indicates a close affinity between the dramatic art and the building art.[31] The inscriptions refer to the *sūtradhāras* and other artisans who

25. P.K. Acharya, op. cit., s.v. *sthapati*, p. 580.
26. *CII.* IV (ii), p. 317.
27. Bhandarkar's List, 1683.
28. *CII,* IV, p. 558, EI, XI, p. 476.
29. Ajantā Cave, No. XV.
30. D.C. Sircar, *Indian Epigraphical Glossary*, pp. 329, 108.
31. R.N. Misra, *Ancient Artists and Art Activity*, p. 37.

were usually engaged towards the conclusion of the process of building. This is apt to create an impression that the artisans (*sūtradhāras*) who were closer to the building activity found mention in them while others, such as the *sthapatis* who, being only the designers, were remote from it, were ignored. Thus, the prominence of the *sūtradhāras* as compared to the *sthapatis* in the execution and designing of buildings is too difficult to establish. A synchronism of roles in theory and practice between the *sūtradhāras* and the *sthapatis* may ultimately have made the latter redundant, although canons continued to beat the line previously established.[32]

QUALITIES OF AN ARCHITECT

Samarāṅgaṇasūtradhāra mentions the requisite qualifications for an architect in *sthapati-lakṣaṇa*. Here *sthapati* says: "I am now going to describe the *sthāpatya* as handed down to us from generation to generation, by the knowing of which the values and defects of the architects are known." The *sthāpatya* is fourfold — the traditional lore (*śāstra*), practical experience (*karma*), intuitive insight (*prajñā*), and righteous conduct and character (*śīla*). These four elements comprising the science of architecture are really the qualities constituting the fundamental equipment which went to make a *sthapati* an architect. According to the same text, a *sthapati* should be an adept builder, a skilled craftsman. A *sthapati* was to be well-versed in Vāstuśāstra, which consisted of the canons of site-planning and layout, planning of the building, laying out gardens and parks, town-planning, regional planning, and all the traditional subject matter of architecture. Apart from *śilpa,* he was to be equipped with the knowledge of carpentry, engineering, and machine-making (*yantra-karma-vidhi*). Moreover, he was to be a skilled mathematician, astronomer, astrologer and master of the *śiras,* the conditions of different places.[33] Another qualification of an architect was practical experience. Hence, the adeptness in action was one of the essential qualities of an architect.[34] Again, whatever degree of mastery and perfection an architect attained in his art, he was not yet a perfect architect if he lacked personal insight (*prajñā*),

32. Ibid.
33. *Samarāṅganasūtradhāra,* Chap. 44, verses 3 and 4.
34. Ibid., verses 8-10.

immediate intuition. Without readiness of judgement in contingencies, he was like a *nirmada,* an elephant without work.[35] *Prajñā* was a great distinction of a true *sthapati.* Over and above all these qualifications, an architect was to possess a character above reproach. The sacred task of architecture could be entrusted only to one who had a high moral character. The *Samarāṅgaṇasūtradhāra* emphasizes this essential qualification of a *sthapati*:

> An architect must strive at all cost to maintain his character and conduct. It is only then that his actions bear fruit, and in their turn, become harbingers of goodness on earth.[36]

MOBILITY OF AN ARCHITECT

The role of the village architect in building-activity is mentioned in an inscription. The Nāgarī Plate of Anaṅgabhīma III (Śaka 1151-52) describes a village of artisans and craftsmen (*śilpī*s) as having several buildings of different types.[37] As regards the building materials and the methods used in the construction of houses, they were in accordance with their means, and the common people of the society constructed their houses themselves. According to Bāṇa[38] and Yogeśvara,[39] they generally lived in huts.

Architects who lived in the towns and cities had more importance and better opportunities to fulfil the requirements of the people. Vāstuśāstra, dealing, among other things, with the planning of a city, mentions 20 types of cities[40] which were created by proficient architects. A large number of cities existed during the period,[41] the buildings of which were made from burnt bricks joined with plasters, and covered with tiles.[42] Apparently hundreds of different kinds of workers, such as

35. Ibid., verses 13-14.
36. Ibid., verses 16-18.
37. *EI*, XXVIII, lines 127ff; XXII, p. 259.
38. *Hcar* p. 228, 230.
39. *Sad*, 2.174.5; 2.173.1.
40. *Viśvakarmā Vāstuśāstram*, Introduction, XVIII. See *Śukra*, I, 425-28, p. 28.
41. A long list of these towns is given in P. Niyogi's *Contributions to the Economic History of Northern India*, pp. 116ff. In *Rājataraṅgiṇī*, we read of sky-touching buildings and temples, *RT*, VII, 608.
42. *JUPHS*, XVII, p. 196. For this see *HIED*, I, pp. 78, 87. Al-Idrisi has said about this.

sthapatis, *sūtradhāras*, sculptors, and masons were engaged in making buildings in cities and towns.

There are references available to mobility of architects from one place to another, and from one kingdom to another. The great Virūpākṣa temple, dated about CE 740, was most likely built by workmen brought from Kāñcīpuram. The temple was an imitation of the Kailāsanātha temple at Kāñcīpuram.[43] The architect of the temple, Guṇḍa, received the title of Tribhuvanācārya. Similarly, in another instance Acyuta, son of Rāma, the main architect, came from Kamboja (north-west frontier) to build the triple-temple of Viṣṇu at Pṛthūdaka.[44] These architects were commissioned by the patrons for building purposes. The extant evidence reveals instances of individual and groups of resident and itinerant architects during the period under review.[45] The demand for efficient and brilliant architects was so high that sometimes they were commissioned at far-off places. According to Coomaraswamy, "the importation of craftsmen and labourers, including quarrymen, who have their own methods of obtaining the large stone beams required, is of interest in connection with the vexed question of the construction of Hindu temples in farther-off India and Indonesia."[46] He again observes that it is far from unlikely that in some cases the whole of the work was done by workmen of Indian birth under the guidance of a *śilpin*, using the principles of India to *Śilpaśāstra*. According to him, such workmen moved from India to Ceylon in large numbers during various periods. He quotes *Mahāvaṁsa* to the effect that "craftsmen and a thousand families of the eighteen guilds" were sent by a Pāṇḍyan king from Madura to Ceylon in the time of Vijaya.[47]

WORKS OF ARCHITECT

The word *vāstu* literally means "place of residence." In the Sanskrit lexicon, it

---

43. A.K. Coomaraswamy, *History of Indian and Indonesian Art*, p. 95.
44. *EI*, I, pp. 242ff.
45. R.N. Misra, *Ancient Artist and Art Activity*, p. 33. See Brajesh Krishna, *The Art Under the Gujara-Pratihāras*, p. 28.
46. A.K. Coomaraswamy, *History of Indian and Indonesian Art*, p. 95.
47. *EI*, I, pp. 42ff.

denotes a house-site or house proper.[48] But it has wider connotations and includes all architectural activity, including digging of wells and tanks and erection of forts, etc.[49]

Construction Work for Water

In the absence of natural supply of water for drinking, washing, and irrigational purposes, the villagers excavated tanks and wells and constructed embankments for storing water. The number of such artificial tanks, wells and embankments in a village depended upon the requirements of the villagers. These artificial sources of water constructed by architects were generally called *puṣkariṇī*,[50] *palvala*,[51] *jalāśaya*,[52] *pokhiri*,[53] *pokhirī*,[54] *sarā*,[55] *taḍāga*,[56] *vāpi*[57] and *kuṇḍa*.[58] *Kuṇḍa*s were natural pools. Wells were dug both inside and outside the village habitat. The inside wells (*kūpa*s) were meant for drinking and washing purposes, while the outside wells served the purpose of irrigation. *Mayamata* also speaks of the provision of wells within a village habitat.[59] A copper plate of the period refers to

---

48. *Aṣṭādhyāyī*, IV.3.73; V.S. Agrawal, *India as Known to Pāṇini*, p. 337; *Brahmajālasutta* (Eng. tr. Rhys Davids), pp. 16-18, fn.; *Āśvalāyanagṛhyasūtra*, II.7.1; *Amara*, II.3. 19; *Halāyudha*, V.290; P.K. Acharya, *Dictionary of Indian Architecture*, p. 548.

49. *Gṛhaṁ kṣetraṁ = ārāmas = setubandhas = taṭakam = ādhāro vāstu*, quoted from A.M. Shastri, *Bṛhatsaṁhitā of Varāhamihira*, p. 372.

50. *JASB*, IX, pt. 11(1840), pp. 766ff., I, 23; *EI*, XXIX, No 1A, 1.31; *EI*, XII, No. 3; II 34-35; *JASB*, LXVI, pt. 1, pp. 113ff, p. 1.3 (obverse), 1.8; *JASB*, LXVI, Pt. 1, pp. 285ff, pt. 3 (obverse), 1.13; *IB*, III, No. XIII, 1.52; *IB*, III, No. 15, II. 60-61; *Kāmarūpa Śāsanavalī*, pp. 1ff., f.132.

51. *Pavanadūta of Dhoyi*, V.20. See, A.K. Choudhary, *Early Medieval Village in North-Eastern India*, p. 57.

52. *IB*, III, No. 4, 1.18; *Maya*, 9. 88.

53. *IB*, III, No. 17, I. 32.

54. *EI*, II, No. 28, 1.57.

55. *IB*, III, No.11, 1.40.

56. *Mānasāra*, 9.81; *Saṁskārāratnamālā*, I, p. 28.

57. *Maya*, 9.88; *JASB*, LXVI, pt. 1, pp. 285ff., Pl. 3. (obverse), 1.13; *Saṁskāratnamālā*, I, p. 28.

58. *IB*, III, I.42; Ibid., I. 35.

59. *Maya*, 9.88.

an external well.[60] The *kuvā* of the Tajpur Grant,[61] signifying a well,[62] was situated in the boundary of a village. Sometimes wells and tanks were made of stone. The Mau Inscription of Candella Madanavarman speaks of tanks and reservoirs being made of hewn and dressed stones.[63] This work was done by professional stone-cutters (*śilākūṭas*).[64]

The inscriptions of Imperial Paramāras refer to channels, tanks and wells which were constructed under the patronage of rulers.[65] Vākapati II got constructed a *taḍāga* named Muñjasāgar of Vākapati (CE 974-995). Bhojadeva also got erected a tank Bhojatala near Cittoṛ and a big lake near Bhopal. Similarly Udayāditya of the same dynasty had constructed Udayasāgar in Udayapur near Bhopal. An inscription of Amera of Naravarman mentions a *taḍāga* built during his time.

The Raipur Museum Stone Inscription of Pṛthvīdeva tells us that a tank named Vallabhasāgar was built by Vallabharāja in a city.[66] It is curious to note that some inscriptions mention the name of the architect by whom the work was accomplished. Maṅglana Stone Inscription of CE 1215 speaks of an architect named Āsala,[67] who constructed a step-well. The same inscription also refers to a mason Jāhada, who shaped the stones for a step-well built by the architect Āsala.[68] Siṅgāli Kārgī,[69] the son of Kālī, mentioned in an inscription of Vanhadaka, erected a tank. Similarly, Bhojuka, a mason, was appointed to build a step-well.[70]

---

60. *JASB*, LXVI, pt.1, pp. 285ff., Pl. 3 (obverse), 1. 11,
61. *JASB*, IX, pt. 11 (1840), pp. 766ff., I. 23.
62. P.C. Chaudhuri, *The History of Civilization of the People of Assam*, p. 391.
63. *EI*, I, p. 202.
64. Ibid., I, pp. I62ff.
65. *The Inscriptions of Imperial Paramāras*, L.D. Series, 73, p. 38.
66. *CII*, IV, Ins. No. 85, Verses 18 and 21.
67. *IA*, XLI, pp. 11, 86 (line 9).
68. *IA*, XLI, pp. 86, 88, lines 9-10.
69. *EI*, X, p. 80.
70. *EI*, XII, p. 46.

Construction of Forts

The art of erecting fortifications by architects is very ancient.[71] Forts were always the mainz base for the defence of our country. Materials like stones, bricks and plasters were used in building different types of forts. The masons of the pre-Aryan time (called Dāsas and Dasyus) were excellent builders of forts. Sambhara, a Dāsa had 99 or 100 forts.[72] It is also probable that the Vedic Aryans built forts for vanquishing the pre-Aryan inhabitants. Architects erected forts of considerable magnitude — we find one described as "broad" (*pr̥thvī*) and another as "wide" (*ūrvī*).[73] The tradition of masons constructing fortifications continued for long, so that in the Jātakas we read of cities fortified with walls and ramparts.[74] The Smr̥tis describe forts as constituents of the state (e.g. of the *saptaṅga rājya*)[75] Kauṭilya considers the fort one of the seven chief constituent elements of the state, and refers to its different varieties.[76] Elsewhere he says that "the heaven of the king and of his army is a strong fort."[77] From these references it is clear that construction of forts by architects was thought a progressive performance. The typical ideas about fortifications expressed in the sources of the period and their importance bear out the efficiency and skill of the architects. The art of raising fortifications as military architecture had varied character during the early medieval period.

The importance of forts is discussed at length in *Yuktikalpataru*,[78] which divides forts under two heads: *akr̥trima* (natural) and *kr̥trima* (artificial). *Kr̥trima* forts were constructed by architects. *Mānasāra* classifies forts under nine heads in accordance with the nature or method of the defence required.[79] According to

71. The towns of Chalcolithic culture were fortified as observed by N.G. Majumdar, *ASI*, No. 48, pp. 89-90.
72. *R̥V*, I, 130, 7; II, 19, 6; II, 14, 6.
73. Ibid., I, 189, 2. For Vedic references to fortifications see Muir, *Original Sanskrit Texts*, II, pp. 378-83.
74. See Kameshwar Prasad, op. cit., pp. 66ff.
75. R.K. Dixit, "Fort in the Smr̥tis," *Uttara Bhāratī*, XII, no. 1, 1960, pp. 109-16.
76. *Arthaśāstra*, II, Chap. 3.
77. Ibid., VI, p. 362.
78. *Yuktikalpataru*, pp. 17ff.
79. *Mānasāra*, X, 78 and 90-91.

Somadeva, "A king without a fort has no refuge, just like a bird let loose from a ship in the midst of the ocean."[80] *Śārṅgadharapaddhati*[81] compares a king without a fort to a snake without poison. Arab writers speak of a number of forts throughout north India.[82] Inscriptions of the period throw considerable light on the forts then in existence.[83] The rulers of the time used to evolve their scheme of defence, and appoint architects for building forts. The newest building technology was invested in erecting forts of different shapes. Presumably stones, bricks and plasters were used for constructing these forts. Thus in the early medieval period in India, construction of forts was thought as important as constructing of civil buildings.

Construction of Monuments and Temples

It is needless to say that the excellence of the architecture of the early medieval period is primarily seen, from the hundreds of extant lofty and beautiful temples of the period.

It is interesting to note that in connection with the establishment of new cities, the plan of the city was made by the *sthapati*s, and the *sthāpaka*s. The latter prepared the plan and erected religious buildings. The former were a combination of town-engineers and secular architects. The *sthapati*s who built the houses for the royal guests were regarded by some sages as heroes. Obviously, they were assisted by the *śilpins*.[84]

Besides the architects there were also some other kinds of workers who prepare the cement-like material for their use, and assisted them in sundry ways. *Bṛhatsaṁhitā* describes several preparations of cements or powders called *vajra-lepa*s (paints or coatings as strong as the thunder-bolt), and *vajra-saṁghāta* (composition as hard as the thunder-bolt).[85] Architects and building workers used these materials in building temples, houses and forts. From the descriptions given

80. *Nītivākyāmṛta*, p. 80.
81. p. 220.
82. *HIED*, II, pp. 28-29; 226-231; 324-25.
83. *EI*, X, 105; IA, VI, 77.
84. *Prācī-Prabhā*, p. 403; A.K. Majumdar, *Chaulukyas of Gujarat*, p. 114.
85. P.C. Ray, *History of Hindu Chemistery from the Earliest Times to the Middle of the 16th Century* CE, pp. 104-05.

for their preparation and use they seem to have been rock-cements and metal-cements respectively. The workers who possessed chemical knowledge prepared different kinds of mixtures of cements. The process for the preparation of *vajra-lepas* consisted in first extracting juices of finely ground fruits, seeds, flowers and barks of plants rich in gummy and resinous substances and concentrating them, and then mixing them with naturally occurring resins and resinous substances to obtain a paste. Sometimes in this process mercury was also used. The paste was heated, and applied to the walls of temples and houses for residential purposes.[86] Different varieties of cements and chemical methods of their preparation given in the sources indicate that cement was used on a large scale. Thus scientific development in making cement gave new trends to architecture. Moreover, it may also be mentioned that the job of an architect was secure. His demand and popularity was based on the degree of his skill in making temples and other kinds of building.

GUILDS OF ARCHITECTS

It may also be surmised that architects had their guilds. These guilds were engaged in building activity in the cities on a large scale. The Kāman inscription of our period refers to the guild of architects *sthapatis*.[87] The task of building edifices was a well organized one. The extant monuments usually indicate a premeditated design and its execution, every single architectural part, including motifs and reliefs, being predetermined by the chief architect and made according to a planned lay-out. The existence of specialized classes in different departments of building activity, indicates that architects were gaining more and more specialization in their craft. In this specialization, many factors, such as acquisition of greater skill through the successive stages of the practice of a craft, or teacher-disciple relationship, or the hereditary transmission of skill contributed a lot. It may be noticed that guilds of architects not only protected their economic benefits and formed rules and regulations for them, but also enabled them to become members of the administrative bodies of the ruling class.

Guilds of architects were obviously more mobile than guilds of weavers or

86. Ibid.
87. *EI*, XIX p.60; I, p. 20.

metal workers, who formed a more integral part of the village system. These guilds moved around in a district, settling down temporarily at the site of construction for as long as was required. In the case of immensely ambitious building plans, such as those of huge temples, the architects were provided houses at the sites of building for a decade or even more. The temples and other such structures constructed with huge blocks of stone throughout India during the period prove that there were expert architects[88] and engineers to design and execute such pieces of art.

The guilds of architects worked for patron who requisitioned their services. In fact, the temples of the period cannot be considered creations of a single man, but rather those of large groups of varied workers, several of whom experts in their profession and each making his finest contribution to the final product.[89]

SOME IMPORTANT ARCHITECTS

With the acceleration of building-activity in the early medieval period the architects came to play an important and creative role in the development of culture. They were so much dedicated to their art that they did not consider it important to engrave their names on the resultant edifice. Their chief aim was to work in the interest of perfection in their art.

However, some inscriptions of our period do give the names of the important architects who acquired an honoured position in their art by their devotion and industry. It is interesting to note that the architects in the early medieval period were free to change their profession according to their free will. It appears that *sūtradhāra*, *sthapati* and the sculptor belonged to the same caste. The Vasantagaṛh Inscription of Pūrṇapāla[90] refers to a mason named Śivapāla, one of whose ancestor was a *sūtradhāra* (a well-known carpenter named Deuka) and another was *sthapati* (a famous architect named Nāga). From this it would appear that both *sūtradhāra*s and *sthapati*s belonged to the same caste and that these were professional titles. Māmariyañci-Tamma was another architect who was a son of

88. Urmila Agarwal, *Khajurāho Sculptures and Their Significance*, p. 188.
89. Vidya Dehejia, *Early Stone Temples of Orissa*, p. 20.
90. *EI*, IX, p. 15.

goldsmith Bandiyoja of CE 1242.[91] Similarly, Anakoja[92] and Kalakoja[93] were two architects who belonged to a brazier family and were sons of Mārāla and Mārāla-Mindoja respectively of CE 1395.

In an inscription we find a mention of an architect named Nāyaka, who was head of the architects. He fashioned the very lofty temple and a *maṇḍapa* of Śiva, with chisel in CE 804.[94] The same inscription also mentions the name of an architect Thoḍhuka, the son of Sammana, who worked on the same temple with Nāyaka.[95] Another qualified architect Naṇṇaka constructed a Śiva temple elsewhere in CE 804.[96]

Acyuta,[97] the son of Rāma, was an eminent architect of CE 882–917. He came from Kamboja to Pṛthūdaka to build a temple. His name is mentioned in an inscription, where he is called "an image of Dhanvantari, an incarnation of the quintessence of learning, a friend of the virtuous, and a bee on the lotus of the heart of his master." Caṇḍī Śiva[98] was the architect of a temple. He was the famed son of Vīrabhadra, knowlegeable like Viśvakarman in the science of building houses (*vāstu-vidyā*). He built the delightful house of Śaṅkara with its chapels (*maṇḍapas*) and beautiful porch (*toraṇa*), which contains all the gods, a veritable portion of heaven made by the Creator Himself. Some architects were the *gurus* of the sculptors of that period. Idamoraka (Indramayūra) Ācārya, an architect, was the *guru* of the sculptor Nataka (Nartaka), who made the image of the cobra on a slab.[99]

Some architects were so brilliant in their craftsmanship that they have been highly appreciated in the inscriptions. According to the Ratnapura inscription of Pṛthvīdeva,[100] one Devanāga was the "crest-jewel among sculptors" and built

91. *EC*, III, no. 85, p. 48.
92. Ibid., V, pt. 1, no. 61.
93. Ibid.
94. *EI*, 1, 107, 111.
95. Ibid.
96. *IA*, XIII, pp. 163-65.
97. Pehowa Praśasti of the Reign of Mahendrapāla, *EI*, I, p. 250, fn. 40.
98. Harṣa Stone Inscription, *EI*, 11, pp. 123-24 and 128 fn. 72.
99. *IA*, XIV, p. 334, fns. 20 and 23.
100. *EI*, I, pp. 49 and 52.

the temple of Śiva (Kāṇaka) Śūlapāṇi.[101] He was the crest-jewel of the guild of Varendra artists (*varendrakaśilpī goṣṭhī-cūḍāmaṇi*), son of Bṛhaspati, grandson of Mānadāsa, and great-grandson of Dharma, lived towards the end of the eleventh century CE. Another architect named Devāditya[102] was the son of Āhlādana who was the architect of Vaidyeśa. He was known to figure among the first rank of architects.

An inscription of the Khajurāho rulers of CE 1116 refers to an architect Chiccha.[103] He built the temple of Pramatthanātha and has been called *vijñāna-viśva-karttri-dharmadhara-sūtradhāra.* The architect Pithe[104] of CE 1155-56 knew all the rules of Viśvakarman (the architect of the gods), and planned, designed and executed a number of buildings, including a temple of Śiva. He also constructed a cloister (*maṭha*) with wonderful floors (*bhūmika*) and a hall of study (*vyākhyānaśālā*).

Not only the architects but sometimes other classes of *śilpīs* are also mentioned in the inscriptions. The Sāṇḍerava Stone Inscription of Kalhaṇadeva Cāhmāna[105] refers to Imdarāka, a *sūtradhāra* who assisted the chief architect Pāhiṇi, the builder of the *maṇḍapa,* and other parts of the temple of Bhīmeśvara. The same inscription mentions Pāhiṇi as the son of *sūtradhāra* Mahaduā. Pāhiṇi was involved in the construction work of the aforementioned temple. Sāmpula was an intelligent artisan who built a temple of Śiva in CE 1189.[106] He has been called the "crest-jewel among the sculptors" because of his mastery over his craft.

In one of the inscriptions it is said that a *paṇḍita* from the Navagrāma-draṅga (watch-station near mountain passes), son of Kālī, was a *sthapati* who constructed a tank.[107] Satyadeva[108] was the son of Pitāmaha, a merchant by birth, who was the Kārāpaka[109] selected by Goṣṭhī to supervise the work of erecting the temple of

101. Deopara Inscription of Vijayasena, *EI*, I, pp. 311 and 315.

102. *EI*, I, pp. 24 and 31.

103. *EI*, I, p. 146.

104. *EI*, II, pp. 13, 17 and 19.

105. *EI*, XI, p. 48.

106. Ibid., I, pp. 49 and 52.

107. Ibid.. V. 11, p. 291.

108. "Vasantagaṛh Inscription of Varmalata", *EI*, IX, pp. 189 and 192.

109. Kārāpaka was the person appointed to look after the construction of the temple, Kielhorn, *IA*, XIX, p. 62, note 53.

goddess Kaṣemāryā. Obviously the architect Satyadeva was a skilled craftsman. In addition, an inscription of CE 1140[110] refers to sculptor Kālidāsa, who was a champion over the proud, a thunderbolt to the rock (*giri*), a titled (i.e. a very eminent) sculptor. He made the *makaratoraṇa* (or the carved headpiece of the lintel). Thus it seems that the construction work on the temples was carried out not only by architects but also by other craftsmen.

There was an efficient architect who was profoundly devoted to his work of constructing temples. Jakanācārya[111] by name, he was the architect of the temples at Halebiḍ and Somanāthapura. Moreover, he was a reputed architect of the magnificent Kait Īśvara Temple. He was also credited with having built all the temples (similar in style) throughout the district. Jakanācārya, having accidentally killed a brāhmaṇa, employed 20 years of life in rebuilding temples between Kāśī and Rāmeśvara with the hope of washing away his great sin.

(Śrī) Gundan[112] was an eminent architect of the western Cāḷukya king Vikramāditya II, who built the temple of the (present) god Virūpākṣa, originally Lokeśvara. He is called *sūtradhārī*, *tribhuvanācārya* and *sarva-siddhi-ācārya*.[113] He is said to have been the creator of many cities and houses.

According to the Vasantagaṛh Stone Inscription of Pūrṇapāla (CE 1042) *sthapati* Nāga was the designer of a fort in the ancient city of Vaṭa.[114] Two *sūtradhāras*, Deuka and his son Śivapāla, also find mention in the same record along with *sthapati* Nāga. The tradition of engraving the names of architects was continued even into later times. The Peshawar Museum Inscription of Vanhaditta (CE 1461) describes *sthapati* Siṅgālī Kārgī, the son of Kālī as the builder of a pond.[115]

It may be concluded that the architect was generally put in the class of the *śilpīs*. He built buildings of various kinds as required by the occasion, and demand of the society of the period Throughout the period under study, brilliant and

---

110. *IA*, I, p. 44.
111. *EI*, V, Part 1, no. 239, tr., p. 275.
112. *IA*, I, p. 44.
113. *IA*, X, pp. 163-66 and 170-71.
114. *EI*, IX, 6, 12-15.
115. *EI*, X, 80-81.

expert architects not only maintained the temple of the previous artistic building activity, but also improved upon it by investing new types of technology in the architectural work. Generally, the architects worked in groups and formed themselves into guilds for their social and economic benefits. Some architects were patronized by the rulers because of their skill and creativity. This provided them respectable social status in their society. The *Śilpaśāstra* of the period specifically refers to the qualifications for architects, rules and regulations for practising *vāstu-vidyā* and so many other important related features. Various terms for the architect like *śilpī, śilpin, sthapati, sthāpaka, sūtradhāra, vardhakī, sūtragrāhin, sūtrakāra, sūtrabhṛt,* and *rūpakāra* are used in the literary works of the period and in inscriptions. This speaks for the varied specialization in the sub-fields of *vāstu-vidyā*. It is important to note that during the period the skill of the architects had reached its fullest development. Architects frequently moved from one place to another, and from one kingdom to another. Sometimes architects engraved their names on the buildings they made, which easily indicates that in the period under study they had reached a supreme level of artistic attainment, and were very much in demand.

Sculptors

A sculptor is a person who creates art objects in the form of sculptures. He uses his imagination to model an actual or an imaginative view. The expression of the sculptor is thought to be of the highest order when it is "round," that is, when it accords with the ancient Indian artistic canons. This expression may be manifested in the form of images, in stone, clay, wood or metal.

The term *rūpakāra* is used frequently in the existing literature to connote a sculptor, just as *citrakāra* is used to signify a painter. *Citra* is the term for sculpture in the round, while for carving in relief, high or low, the appellation is *ardhacitra*. Painting, which in many ways bears semblance to sculpture, the third dimension or depth being expressed by the technique of light and shade, is called *citrābhāsa*, literally meaning semblance of sculpture.[116] Treatises on iconography clearly indicate that the term *citrakāra* was also taken to mean a sculptor.[117] As said

116. C. Sivaramamurti, "Classical Painting and Sculpture", in *The Indian Experience*, p. 41; also see Bhandarkar's List, 559.

117. T.P. Bhattacharya, *The Canons of Indian Art*, pp. 37ff. Also see R.N. Misra, *Ancient Artists and Art Activity*, p. 52.

above, the word *rūpakāra* traditionally signifies a sculptor,[118] but in ancient epigraphs we also find the term "*śilāśrī* (a sculptor, "one who imparts beauty to stones"). The various extant literary works employ a number of other terms too, such as *sūtradhāra, rūpadakṣa, śailavardhakī, aveśani, takṣaka, kārmika* (*kammina, karmin*), *rūpaṭaka, śilpin, śilākūṭa, śilāvaṭa* and *śilpī*. The word *sthapati*[119] denotes architect as well as sculptors. All these descriptions indicate the proficiency of the concerned category of artisan in the art of creating, sculptures, i.e. in *śilpa-vidyā*.

An earlier text *Mahāvastu*[120] refers to various classes of artisans and craftsmen and the specialized groups they constituted. They are: *citrakāra* (painters); *vardhakīrūpakāra*s (carpenters); *kārūpatrika*s (carvers); *pustakāraka*s (modellers of clay); *pustakarmakāraka*s (plasterers); *lepaka*s (decorators); and *sthapati-sūtrakāra*s. The hierarchy of these artists is not made clear in the text and the same state seems to have continued up to the medieval period.

Sometimes artisans and craftsmen acquired skill in more than one art. This is confirmed by the evidence furnished by the epigraphs and the texts of the period. The knowledge and skill of a sculptor was communicated from father to son or from master to disciple.

A few works assert that sculptors earned their livelihood by selling images produced by them. Probably images of gods, deities, animals, and human beings were made in different materials and sold by them. That making of images was a source of livelihood is indicated by Pāṇini and a commentary on this work.[121] Patañjali refers to the Mauryas' involvement in making images for monetary return.[122]

---

118. Bhandarkar, op. cit., p. 559.

119. BS, LII.97, 103, 108; LV. 30, LIX. 18. See A.M. Shastri, *India as Seen in the Bṛhatsaṁhitā of Varāhmihira*, p. 311.

120. *Mahāvastu* (tr.), J.J. Jones, III, p. 112. See pp. 443-44.

121. Pāṇini, V, 3.99. See J.N. Banerjea, *Development of Hindu Iconography*, p. 391.

122. J.N. Banerjea, ibid., p. 40.

MATERIAL USED BY THE SCULPTOR

The rural and urban sculptors used different types of material for their products, the stone, clay, wood and metal being available there.

Varāhamihira divides images and *liṅga*s into seven categories on the basis of the material of which they were made: (1) *dārumayī* (wooden), (2) *mṛṇmayī* (made of clay), (3) *maṇimayī* (made of precious stones), (4) *sauvarṇī* (made of gold), (5) *rajatamayī* (made of silver), (6) *tāmramayī* (made of copper), and (7) *śailī* (made of stone).[123] With slight modifications this classification is found in *Matsya Purāṇa*, *Śukranītisāra* and *Samarāṅgaṇasūtradhāra*.[124] It is noteworthy that from the very early times sculptural materials like copper,[125] crystal,[126] sandalwood,[127] shell or iron,[128] gold,[129] silver,[130] iron,[131] precious stones,[132] and bronze[133] were prescribed for making icons of the Sun, Moon, Mars, Mercury, Jupiter, Venus, Saturn, Rāhu, Ketu respectively.[134] Similarly, wood, gold, iron, silver, white clay, and cow's skin were regarded as particularly suited for carving figures of Indra, Yama, Varuṇa, Vāyu, Kubera and Śiva respectively.[135]

---

123. *BS*, LIX, 4-5. See A.M. Shastri, op. cit., pp. 409-10.
124. G.O.S., II.1.1.
125. *YY*, VI, 4; See *BY* XVIII, 3-5.
126. *BY*, XVIII, 6-8.
127. *BY*, XVIII, 11-13. According to *YY*, VI, 9, however, it should be made of Rudhirakhya-maṇi.
128. *BY*, XVIII. 11-13. According to *YY*, VI, 17, it should be fashioned in gold.
129. *BY*, XVIII, 14-15. *YY*, VI, 18 prescribes *vimalaka-maṇi* for Bṛhaspati's image.
130. *BY*, XVIII, 16-17. But also see *YY*, VI, 7 (*citra*).
131. *BY*, XVIII, 18-20. *YY*, VI, 13 prescribes blue glass (*nilakācha*).
132. *BY*, XVIII, 21-22. The meaning of Nasa is not clear. According to *YY*, VI. 11, Rāhu should be fashioned in *devadāru* (wood).
133. *BY*, XVIII. 23-24.
134. See *Yāñavalkya-smṛti*, I. 296-98, as also *Bṛhajjātaka*, II, 12; which associates copper, precious stones, gold, alloys of metals, silver, pearls and iron to the seven planets beginning with the sun.
135. *YY*, VI, 4, 8, 12, 16, 18.

Śukranītisāra[136] generalizes that sculptures made of sands, pastes, paints, enamels, earth, wood, stone and metal were thought to be in an increasing order of strength and durability.

Al-Beruni[137] specifically mentions the material from which sculptures were made. According to him, a statue made of precious stones was superior to one made of wood, and one made of wood superior to one made of clay. He also says that a statue of precious stones was equally superior for all the men and women of the empire.

According to *Agni Purāṇa*[138] an image made of wood had greater merit than one made of clay; one made of terracotta was held better than one made of wood, and one made of stone was thought superior to one made of terracotta. Thus it is clear that the superiority of stone images was widely accepted. Stone images were held durable, particularly because they could easily be transferred from one place to another without any fear of breakage. In the same text[139] elsewhere states that phallic emblems were made of materials like common salt, clarified butter, pieces of cloth, clay whether soft or burnt, wood, stone, pearls, gold, iron, silver, copper, brass, zinc, mercury, mercury-iron, and metals combined with gems.

Al-Beruni talks of the proportion of idols and their parts.

> If the artist keeps the right measure, and does not make anything too large or too small, he is free from sin, and can be sure that the being represented by him will not visit him with any mishap. However, if he makes the idol one cubit high (together with the throne two cubits), he will enjoy health. If he makes it higher still, he will be praised, but he must know that making the idol too large, especially that of the sun, will hurt the ruler, and making it too small will hurt the artist.[140]

The art of making idols was specially supervised by the rulers. According to Al-Beruni, if the artist gave the idol a thin belly, it would cause famine in the country

136. Sukra, Ch. IV, Sec. IV.

137. Sachau, *Al-Beruni's India*, pp. 120-21.

138. *Agni Purāṇa* (tr. M.N. Dutt), pp. 32-33.

139. Ibid.

140. Sachau, *Al-Beruni's India*, I, pp. 120-21.

and if he gave it a lean belly, it would lead to ruin of property. If the hand of the artist slipped and produced something like a wound, he would have a wound in his own body which would kill him. If the idol was not completely even on both sides, say if one shoulder was higher than the other, the artist's wife would perish. If the artist turned the idol's eye upward, would go blind for the rest of his life, and if he turned it downward, he would be hounded by troubles and sorrows. In other words, the extent of the dedication and proficiency of the artist was assessed through his creation. If the idol did not appear complete in all aspects, both the artist and the ruler were responsible for its deficiencies.

STONE SCULPTURES

Thousands of stone images of different gods and goddesses were installed in a large number of temples in the period under review. These images were carved out of firm rock with the sculptor's chisel (*ṭaṅka*).[141] The construction of these sculptures indicates the high degree of technical skill and mastery in stone carving achieved by sculptors in the period. Mostly religious in nature, the stone sculptures of the period reflect the experience of many centuries. This experience was not the experience of an individual, but of the entire class of sculptors. Iconographic canons had also been evolved to provide guidelines to sculptors in making religious images, though the sculptor was free to express his feelings and skill in the embellishment of the temples. The iconographic texts must have originated after the emergence of image-worship, which was definitely in vogue in the later Vedic period.[142] An earlier text *Śilpa-Prakāśa* mentions the art of moulding images for religious purposes.[143] The importance of sculptures is specially stressed in this text. It is said that Viśvakarmā, master of the 64 arts explained to the craftsman the rules and regulations of constructing images. The sculptor was to strictly follow the rules in the case of religious images and this practice continued through the ages. The role of the sculptors have been very important from time to time. They created anthropomorphic, therio-anthropomorphic, theriomorphic and other forms. Almost all the religious icons were based on the Indian mythology,

141. *ASK*, pp. 13-15, 53, 118; *DKC*, pp. 206-07.

142. Nihar Ranjan Ray, *CA*, pp. 525ff.

143. T.P. Bhattacharya, op. cit., p. 324.

and some of them were made highly ornamented. These sculptures could be used in the society of the period for veneration, for the sculptors formed them according to the scriptures. The art of sculpture was, thus, a work of religious merit for the sculptor also. After establishing his sculpture in the temple the chief *śilpin* used to take his bath with great devotion in the water of a nearby tank or river. It was said that Viśvakarmā himself explained the ceremonies to be observed by a sculptor after establishing the icon.[144]

The stone sculptures collected from different parts of north India have been found aesthetically very superior. They are carved in stone by chiselling with an axe, and are highly ornamented. It appears that the period from the seventh to the twelfth century CE saw an extreme flowering of the Indian sculptural art, the fulfilment and culmination of the trends and tendencies of many centuries. Even after the collapse of the Gupta imperial fabric, the greater part of north India remained influenced by the Gupta period classical aesthetic ideals, and the high calibre of achievement in stone sculpture was maintained even during the following period, till about the middle of the eighth century CE.[145] During the earlier centuries of our period the sculptors began to also take into account the local tastes and prejudices in fashioning the images. In the field of art this regional outlook led to the first manifestation of provincial schools, which gradually and clearly came into being about the middle of the eighth century CE.[146]

The sculptors of the tenth century CE carved stone images with a close affinity to the metal images of that time. The charm and delicacy in modelling, attained by the artists through experiment of generations can be seen in the images of this period.[147] In the twelfth century CE a kind of cultural stagnation and rigid and petrified religious outlook changed the general attitude of people to the art of sculpture, and led the artist to find fulfilment and solace in intricate ornamentation and representation of the complicated pantheons sought and prized by the society of the time.

---

144. Vidya Dehejia, *Early Stone Temples of Orissa*, Appendix (Extracts from the *Śilpa-Prakāśa*), pp. 189-98.

145. S.K. Saraswati, *Survey of Indian Sculpture*, pp. 149-50.

146. Ibid.

147. For details see S. Kramrisch, *Pāla and Sena Sculptures*.

TERRACOTTA SCULPTURES

For the study of the terracotta figurines we have to depend mainly on archaeological remains. It is discovered that terracotta images were made on a large scale in the Gupta period, but there is no paucity of this industry during our period either. Excavations at numerous sites in north India reveal remains of brick temples belonging to the early medieval period, which indicates a broad geographical spread for the medium of terracotta. It appears that in the early medieval period bricks were frequently used, but they being more perishable, the temples made of bricks were destroyed far more easily than buildings in stone. Many of the extant brick temples of the period under review are situated in Kanpur, Fatehpur, Sitapur and Hardoi districts of Uttar Pradesh. This part of north India has had a long tradition of brick temples. The famous brick temple Bhītargāon of the earlier period still stands there. Brick temples of the Pratihāras are also known to have existed in Kalayat (district Jind, Haryana), which clearly indicates wide prevalence of brick architecture.[148]

The terracotta figurines are important from the economic point of view, for quite a number of people seem to have earned their living by making and selling them. These gifted clay-modellers created things of real beauty in the modest medium of clay, and satisfied a popular demand at the cheapest possible rate. Thereby, they served the interest of the poorer section of the society, who could not afford to buy precious metallic or stone statues.

The clay figurines were much in demand for both religious and secular purposes. On festive occasions and in fairs terracotta figurines of exquisite form and beauty were specially in great demand. Craftsmen of clay-modelling prepared terracotta human and animal figurines, toys, toy-carts, beads, ornaments, decorative pieces, etc. At the time of Rājyaśrī's marriage multitudes of modellers (*lepyakāras*) were engaged in moulding clay figurines of fishes, tortoises, crocodiles, coconuts, plantains, and betel plants.[149] Terracotta toys for children were also very popular. There is a reference to Rohasena's clay toy-cart in the Mṛcchakaṭika.[150] In the

148. See Brajesh Krishna, *The Art Under the Gurjara–Pratihāras*, pp. 105-09.

149. *Hcar*, IV, p. 142.

150. *Mṛcchakaṭikam*, VI, p. 178 .

later period many terracotta objects continued to be produced different purposes in the society. A terracotta plaque from Mahāsthān representing Mithuna and the dream of Triśalā is a Pāla piece of great beauty.[151]

PREPARATION OF CLAY SCULPTURES

The medium of terracotta was so important that quite a few literary works describe the method of making images in terracotta. *Samarāṅgaṇasūtradhāra* contains a description of the preparation of terracotta images by sculptors.[152] Earth was first to be collected from tanks, wells, etc. or from the roots of trees, or from banks of rivers and kneaded. The potter, as an artist, was then to model the image according to his skill and craft. Thereafter different colours were given to these images. The work also gives the formula for the preparation of *lepya*.[153] Another work *Śilparatna* also contains several instructions for the preparation of the clay to be used in image-making. One kind of clay was called *mṛtsnā*, which was the same as the clay prepared for brick-making.[154] This clay was to be free of husk, charcoal, bones, stones, sand, wooden pieces, or pieces of bricks, and made homogeneous by being stirred with foot again and again, and mixed with extracts of barks of some trees and *triphalā* water for three months. Then this clay was ready for making images. This preparation of clay with scientific care indicates the skilled workmanship of the craftsmen. The clay for images thus was made very strong, so that the sculpture might last long. Other similar methods for preparation of clay are prescribed in *Śilparatna*.[155] Different colours for different castes are mentioned in these texts. The artist is instructed to collect the earth of the right colour (white, red, yellow or black according to the caste) from the prescribed places, and to stir it in a vessel, filter it through a piece of new cloth and when it is free of water and after being dried in the sun, rub the resultant earth with decoration of bark of *lākṣā* and *kṣīra* trees, dry it again and mix it with a decoration of *khadira* and *arjuna*. He is to rub and let it dry till the mud becomes a *piṇḍa*, mix it with *triphalā* water and let it dry till very little water is left, then

151. C. Sivaramamurti, *Indian Sculpture*, pp. 113-14.
152. Tarapada Bhattacharyya, op. cit., p. 429.
153. *Śilparatna*, Chap. 14, p. 118.
154. Tarapada Bhattacharyya, op. cit., pp. 430-31.
155. Ibid.

again make a lump of it and divide it into four parts. Take one part of it, mix it with mud again, and rub it with *triphalā* water for 7 to 10 nights, then, pound it along with equal quantity of barley, wheat, *māṣatasi* leaves. The artist is then to take 1/8th part of the clay and mix it with coconut water and let it lie for 10 days, then mix juice of *śrīveṣṭa, guggulu, kundurika,* and *sarjā* in equal parts and rub it with 1/16th part of the mud along with curd. In this way the preparation of clay is described as a long process. However, sometimes the artists also made sculptures of pure clay.[156]

Clay images were of two kinds: those made of pure clay and those others (called *lepya* images) made of clay coated on straw, etc.[157] Both these kinds of clay, however, were to be specially prepared. *Atri Saṁhitā* refers to preparation of *ghaṭa* (*kaṭa*) *śarkarā* to be coated on stone images. About clay images it prescribes that earth was to be collected and mixed with *auṣadhas*, *cūrṇa* of *kaṭaśarkarā*, extract of *kapithva* and river water, and was to be left over for a month or 1½ month,[158] and then used for making images. The production of such images was possible only on a small scale, and artists working in this industry could only satisfy the local needs of the society. The history of terracotta in India suggests that its large scale production started only with the rise and growth of towns.[159]

WOODEN SCULPTURES

Carving on wood has been a very important craft since ancient times. The period under review was no exception. In the medieval times wood-carvers fashioned wooden sculptures in order to cater to the needs of the society in respect of various rituals and other purposes.[160] According to J.N. Banerjea, like early architectural remains, the extant early stone sculptures in the round and relief-carvings may have been influenced by their wooden prototypes in respect of their form and

156. Ibid., p. 431.
157. Ibid., Appendix H, p. 428.
158. Ibid., p. 429.
159. Devangana Desai, "Terracottas and Urban Culture of Ancient India (*c.* BCE 600-600 CE)", Paper presented to the Symposium on Art and Society held at the Calicut Session of the Indian History Congress, 1976.
160. *BY*, XVIII, 9-10; According to *YY*, VI, 9, however, it should be made of Rudhirākhyāmaṇi.

technique.[161] *Bṛhatsaṁhitā* refers to the wood from which the images and *liṅgas* were fashioned.[162] In this text one whole chapter is devoted to describing in detail the art of making wooden images. The procedure of selecting wood for making images is also described in *Matsya Purāṇa*,[163] *Viṣṇudharmottara Purāṇa*[164] and *Bhaviṣya Purāṇa*.[165]

Daṇḍin mentions wood carving,[166] and furnishes an interesting reference to the figures of horses and elephants formed out of the timber of the *vidruma* tree.[167] This art is also referred to in the works of Bāṇa.[168] It appears that images of wood were not fashioned on a mass scale; they were carved for royal palaces and in the houses of the rich people.[169] The art of carving sculptures in wood was a very fascinating work, and it appears that a large number of artisans and craftsmen were engaged in it. Small sculptures and articles like toys of exquisite form and beauty were prepared by artists according to the requirements of people. There is a reference in *Avantīsundarīkathā* to carvings of figures on wooden archways and pillars.[170]

In the present Kashmir[171] and Himachal Pradesh temples and houses were built of wood during the period under survey. Evidently, wood workers carved sculptures on the bas-reliefs of these temples for decorative purposes. Judging by the present Lakṣaṇā Devī temple of Caurāsī and the Śakti Devī temple at Chatrahī, parts of both of which belong to the original structures, one can surmise that Śiva temples and Gaṇeśa temples were largely made of wood. According to Goetz carved wood columns and façades of such temples date back to Meruvarman's

161. *Development of Hindu Iconography*, pp. 211-12. See *PIHC*, 3rd Session, pp. 176-84.

162. *BS*, LIX. 4-5.

163. *MP*, Chap. 257.

164. *VDP*, III, Chap. LXXXIX.

165. See *Brahmaparvan*, Chap. 131.

166. *ASK*, pp. 91, 107; *DKC*, p. 135.

167. *ASK*, p. 91, 107.

168. *Hcar*, pp. 138ff; *Kād*, para 28.

169. *Ragh*, VI, p. 32; *Hcar*, pp. 138-39, 232; *Kād*, Para 28.

170. p. 104. See regarding pictorial representations on Walls Kād, Para 64.

171. *RT*, VIII, 2390.

time.[172] Some iconographic signs of the period have also survived. The seventh- and eighth-century wood carvings of Cambā include the four-bracket figures and two images of the seventh century preserved in the Doca-Moca temple at Gajan in the Kullu district.[173] Ācārya Nemīcandra refers to wooden figures of elephants, etc.[174] Some, wooden sculptures belonging to tenth-eleventh century CE discovered at Sonarang (Dacca, Bangladesh) present the figure of Viṣṇu in the *yogāsana* pose.[175] An exquisitely carved image of standing Viṣṇu, with all the usual attributes of the deity and flanked by his consorts Śrī and Sarasvatī, reveals great artistic skill of the master-sculptor and the wood workers of Bengal.[176] Equally capturing is the fine statue of winged Garuḍa, the celestial vehicle of Viṣṇu, found during the excavations at Raghurāmpur and now displayed in the Dacca Museum.[177]

REPUTED SCULPTORS

It is curious to note that in ancient India the sculptor dedicated himself to his art but very rarely inscribed his name on the art objects that he created. The sculptor had a vast knowledge of his art, and followed the iconographic texts. He worked on various types of material, depicting his ideas in his art. There are only a few scattered references to the names of the sculptors, their genealogies and their activities. Some sculptures of the early medieval period are important because they reveal the names of the sculptors who created them.

The Candella monuments give us some names of the sculptors of Khajurāho. There are 30 temples at Khajurāho erected by the Candellas, and they were all completed between c. CE 900 to 1050.[178] The Brāhmaṇical, Jaina and Buddhist

172. M. Postel; A. Naven; K. Mankodi, *Antiquities of Himachal*, p. 47. See H. Goetz, *The Early Wooden Temples of Chamba.*
173. M. Postel, Ibid., pp. 65-69.
174. *Āmk*, of Ācārya Nemīcandra, 84, 190.
175. R.D. Banerji, *Eastern Indian School of Medieval Sculpture*, pp. 109-24, PI. 145A; N.K. Bhaṭṭaśāli, *Iconography of Buddhist and Brāhmaṇical Sculptures in Dacca Museum*, p. 228, pt. 174.
176. R.D. Banerji, ibid., PI. 476; N.K. Bhattasali, ibid., pp. 82f, Pl. 28.
177. N.K. Bhaṭṭaśāli, ibid., p. 109, Pl. 41, Fig. 2. See B.N. Sharma, *Social and Cultural History of Northern India*, p. 144.
178. R.C. Mazumdar, *Hindu Temples*, Preface.

monuments of this period are known for their wealth of beautiful images. Numerous sculptures are found carved on the bas-reliefs of temples. A most famous Candella sculptor was *citrakāra* Śrī Sātana.[179] His son Citanaka fashioned the famous Bodhisattva Siṁhanāda image found at Mahobā. It is mentioned in the inscription of the image that Citanaka was a *citrakāra*, by caste, and quite well versed in all the fine arts: *citrakāra śrī sātanastasya putraḥ sakalaśilpavidyākuśalaḥ cittanakas tasyeyam*.[180] The inscription incised on the pedestal of Mahobā Jaina image of Nemīnātha was made by *rūpakāra* Lākhana in the reign of vs 1211. Madanavarmadeva records the dedication of the image.[181] Sculptors Rāmadeva,[182] Devarāja,[183] Somarāja[184] and Rāma[185] are also mentioned in the Candella inscriptions. These sculptors made beautiful images with inscriptions engraved on their pedestals. According to the Candella records, there was *rūpakāra* Lahaḍa, the son of Rāma. Lahaḍa is said to have made a beautiful image of Nīlakaṇṭha-Śiva.[186]

The Pālas, who held sway in eastern India during the period from CE 730 to 1119, gave a fillip to the art of sculpture by extending royal patronage to it. Mahābodhi inscription records the religious work of a sculptor. The stone slab carrying the inscription indicates that the four-faced Lord Śiva was established in the place of worship called Campaśa (Campeśa) by Kesaba, the son of sculptor Ujjala.[187]

---

179. B.L. Dham, *A Guide to Khajurāho*, Preface. See Keshvachandra Mishra, *Chandel and Their Political Period* (in Hindi), p. 239.
180. See C. Sivaramamurti, op. cit., pp. 5-6.
181. Cunningham, *ASR*, XXI, p. 73.
182. Khajurāho Jaina Image Inscription (vs 1215), Kielhorn, *EI*, pp. 152-53.
183. Mahobā Stone Inscription (vs 1240); Cunningham, *ASR*, XXI, p. 72; Smith, *PASB*, 1879, pp. 143-44.
184. Ibid.
185. Kālañjar Rock Inscription (vs 1188), *ASR* Maisey.
186. *EI*, XXXI, p. 166; A. Cunningham, *ASR*, XXI, pp. 34-35, Pl. XC.
187. The Mahābodhi Inscription of the time of Dharamapāla, A. Cunningham, *Mahābodhi*; Pl. XXVIII, 3, *Journal and Proceedings of the Asiatic Society of Bengal*, IV (New Series, pp. 101-02; *Gauḍalekhamālā*, p. 31. See R.R. Mukherji and S.K. Maity, *Corpus of Bengal Inscriptions*, pp. 110-14 in *JASB* (1848), p. 321; Re-edited by A. Cunningham in *ASR*, XXI, pp. 34-35.

Instances of expert *rūpakāraṣ* have also been noticed in the inscriptions of Bengal. The inscription on a Sūrya image of Bengal of the tenth century CE mentions that the stone image was carved by the "wise and good" *śilpī* Amrit, a pupil of Indranīlamaṇi.[188] The inscription of Vijayasena, engraved by a famous artist mentions his name as Śūlapāṇi. He was the chief of the *goṣṭhī* (guild) of the *śilpīs* of Vārendra. The inscription also mentions his parentage.[189] The long list of his ancestors given there reveals that he was very famous among the sculptors and was the chief of his corporation. The inscription gives the name of his father as Bṛhaspati of his grandfather as Mānadāsa, and of his great-grandfather as Dharma.

The Imperial Paramāras continued the tradition of graceful sculptures. The famous Vāgdevī (Sarasvatī) image, now in the British Museum, has an inscription on its pedestal mentioning not only the fact of the installation of the image of the goddess of learning by Bhoja in his city of Dhāra, but also the name of the sculptor of the image as *sūtradhāra* Manathala, the son of Sahira (*sūtradhārasahirasuta manathalna ghaṭitam*).[190] Another inscription from Dhāra mentions the titles *śilpī* and *rūpakāra* for sculptors which clearly reflects their skill and mastery over their art. *Śilpī* Rāmadeva and his father *rūpakāra* Sīhaka[191] are mentioned in the Dhāra Praśati. The references to the *rūpakāras* who worked for the Paramāras include those to Sīhaka and Kānhaka (or Kānhaḍa).[192]

The famous architect of the Mount Ābu temples, Śobhanadeva, who was greatly encouraged by the wife of a great minister, is known to us from an inscription on one of the temples. The sculptor extremely was clever in his art, and once he fashioned the portrait of the minister's mother so realistically that tears welled up in the latter's eyes to see it.[193]

188. R.P. Chanda, *Indian Sculpture*, p. 66, Pl. XX.

189. C. Sivaramamurti, op. cit., p. 6.

190. Ibid., p. 5.

191. Bhandarkar's List, 1660.

192. *EI*, XXXII, p. 156; Bhandarkar's List 559; Sīhaka's son Rāmadeva is also mentioned as *Śilpī* in the inscription. A *Sūtradhāra* Rāmadeva is referred to in the Candella record. See *EI*, XXXI, p. 166, which records that this *sūtradhāra* added a *maṇḍapa* to the Nīlakaṇṭha temple at Kālañjar. A. Cunningham, *ASR*, XXI, p. 350, also refers to *rūpakāra* Rāmadeva of Khajurāho; See R.N. Misra, *Ancient Artists and Art Activity*, p. 51.

193. C. Sivaramamurti, op. cit., p. 7.

A Kaḷacuri inscription tells us that the temple of Bilvapāṇi was constructed by Devagaṇa, described as *rūpakāra śiromaṇi*. It is seen here that a *rūpakāra* was regarded as superior to a *sūtradhāra*.[194] In another inscription of a slightly later date Sāmpula is mentioned not as a *sūtradhāra* but as a *rūpakāra* and eulogized as *aneka-śilpa nirmāṇa-payodheḥ pāradr̥śvanā*, "One who has seen farther shores of the oceans of various crafts."[195] Hāsala,[196] Lakṣmīdhara, and his sons Dharaṇīdhara and Cāndārka also find a mention in the Kaḷacuri's inscription.[197] They are described as intelligent and repositories of all *śilpa-vidyā*. The Jabalpur plates of the Kaḷacuri Jayasiṁha[198] mention *rūpakāra* Talhaṇa, the son of Palhaṇa, belonging to the reputed Kokāsa family of artisans.

Hoysaḷa sculptures, though belong to south India, are important in this regard. An important general feature of the Hoysaḷa sculptures is that most of the individual sculptures are signed. Possibly, the self-praise found in many of them is the most logical explanation of it. This feature only reflects the artists, pride in their accomplishments.[199] Pāka is the earliest of the known sculptors of Paṭṭaḍakaḷ. He worked on the Saṅgameśvara temple, built by Vijayāditya in the beginning of the eighth century CE.[200] A number of sculptors worked on the Lokeśvara temple under Guṇḍa. Anivāritācari and Sarvasiddhi Ācārya headed the guild of the artisans among whom were Baladeva, Dāmodara, Revaḍi, Ovajja, Ceṅgamma and Pullappa.[201] The Hoysaḷa temples at Beḷur, Somanāthapura and Aihoḷe have several sculptures giving not only names of their creators but also the attainments of the later in their field. An inscription of the eleventh century CE Sovarāśi, containing beautiful patterns of swans and peacocks deftly entwined with letters is now preserved in the Indian Museum.[202] It is a very interesting inscription, for

194. R.N. Misra, op. cit., p. 55.

195. *CII*, IV (ii), pp. 490-515.

196. *CII*, IV, 401-07.

197. Ibid., pp. 477, 461, 483, 194 and 631.

198. *CII*, IV (i), p. 329.

199. In praise of Hoysaḷa Art, *Mārg*, XXXI, no. 1, (December 1977), p. 43.

200. A.M. Annigeri, *Paṭṭaḍakaḷa Guḍigaḷu*, Dharwar, Kannada Research Institute, 1960, no. 21. See S. Rajasekhara, *Early Chalukya Art at Aihoḷe*, p. 31.

201. A.M. Annigeri, ibid., no. 2, See S. Rajaśekhara, op. cit., p. 28.

202. C. Sivaramamurti, op. cit., p. 4.

it indicates, the sculptor's skill not only in carving figures but also in engraving words artistically. There were many other artists who were known to be masters of the crafts of sculpture and architecture. The practice of providing information regarding the origin and position of the artist along with his name was common in the case of the sculptures of the Hoysaḷa craftsmen.[203] At Beḷur there are several names of sculptors like Cāvana, Dāsoja, Padari Malloja, Cikkā, Hampā, Keñcā, Malliyannā, Masada and Nāgoja. The title of Dāsoja is given as *birūdaruvāri-gaṇḍalabaḍiva*, meaning "the smiter of the crowd of titled sculptors," while his son Cāvana is called *birudarūvāri-madanamaheśa* "a Śiva to cupids, the titled sculptors."[204] Other titles, meaning "champion over rival sculptors," "tiger amongst sculptors," "thunder-bolt to the mountains," "the rival titled sculptors," are also mentioned for extraordinary skilled sculptors.[205] Sculptors of this period not only mentioned their names and titles on their works but also put their signatures to them.[206]

Thus, it may be concluded that the sculptor played a creative role in the socio-economic life of the period under review. The highest expression of the sculptor emerged as sculpture which was thought "round" according to the Indian canons. His work, whether in stone, clay, wood or metal, was a mirror to the society of the period. The sculptor had a comprehensive knowledge of his craft, and he followed the iconographic texts. He was totally dedicated to his craft, and earned his livelihood by selling or merely fashioning the sculpture. A few scattered references to reputed individual sculptors of the period have been found available.

Engravers

The artisans who engraved inscriptions on stone and copper plates are known as *śilpin*s in the epigraphs of the early medieval period. The act of writing letters on

---

203. S. Settar, "Peregrination of Medieval Artists", *Journal of Indian History*, Golden Jubilee Volume, Trivandrum, 1977, pp. 419-36. This article is based on a section of Setter's dissertation. The Hoysaḷa Styles of Temple Architecture and Sculpture, XI to XIV centuries Cambridge University (unpublished), 1970.

204. C. Sivaramamurti, op. cit., pp. 4-5.

205. In Praise of Hoysaḷa Art, *Mārg*, XXXI, no. 1, December 1977, pp. 44ff.

206. See C. Sivaramamurti, op. cit., pp. 2ff.

stone, metal, terracotta and seal was called *utkīrṇana*.[207] Evidently, the custom of engraving inscriptions was in vogue before the early medieval period. It was a well-planned process performed by the state or some patrons of the time. The engraver had only to chisel the drafted matter given to him by the royal court or a patron.

As noted earlier, the term *śilpin* has a wide connotation. In general it denotes an artisan class which was engaged in working on stone or metal, or in building activity. However, in some of our epigraphs the term *śilpin* has been used specially for engravers. The Deopārā Inscription[208] of Vijayasena of the last quarter of the eleventh century CE uses it for engravers. The engraver Vāmana of the Sārnāth Inscription of Kumāradevī of the twelfth century CE is called a *śilpin*.[209] Similarly, Someśvara[210] and Mahīdhara[211] have been mentioned in the inscriptions of Bengal as *śilpins*. Some of the epigraphs of central India mention Citaku[212] and Palhaṇa[213] as reputed engravers of their time, and epithet *śilpin* has been used with their names.

MATERIAL USED BY THE ENGRAVERS

Engraving of inscription on stone can be traced back to thousands of years ago. The earliest available inscriptions belong to the Mauryan period, and were inscribed by the engravers under the royal patronage of Aśoka. The inscriptions are inscribed either on rocks or on pillars which were specially got erected by the king for the purpose. The engravers of ancient India had also the opportunity to show their skill of inscribing letters on metallic surfaces, bricks, shells, ivory plaques, tablets, earthen pots, etc.[214] It is noteworthy that in the period under

207. In the inscriptions the terms like *utkīrṇana, utkirnnā* and *utkīrnnam* are used for engraving. See *EI*, XXXIV, pp. 235ff, 152ff; XXXII, pp. 147ff; IV, pp. 199ff.

208. *EI*, I, p. 305f.

209. Ibid., IX, p. 319f.

210. Ibid., XIII, p. 42.

211. Ibid., XIV, p. 323.

212. Mirashi, *CII*, IV, p. 557.

213. Ibid., p. 329.

214. For details see D.C. Sircar, *Indian Epigraphy*. pp. 70ff.

study, engraving was done not only by the *śilpin*s but also by other classes of artisans and craftsmen.

Metal engravers used copper, gold, silver, bronze and iron for inscribing the texts going with the grants made by kings and subordinate rulers. Among metals, copper was the most popular material for purposes of engraving. Official donee title deeds called *tāmra-patras*, *tāmra-śāsanas*, *tāmra*, etc.,[215] were frequently engraved on copper.

The word *śāsana* meant *rājaśāsana* (royal charter), and *tāmra-śāsana* denoted a royal charter graved on copper.[216] Royal charters or *rājaśāsana* may be classified as *dāna-śāsana* (recording gifts); *prāsāda-śāsana*s (recording various kinds of favours); and *jaya-patra*s declaring the victory of one of the parties in a dispute.[217] A *tāmra-śāsana* was sometimes called *tāmra-paṭṭa*.[218] Again, sometimes *tāmra-śāsana*, the term denoting a deed or charter stood for the land granted by means of such deed or charter.[219] Land thus bestowed, and thus revenue-free was often called just *tāmra*,[220] or *śāsana*.[221] The word *śāsana* in this sense is widely used not only in the medieval records of Orissa but even in Modern Oriyā.[222] Revenue-free lands granted by the rulers in favour of persons, deities or religious establishments were usually endowed with a deed engraved on durable *tāmra-paṭṭa*, i.e. a plate (or plates) of copper. In the period under study, plates of copper were fashioned by metal workers for this purpose on a large scale.

Plates were also engraved by *pītalakāra*s (braziers),[223] *lohāra*s or *lohakāra*s

---

215. For details, see D.C. Sircar, op. cit., pp. 97ff.
216. Ibid., pp. 102ff.
217. "Vyavahārakhaṇḍa," *Kṛtyakalpataru*, pp. 157-60.
218. D.C. Sircar, *Select Inscriptions*, p. 352.
219. Ibid., p. 353.
220. *IHQ*, XIII, p. 240; *EI*, XXVIII, pp. 308, 311; IV, pp. 128 and 131.
221. N.G. Majumdar, *Inscriptions of Bengal*, III, p. 74, *EI*, XXIV, p. 298; XVII, p. 330.
222. D.C. Sircar, op. cit., p. 104.
223. *EI*, XXXII, pp. 123-25; Ibid., IV, pp. 153-70.

(blacksmiths),[224] *suvarṇakāras* or *sunāras, hemakāras* (goldsmiths),[225] *rūpakāras,*[226] *sthapatis,*[227] *śilpins* or *vijñānins* or *vijñānikas* (sculptors)[228] and *sūtradhāras.*[229] It is interesting to note that the work of engraving was not confined to only these artisans, who probably belonged to the lower class of the society. The people of upper classes also engraved some copper-plates. We find mentions of brāhmaṇas,[230] kṣatriyas[231] and kāyasthas[232] as having engraved on copper plates. It is clear that engraving on plates was neither done by a particular caste nor as a hereditary profession.

It seems that some goldsmiths were engravers by profession, and they enjoyed high status in the society. Kaṭṭaya was a foremost goldsmith, who engraved the Masulipaṭam Plates of Vijayāditya III of CE 844-88.[233] Sedhaka, who ornately engraved the Pratihāra Grant Plate of Naravarman of CE 1240,[234] was a goldsmith. Another engraver Kāmadeva, who engraved the Nāga inscription,[235] calls himself an active goldsmith. We also have an account of a goldsmith who engraved the Koṭṭayam Plate of Vīra-Rāghava[236] and with whose signature the inscription closes. This artisan boasts of his title *Śeramāṉlokapperundattān,* meaning "the great goldsmith of the world." Apparently, goldsmiths had an economically sound position in the society. They were jewellers and master-craftsmen who often employed junior craftsmen to produce separate sections of inscription which were assembled into the total engraving.

---

224. Ibid., IV, pp. 97-129.
225. Ibid., XXX, pp. 143-52; Ibid., XXX, pp. 237-42. For these engravers, IA, XVII, pp. 227, 230, 236 and 314.
226. *EI,* XXXII, pp. 139-56.
227. Ibid., IV, pp. 221-25.
228. Ibid., XXVIII, pp. 312ff; *IA,* XVII, p. 234; XVI, p. 208.
229. *IA,* XV, p. 360; *EI,* XXXIII, pp. 31-36; Ibid., II, pp. 40ff.
230. *EI,* XIX, pp. 69-75; *JAOS,* VII, p. 24.
231. Ibid., XXXIV, pp. 31-32; Ibid., XXVIII, pp. 1-11.
232. *EI,* XXI, pp. 41-50.
233. Ibid., V, pp. 122-26.
234. *EI,* XXX, pp. 143-52.
235. Ibid., XXX, pp. 237-42.
236. Ibid., IV, pp. 290-97.

PURPOSE OF ENGRAVING

The epigraphs engraved by *śilpins* in the period under study record variously the grant of a village (or villages) to brāhmaṇas or in favour of some deity; construction or renovation of a temple; installation of the image of a deity; provision for the burning of a lamp in a temple; endowments for the benefit of monks; execution of works of public welfare like digging of tanks, building of religious colleges and dwelling places for monks, etc.

NAMES AND THE GENEALOGY OF ENGRAVERS

A large number of inscriptions of our period clearly mention in the end of the record the names of the engravers, their genealogy, their caste and their village. These artisans (*śilpins*) were protected by the royal authority. They engraved their orders with the help of chisel and hammer. They were proficient in the art of chiselling letters on the given material. It is obvious that an engraving was accomplished not by the engraver alone, but jointly by the executor (*dūtaka, dūtak*) the author, the writer or scribe, and the engraver. For example, Paṇḍita Śūdraga was the author of the Paldi Inscription of Guhila Arisiṁha of CE 1116[237] which was written on the stone slabs by Paṇḍita Hariścandra, the scribe. Keśarin was the engraver of the same inscription. The installation and sanctifying ceremony were conducted by the learned astrologer Yaśodeva. Rājaputra Salakhaṇarā, son of Ūpalarā of the Solaṅkī race, was the officer-in-charge of all the concerned arrangements.

Sometimes the genealogy of the engravers was also given in eulogistic compositions. The engraver of the inscription of Deopārā of Vijayasena[238] gives a list of his forefathers. It was engraved by Rāṇaka Śūlapāṇi, the foremost of the guild of artists of Vārendra and a son of Bṛhaspati, grandson of Mānadāsa and great-grandson of Dharma. The edict (*śāsana*) of Vijayāditya III (CE 844-88)[239] was engraved by the foremost of goldsmiths, Kaṭṭaya, the son of Mādhava and grandson of Īśāna. Similarly, Tataṭa, the son of Subhaṭa and grandson of Bhogata, was the engraver of the Khalimpur Plate of Dharmapāladeva.[240]

237. *EI*, XXX, pt. 1, pp. 8-12.

238. *JASB*, 34, pt. 1, pp. 128-54.

239. *EI*, V, pp. 122-26.

240. Ibid., IV, pp. 243-54.

It is interesting to note that in some records the name of the engraver is not given, while his father's name is given. This means that some engravers incised inscriptions with ritual formalities or took their work in the spirit of an auspicious rite. Here it may also be assumed that in such instances the elders of the engravers were so famous in their profession, that the engraver of a particular inscription would not like to stand in competition with them in eminence by chiselling his own name. This care has been noted in an inscription engraved by the son of Lakṣmīdhara.[241]

We have references in which the object of the inscription was a ritual which was performed jointly by the donor or donors and the engraver. Donor Nandana was involved with his wife Rohiṇī and six sons in this activity.[242] The whole family composed the *praśasti,* which was engraved and set up at the temple by the engraver. Vāhari, kṣatriya by caste, was a learned mason, and his son named Vāhila of a place called Dhūlāvāsa engraved the *praśasti* in well-formed letters along with a beautiful circular diagram. Similar kind of statement has been noted elsewhere.[243] Kṣatriya Durgāditya, the son of Candra, engraved in an inscription of Svāmīrāja for the attainment of religious merit.

There is available evidence to the effect that in certain cases writing and engraving were done by the same person. Vinayacandra, son of Bhānucandra, was the writer and the engraver of the Ponnutūru Plates[244] of Gaṅga Sāmantavarman. Again, it was he who wrote and engraved the grants of the early Gaṅga kings of Kaliṅga till the 91st year of the Gaṅga era.[245]

There are accounts in which an inscription is engraved by two persons. The engravers named Ruvāri, Sovoja and Honnoja engraved an inscription of Cāḷukyas at Ablur.[246] A person named Siddha Sārasvata of the Kāśyapa appears to have

241. Bilaigaṛh Plates of Kaḷacuri Pṛthvīdeva of CE 1144, *EI*, XIX, pp. 195-96.

242. *EI*, XXXIV, Part 11, pp. 77-90.

243. *EI*, XXVIII, p. 11f.

244. *EI*, XXVI, pp. 216-20.

245. Ibid.

246. Ibid., V, pp. 213-31.

cut the stone for the same inscripition, where in the last verse it is stated that the honorofic dedication (*praśasti*) was incised by sculptor Hemadeva.[247]

Of course, there are also exceptions to the rule. Sometimes inscriptions are closed with verses of writers and engravers. One of the trends was to inscribe the names of the composer and the writer but not the name of the engraver. On the contrary in some cases the name of the engraver is given, but not that of the writer. In two plates of Govindacandra of Kanauj, the engraver Someka inscribes his name, but not the name of the writer.[248]

MASTERY IN ENGRAVING

The engravers had a sound knowledge of the script in which they inscribed a record. Specialization in engraving made the *śilpin*s prosperous. The engraver subscribed his name to inscriptions in more than one capacity. Thus, many plates of the Candella king Paramardideva have been engraved by Palhaṇa, who interestingly describes himself as a *pītalakāra* (brazier).[249] In the Semra Plate of CE 1165, and five later years, in the Icchawar Plates of CE 1170[250] represents himself as a *śilpin*,[251] and after two years more, in CE 1172, in the Mahobā Plate calls himself a *vijñānin*.[252] In the later Pachar Plates[253] of the Candella king he figures as a *vaidagdhi-viśvakarman* (master of art and craft). Clearly Palhaṇa was patronized by the Candella king Paramardideva, and his rank was promoted from time to time due to his increasing skill and experience. Presumably, Palhaṇa had reached a stage in his career when his knowledge was not confined to the bare technicalities of the craft, but it, under the patronage of the royal king, embraced a wider field, including the aesthetic aspect of the craft.

---

247. "Methi Inscription or Yādava Kṛṣna," *EI*, XXVIII, pp. 312ff.
248. *EI*, IV, pp. 97, 129.
249. *EI*, IV, pp. 153ff; *IA*, XXV, pp. 205ff; *EI*, XVI, pp. 9ff; X, pp. 44ff; XX, pp. 128-29.
250. See S.K. Mitra, *The Early Rulers of Khajurāho*, p. 181.
251. The epithet *śilpin* was probably not applied to a craftsman when he had become an expert in his line.
252. The *vijñānin* was apparently superior to the *śilpin*.
253. *EI*, X, pp. 44ff.

Boppanāga, son of the *akṣaśālikā* (goldsmith) Yotranāga, engraved two inscriptions of King Tivara.[254] Some plates of Jayarājas, are engraved by Acalasiṁha.[255] Similarly, Lokāyi is the engraver of the four plates of Rājarāja III,[256] and *śilpin* Nandabhadra of the two plates discovered from Pāṇḍukeśvara.[257] Again, Pāṇḍaya, who was proficient in the art of engraving, inscribed some Kaḷacūris inscriptions.[258]

Thus, it would appear that engravers had a command over the art of inscribing letters, and they mostly dominated the writers. Karṇabhadra was a highly intelligent, modest and good artist who engraved the copper plate of Vidyādeva of Kanauli.[259] This inscription was written by Nīlakaṇṭha at the command of *sūtradhāra* Sūraka. It reveals the domination of the engraver over the writer. The skill of an engraver named Nāthū is attested by an inscription which represents him as "clever in the art of engraving."[260]

Apparently *śilpins* were engravers belonging to many classes. Thus, engraving was not done by a particular professional caste. It is discovered that every *śilpin* does not have a full command over the art of chiselling words on a given material. Many inscriptions are not ornate, and many others are not inscribed neatly.

The social status and economic condition of the engravers are not well known to us because of the meagreness of information. In some of the inscriptions their names are incised at the end of the record. In some cases, the corners of the epigraphs have broken down, so that even the names of the engravers are lost.[261]

---

254. *EI*, XXXIV, pt. III, pp. 111-16; VII, pp. 106ff.
255. Ibid., XXXIV, pp. 28-31.
256. *EI*, XXXI, pt. VI, pp. 249-62.
257. Ibid., XXXI, pt. VI, pp. 277-98.
258. Ibid., XXXI, pt. V, pp. 227-32.
259. Ibid., XXI, pp. 148-53; See R.R. Mukherji and S.K. Maity, *Corpus of Bengal Inscriptions*, pp. 370-85.
260. *EI*, XXVI, pp. 159-65.
261. K.K. Thaplyal, *Inscriptions of the Maukharis, Later Guptas, Puspabhutis and Yaśovarman of Kanauj*, p. 9.

VILLAGES OF ENGRAVERS

Since ancient times the artisans and craftsmen had their own villages.[262] An important feature of the early medieval period is a considerable increase in the number of the artisan class. We learn from the inscriptions that those who engraved them in some cases belonged to the same village. Thus, engraver Puṣyāditya, son of Candrāditya, hailing from the village Poṣali, incised the Plate of Malupāla I,[263] and the artisans of Poṣali are known to have also engraved some other records of the Pāla kings.[264] Pṛthvīdeva, son of Haradeva, who engraved the plate of Vigrahapāla III, hailed from the village of Jinnidī.[265] The engraving of a Paramāra Inscription of CE 1059, was done by Āśarāja, son of Kāyastha Śrīdhara, who belonged to the village of Valabhi.[266] *Śilpin* Someśvara, the resident of Magadha, engraved the inscriptions of Bengal.[267] Kaṇṭācārya of Śrīpiṭhapuram engraved three inscriptions of Mallapadeva, a Cāḷukya ruler.[268]

The engravers hailed from the artisan class, and artisans and craftsmen were śūdras, that is from the lower level of the society. A large number of inscriptions chiselled by these people, among other things, mention their profession and community. The engravers are referred to variously as the *sūtradhāra*, *rūpakāra*s, *sthapati*s, *pītalakāra*s, *lohāra*s, *rītikāra*s, *akṣaśālika*s, *śilpin*s, *suvarṇakāra*s, *koṭṭali*s, *kolche*s, *takṣaṇ*s, *ācāri*s, artist, *sela-vadhakī*s, etc. K.K. Thaplayal states that the *sūtradhāra*s, those who engraved inscriptions, were generally śūdras.[269] It is seen that in inscribing an engraving separate communities were engaged was an official or a courtier of the king. Presumably the engraver had to write under his supervision, and was not free to express his own ideas.

---

262. *Jātaka*, II, 232; II, 156; III, 387, 408; *Mānasāra* and *Mayamata* also make provision for the artisan class; *Mānasāra*, 9, 72-78 and 116-27; *Mayamata*, 9, 88-96.

263. *EI*, XIX, pp. 1-9.

264. Ibid., XXVIII, pp. 47-59; II, pp. 57-58; XXIX, pp. 48ff.

265. Bangāon Plate of Vigrahapāla III, *IA*, XIV, pp. 166-68; XXI, pp. 97-101; *Gauḍalekhamālā*, pp. 123-26; See Mukharji and Maity, op. cit., pp. 192-97.

266. *EI*, XXXII, pp. 41-45.

267. Ibid., XIII, p. 42.

268. Ibid., IV, pp. 226-42.

269. K.K. Thaplyal, op. cit., p. 110.

3

Goldsmiths and Metal Workers

Goldsmiths

JEWELLERY and ornaments must have originated from man's innate desire to decorate his person. Objects taken from nature — flowers, wild berries, leaves and feathers were used for ornamentation. Golden ornaments and jewellery have also been discovered from Haṛappan culture sites.[1] Haṛappans were fond of ornaments, and their urge for wearing various kinds of ornaments was fulfilled by the professional class of ornament makers. Ornaments of *hiraṇya* (gold), such as *karṇaśobhana*[2] (ornament of ear), *niṣka*[3] (ornament for neck), *rukma*[4] (breast ornament) and *maṇi*[5] (jewel for neck) were used by the Vedic people.

In the cities the ornament-makers produced their goods on a large scale, and gained importance in the society. Mathurā during the period BCE 300 to CE 300 became an important centre of arts and crafts. The *suvarṇikas* (goldsmiths) are mentioned in the inscriptions of the period.[6] Different types of ornaments are profoundly represented in sculptures discovered at Mathurā.[7] Patañjali mentions four kinds of ornaments which could be made out of a lump of gold without disturbing the substance *rūchakas*, *kaṭakas*, *Svāstikas* and *kuṇḍalas*.[8] The literary

1. Bridget Allchin and Raymond Allchin, *The Rise of Civilization in India and Pakistan*, p. 222.
2. *Ṛ̥V*, VIII, 78, 3.
3. Ibid., II, 33, 10, etc.
4. Ibid., I, 66, 10, etc.
5. Ibid., I, 33, 8; I, 122, 14.
6. Luder's List, Nos. 95, 150, 168.
7. V.S. Agarwal, *JUPHS*, XXI-XIII.
8. *Māhabhāsya*, I, 1, 1, p. 7; 15f; See B.N. Puri, *India in the Time of Patañjali*, pp. 104-05 (*akṛtir anyā ca anyā ca bhavati dravyam punas tad eva*).

texts and archaeological sources of the Kuṣāṇa period also bear out the craftsmanship of goldsmiths and jewellers in making different kinds of ornaments. The skillness of goldsmiths is referred to in *Saundarānanda*.[9] Goldsmiths (*suvarṇakāras*)[10] and jewellers (*maṇikāras*)[11] as separate classes are frequently mentioned in the inscriptions of the Kuṣāṇas.

Vātsyāyana includes making of ornaments (*būṣaṇa–yojanā*) in the list of 64 arts (*aṅgavidyās*).[12] In the Gupta period ornament industry achieved considerable progress. Goldsmiths and jewellers produced different kinds of ornaments for the rich and the poor people. According to the texts of the Gupta period, they used emerald,[13] ruby,[14] pearls,[15] pearl oyster,[16] conch-shell,[17] coral[18] and small and big shell[19] for ornaments. Precious stones, *maṇi*,[20] such as diamond,[21] topaz,[22] sapphire[23] and lapis-lazuli[24] are mentioned by Kālidāsa. The jewellers and the goldsmiths acquired a sound economic position in the society. *Bṛhatsaṁhitā* mentions workers in gold, silver and base metals.[25] Daṇḍin speaks about a young maiden Gominī who bids her nurse to sell the bran of rice to the goldsmith in lieu

9. *Saundarānanda*, XV, pp. 68-69.
10. *EI*, X, p. 118; II, p. 2051; XIX, p. 68.
11. Ibid., I, p. 383.
12. See *BS*, I, 3, 16.
13. *Amara*, 9, 92, p. 221.
14. Ibid.
15. Ibid., *Ragh*, IV, 50.
16. Ibid., 9, 23, p. 65.
17 Ibid., 3, 133, p. 301; 9, 23, p. 65.
18. Ibid., 9. 93, p. 229.
19. Ibid., 9. 23, p. 65.
20. *Ragh*, III, 18; XIII, 53, 59; XVIII, 42; XIX, 45; *Kum*, VIII, 75.
21. *Ragh*, VI, 19.
22. Ibid., XVIII, 32.
23. Ibid., XIII, 54; XVI, 69; XVIII, 42; *Megh*, Sec. II, 16.
24. *Ṛtu*, Sec. II, 5; Legge, p. 79.
25. *BS*, XIII, 33; XV, 7.

of his cleaning her jewellery.[26] High degree of craftsmanship of the goldsmiths is attested by the gold and silver coins of the Gupta period.

GOLDSMITHS IN THE EARLY MEDIEVAL PERIOD

During the period under review texts like *Abhidhānacintāmaṇi,*[27] *Rāmacarita,*[28] *Triṣaṣṭiśalākāpuruṣacarita,*[29] *Samayamātṛkā,*[30] *Naiṣadhacarita,*[31] *Deśīnāmamālā*[32] and *Rājataraṅgiṇī*[33] frequently mention jewellery which was used by the kings, rich people and common people of the society. *Mānasollāsa,* and the works of Rājaśekhara elaborately explain the love of men and women for ornaments.[34] The importance of goldsmiths and jewellers in the society because of their craftsmanship in making ornaments is extensively described by contemporary writers. Moreover, the accounts of Muslim writers give us an idea of the ornaments which were worn by Indians in the period under study.

Contemporary inscriptions furnish valuable information about the ornaments of the period under study. The material used for making ornaments was chiefly gold, silver or precious stones. The art of making jewellery was highly developed and goldsmiths had attained a recognized economic position in the society. Our inscriptions refer to moulding of gold,[35] ear-ornament,[36] jewelled-girdle,[37] jewelled

---

26 D.K. Gupta, *Society and Culture in the Time of Daṇḍin,* p. 313.

27 *Ab Chin,* III, 313-29.

28. *Rāmacarita,* III, 33-34.

29. *Triṣaṣṭiśalākapuruṣacarita,* I, 229.

30. *Samayamātṛkā* VII, 14-17.

31. *Naiṣadh,* I, 38; VII, 80; IX, 104; X, 116; XV, 33.

32. *Deśīnāmamālā,* III, 8; I, 110; V, 1.

33. *RT,* III, IV, VII, etc.

34. *Mānasollāsa,* Ill, 7, 1042-47; 8, 1049-1129, II, 1163-1177; V, 1091 to 1098; 1104 to 1108.

35. *CII,* IV, Ins. nos. 103-04, verse 3.

36. Ibid., Ins. nos. 66 and 107.

37. Ibid., Ins. nos. 54, verse 4; Ins. no. 77, verse 11.

ear ornament,[38] jewels in crown,[39] bracelets,[40] necklaces,[41] pearl necklace[42] and golden jar.[43]

MATERIAL FOR ORNAMENTS

Gold and silver were the metals generally used by the goldsmiths for making different kinds of ornaments. Precious stones were embedded in metal to make ornaments more charming and costly. According to *Amarakośa*, gold, silver and other metals were mined from a mountain in north India.[44] *Mānasollāsa* provides names of the places from where gold and jewels were obtained.[45] A river in Kāmarūpa might have contained dusts of gold.[46] Sulaiman and Masudi had heard of the existence of gold and silver mines in the kingdom of the Gurjaras, but they thought that mines of these metals definitely existed in the kingdom of Rahma.[47] The gold coins of Cedi kings Gāṅgeyadeva[48] and Harṣa (CE 1089–1101), and certain other central Indian dynasties initiated gold coins,[49] which indicates that there certainly were some sources of gold. It appears from archaeological findings that Mayurabhañja was the region from where gold was obtained.[50] Thus it may be thought that gold and silver were mined on a small scale in some parts of north India, but they were of poor quality, and that mostly gold was procured from Mount Meru[51] in south India[52] and abroad. *Dohākośa* says in this context that the

38. Ibid., Ins. no. 93, verse 3.
39. Ibid., Ins. no. 54, verse 11.
40. Ibid., Ins. no. 114, verse 4.
41. Ibid., Appendix 3, verse 20.
42. Ibid., Ins. no. 45, verse 71; Ins. no. 93, verse 9; Ins no. 50, verse 9; Ins. no. 67, verse 51.
43. Ibid., Ins. no. 42, verse 21; Ins. no. 58, verse 16.
44. *Amara*, p. 41.
45. *Mānasollāsa*, III, pp. 91ff.
46. Sushil Malti Devi, *Economic Condition of Ancient India*, p. 120.
47. Ibid.
48. Cunningham, *CMI*, p. 72.
49. Ibid., pp. 72ff, 76, 85, 87.
50. Murray, *JRASB*, VI, 1940, pp. 82-83.
51. *Triṣaṣṭiśalākāpuruṣacarita*, II, p. 354.
52. According to Kauṭilya, during the Mauryan time, gold was imported from the south and abroad (II, xii). Even today gold is mined at Kolar in south India.

gold of Jāmbunada was of no use.[53] *Hudūd-e-Ālam* (CE 982-83) informs us that Arabia imported gold from Assam, and during our period, possibly goldsmiths brought it from their native land.[54]

It would appear that precious stones were obtained from the north Indian hills. In the *Śiśupālavadha,* Raivataka mountain is said to have been the abode of the moonstone.[55] Rājaśekhara describes the places from where these stones could be found. According to Kalhaṇa, precious stones were also obtained from the foothills of the Himalayas. According to the Buddhabhaṭṭa,[56] some precious stones were mined near Hazārībāgh in Bihar. The jewellers tested precious stones taking into account the mine, the size, the colour, and the merits and demerits concerned. *Mānasollāsa* mentions six semi-precious stones, namely *vimalaka, rājamaṇi, cankshell, brahmamaṇi,* jasper and *saśyaka.*[57] According to some Arab writers, precious and semi-precious stones were collected on a large scale, and exported to other countries. Ibn Khurdādbeh of the tenth century CE[58] speaks of stones like ruby, pearls, beryl, and corundum being exported from Malabar, some stones from Kannauj,[59] and rubies and diamonds from other parts of India exported on a large scale (*Hudūd-e-Ālam* of CE 982-83 and *Musair bin Muhalhil*).[60] It seems that some artisans and metal workers were in addition to their own occupation, engaged in supplying raw material for ornaments to the goldsmiths.

PROCESS OF ORNAMENT MAKING

Although our sources do not directly speak of the process of making ornament, yet it is surmisable that in our period the goldsmiths were well known for melting

53. *Dohākośa*, p. 341, 116.
54. V. Minorsky, *Hudūd-e-Ālam*, p. 86ff.
55. *Triṣaṣṭiśalākāpuruṣacarita*, I and II-IV, pp. 100, 111, 148, 149, 185, 123, 227, etc.
56. Finot Louis, *Les Lapidaires Indiens, Paris*, 1896, pp. 17, 42-43; See Motichandra, *Trade and Trade Routes in Ancient India*, pp. 208-09.
57. *Mānasollāsa*, II, 6, 17-20.
58. See Motichandra, op. cit., p. 203.
59. V. Minorsky, *Hudūd-e-Ālam*, p. 86ff.
60. Sayyad Suleman Nadvi, *Arab Aur Bhārat Ke Saṁbandha*, pp. 57-58.

and mixing of different metals. *Śukranītisāra*[61] and *Śaiva Tantra*[62] both employ the term *Dhātuvāda*, signifying combination and purification of metals. *Rudrayāmala-tantra* contains a separate chapter on metallurgy (*dhātumañjarī*).[63] Metal workers used special crucibles (*jāmāya-yantram*) for oxidizing metals.[64] After purification the gold or silver was shifted to the workshops of goldsmiths. They melted the metal and converted it into different shapes according to the taste and requirement of people. During the process precious stones were embedded in the metal to make the ornaments appear more beautiful.

Works of Goldsmiths

ORNAMENTS OF KINGS AND NOBLES

It is certain that some goldsmiths and jewellers were engaged in fulfilling the demands of the kings and nobles. They were patronized by the rulers, and their status in the society was high. It seems that during our period the jewellery of the kings and grandees was very extraordinary. Says Huien Tsang about the Harṣa times that garlands and tiaras with precious stones were their head-ornaments, and their bodies were adorned with rings, bracelets and necklaces.[65] Elsewhere it is said by him that Harṣa used necklaces of gems, ear-rings, bracelets, chaplets, neck-jewels, bright head jewels, and that in Prayāga conference he gave away all these as part of his renunciation.[66] The expert craftsmanship of the north Indian goldsmiths is also described by Ābu Zeid of the ninth century CE. He writes that the kings of the Indies were accustomed to wear ear-rings of precious red and green stones. According to him, pearls were held in the greatest esteem, and were keenly sought after.[67] There is yet another description: "The kings of India are accustomed to wearing ear-rings of precious stones mounted in gold. They

61. *Śukra*, IV, III. 145-49 and n.3.
62. Monier-Williams, op. cit., pp. 336.
63. See P.C. Ray, *History of Hindu Chemistry from the Earliest Times to the Middle of the 16th Century* CE, II, p. 126.
64. *Rasārṇava*, IV, 7; *Rasaratnasamuccaya*, X, 5, 6.
65. T. Watters, *On Yuan Chwang's Travel in India*, I, p. 151.
66. S. Beal, *Life of Hiuen Tsang*, p. 180.
67. See E. Renandot, *Ancient Accounts of India and China*, pp. 98-99.

also wear necklaces of great value, formed of the most precious red and green stones."[68] It is said that King Jaipal had one single necklace of the value of 200,000 *dīnāras* which was made of pearls and shining gems and rubies set in gold. His armymen also wore necklaces the prices of which in some instances estimated at 400,000 *dīnāras*.[69]

Rāmacarita of Sandhyākara Nandī,[70] among other things mentions court jewellery. He refers to anklet-bells, charming ornaments studded with diamonds, lapis-lazulis, pearls, emeralds, rubies and sapphires, and necklaces with central gems and pure pearls of round and big shape, which were used by princely families. King Ananta's crown had "a diadem adorned with five resplendent crescents."[71] *Agni Purāṇa* mentions no less than 33 kinds of gems, and analyses the virtues of diamonds, emeralds, rubies, pearls, sapphires and *vaidūryas*.[72] Apparently, extraordinarily precious jewellery was meant only for the kings and nobles. Inscriptions of the period refer to necklaces of pearls worn by the ladies of the royal blood.[73] According to the *Pṛthvīrāja-Vijaya*, Cāhamāna (Cauhān) king had a crown set with gems, a pearl necklace, ear-rings with pearls and pairs of armlets and *aṅgadas*.[74]

UTENSILS

Goldsmiths and silversmiths manufactured utensils of precious metals for persons connected with the royal court, and for the rich people. Kalhaṇa tells us that cups and saucers of gold and silver made by the goldsmiths were used by the kings and nobles.[75] Bhoja, the author of *Yuktikalpataru*, mentions drinking cups of gold, silver, crystal and glass.[76]

---

68. *HIED*, I, p. 11.
69. Ibid., II, p. 26.
70. *Rāmacarita*, Ill, 33-34.
71. *RT*, VII, 195.
72. *Agni Purāṇa*, CCXLVI, pp. 1f.
73. Naihāṭī Plates of Vallālsena, IB, III, pp. 68ff.
74. II, 17-30.
75. *RT*, II, p. 265.
76. Similar description is given by *Mānasollāsa* (III, *viṁśati*).

Articles of gold and silver were also used for decoration and some other purposes. Religious-minded people used them in temples and monasteries. Idols of gods and goddesses and the figures of their attendants were also made of gold and studded with precious and semi-precious stones. A golden statue of the Buddha "of the same height as the king himself" was made by goldsmiths, during the Harṣa time.[77] *Rājataraṅgiṇī* mentions idols of gold and silver decorated with precious stones preserved in the temples of Kashmir.[78] The writer of *Tabaqāt-i-Nasirī* informs us of five idols of gold in a temple of Mathurā, five *gaẓa* in height, the eyes of one of which were formed of rubies, and of another of sapphires.[79] The same writer mentions numerous idols of gold and silver, and one very large golden idol in a temple in Kāmarūpa which exceeded two or three thousand *miśkal*s in weight.[80] The high order of craftsmanship of the goldsmiths of our period is, as is seen above, taken notice of by Muslim writers. It is stated elsewhere[81] that a hundred idols of gold and silver, and one gold image weighing one million *miśkal*s were plundered by Sultān Mahmūd from the fort of Bhīma. A stone inscriprtion of Dhaṅga refers to a *liṅga* of emerald, which was erected by King Dhaṅga.[82]

ENGRAVING

Some goldsmiths engraved on copper plates which were issued by the rulers. There are numerous copper-plate grants carrying the names of the *suvarṇakāra*s by whom the engraving was done.[83]

As we have got references that those who worked on precious metals and jewels do not seem to have been always honest.[84] *Śukranītisāra* provides methods

---

77. Beal, *Si-yu-ki*, p. 218.
78. *RT*, VI, 1083, 1091; See Bamzai, *A History of Kashmir*, p. 221.
79. *Tabaqāt-i-Nasīrī of Minhāz*, p. 85.
80. Ibid., p. 564; *HIED*, II, p. 312.
81. *HIED*, III, p. 63.
82. *EI*, I, p. 137.
83. *EI*, XXX, pp. 143-52; Ibid., XXX, pp. 237-42; ibid, V, pp. 122-26; Ibid., IV, pp. 290-97; for details, see the "Engravers" above.
84. *Triṣaṣṭiśalākā*, I and II-V, pp. 100,111, 148-49, 185, 227, etc.

of testing the purity of metals and jewels.[85] It reveals that it was because of the dishonesty of artisans and manufacture by them of artificial jewels that the state codified laws against them. Similar assertions about their mischief of making artificial ornaments and jewellery are also furnished by other texts.[86] *Ratnaparīkṣā* is known to have helped the intending purchasers to distinguish between the pure and the impure metals and jewels.[87] This may lead one to suppose that in our period the purchasers must have been misguided in procuring genuine metals and jewels for their use. Unethical activities cost them their social status in the society. No wonder that the attitude of the Smṛtis toward *suvarṇakāra*s was much the same as toward the śūdras. Manu, Yājñavalkya, and Śaṅkha quoted by Aparārka (CE 1100-30) and Bhavadeva and Hemādri place them on a level with *karmakāra*s, *niṣāda*s, washermen, actors, *kaivartta*s, tailors, *meda*s and *bhīla*s.[88] The main reason for assigning them to the lowest class, was theft of gold.[89]

Thus during the period under study the urge of the north Indian people for wearing different kinds of ornaments was fulfilled by the professional class of goldsmiths. Terms like *suvarṇakāra*, *sauvarṇika* and *maṇikāra* are used in our sources alike for the goldsmith and the jeweller. Different kinds of ornaments of various metals and materials used on every part of the body are described in our literary and epigraphical sources. Some more proficient goldsmiths and jewellers satisfied the demand of the kings and nobles and were patronized by them. Utensils, engravings and decorations by gold and silver objects were also prepared by the goldsmiths. Economically, the goldsmith class was quite sound, for it satisfied a real and widely-felt need of the society.

Metal Workers

The growth and development of a civilization directly depends upon its natural resources. Industrial workers utilize these resources for productive purposes, and thereby play an important role in the growth of a country's economy. Metal,

85. *Śukra*, IV, ii, 79-129.
86. *Kuṭṭanīmatam*, p. 4, sl. 12, V, 717; *Kathākośaprakaraṇa*.
87. *Kuṭṭanīmatam*, V, 947; *Prabandhacintāmaṇi*, III, 110.
88. *HDS*, II, Pt. 1, p. 98.
89 B.P. Majumdar, *Socio-Economic History of Northern India*, p. 109.

which is a natural gift, has through the times, revolutionized the life of people in India, as also elsewhere. The growth of agricultural products has also been based on new types of implements of metal. Metal workers have used different qualities of metal for different kinds of implements for productive purposes. The metals which were generally used for different purposes in India were gold (*hiraṇya*), silver (*rajata*), copper (*tāmrāyas*), iron (*lohā*), lead (*śīsā*) and tin (*trapu*).

In the early medieval period metal work was pursued with as much success as in the preceding epoch. It may be mentioned here that the metallic art has a significant place among the sixty-four arts listed in the *Kāmasūtra*.[90] Mention is made by Varāhamihira in *Bṛhatsaṁhitā* of mines (*ākara*) and miners (*ākarika*) productive of the country's prosperity (*ākarāḍhyā*). He gives us a long list of metals (*dhātus*), including gold (*kāñcana, cāmīkara niṣka, suvarṇa, hiraṇya, hema, śātakumbha*), silver (*rajata, rūpya*), copper (*tāmra*), iron (*kṛṣṇāyasa, kṛṣṇa-lohā*), lead (*śīsaka*), bell metal (*kāṁsya*) and iron rust (*rītikā*).[91] Yuan Chwang's account tells us that gold, silver, bronze, etc. were very abundant in India in the early medieval period.[92] Among all the metals iron was the most useful in everyday life. However, not only iron, but also other metals are mentioned in the contemporary literature,[93] including copper, bell-metal (or brass), lead, tin, silver and gold.

It appears that during the period under survey the metal workers were highly proficient in melting, casting and other operations of metal industry. There are numerous copper-plate grants which can serve as evidence in this connection. Sometimes they mention the designation of the professionals in the metal working community, e.g., *ayaskāra*,[94] *tāmrakāra*,[95] *kāṁsyakāra*,[96] *pītalakāra*,[97] *pītalahāra*,[98]

90. *Kāmasūtra*, I, 3, 16.
91. *BS*, I, p. 73; XIX, 6, 17; XVI, 14, XL, 7; XLI, 4; XCIV, 20; CIV, 7, 8; V, 74; VII, 20; for detail see, Ajay Mitra Shastri, *India As Seen in the Bṛhatsaṁhitā of Varāhamihira*, pp. 227-36.
92. T. Watters, op. cit., vol. I, p. 178.
93. *Ab Ratna*, II, 15-19.
94. *IA*, XVII, 1888, p. 236; 1, 48, p. 227; 1, 19 (*lohakāra*); *EI*, IV, 97-129.
95. *EI*, IV, Semra Pls.
96. Ibid., XXIII, 229; *IA*, XLI, 20ff.
97. Ibid., IV, 153ff.
98. Ibid., XXXII, 123-25; IV, 153-70.

and *suvarṇakāra*.[99] On the basis of the five inscriptions of Paramardideva, it may be deduced that the engraver Palhaṇa got a gradual promotion from the position of the *pītalakāra* to that of the *śilpin*, the *vijñānin* and then to the *vaidagdhi*.[100] Evidently, this marks the growth of the craftsman in his professional skill. Sometimes *dhūrin* and *cūḍāmaṇi* ranks were also given to metal workers.[101] The terms *lohakāra, suvarṇakāra,* etc. are described in the work of Rajaśekhara.[102] *Bṛhaddharma Purāṇa* also refers to *karmakāras* and *kāṁsyakāras*.[103]

A few sculptural representations of the period also support the social importance of the metal workers. A relief on the back of the Mīrā Temple at Āhāri depicting blacksmiths at work is a remarkable illustration.[104]

SOURCES OF RAW MATERIAL FOR THE METAL WORKERS

There are two terms, viz., *ākara*,[105] and *khani*[106] which have been used in literature for mines. Both terms also occur in the inscriptions.[107] According to *Rājataraṅgiṇī*, earth and mountains and rocks are the sources from where minerals and jewels are extracted.[108] Medhātithi takes the term *ākarakarmānta* to mean "places where gold, silver and other precious metals are dug out." *Amarakośa* mentions among others, the names of the following metals and minerals found in a mountain : *suvarṇa, raupya, tāmra, hārītaka, manassila, śīsā, lohā, vanda, hiṅgula, gandhaka* and others. He uses the term *khani* for mining of minerals.[109] The author does not mention the exact name of the mountain from where the process of mining was done.

99. Ibid., XXX, 143ff; Ibid., 237-42; V, 122-26; *IA*, XLI, 20ff.
100. See S.K. Mitra, *The Early Rulers of Khajurāho*, p. 181.
101. *EI*, I, no. 16.
102. *Kāv*, p. 35.
103. R.C. Majumdar, *History of Bengal*, 1, pp. 568-69.
104. Quoted by B.N. Sharma, *Social and Cultural History of Northern India*, Pl. XXVIII, fig. 1., R.C. Agarwala, *Arts Asiatiques*, XI, 22, pp. 63-64, figs. 4 and 7.
105. See Monier-Williams, *A Sanskrit–English Dictionary*, pp. 33ff.
106. *Ab Chin* IV, 102.
107. *EI*, XX, No. 148, 11, 17-19.
108. *RT*, IV, 39-41.
109. *Amara*, pp. 41-42.

It appears that sometimes mining was a state monopoly. *Rājataraṅgiṇī* tells us of copper deposits discovered in Kashmir and captured by the ruling king.[110] However, in the area which was donated by the king to the brāhmaṇas, the donees had the right over the mineral wealth. Thus metal workers obtained their raw material from *khani* or *ākara* which were either under the control of the state or individual citizens. The process of mining was done by the professional workers, and terms like *khanaka* (a digger[111] or miner),[112] *khanakī* (a female digger)[113] and *khanitra* (an instrument for digging, a spade or a shovel)[114] have been used in the literary sources. *Ākarādhikārapuruṣa* was the officer-in-charge of mines.[115]

INDUSTRIAL CENTRES

It is important to note that certain centres of metal industry in India were famous in the early medieval period. From the synonyms given in *Abhidhānaratnamālā* we learn that Saurāṣṭra was famous for bell metal, while Vaṅga was well known for tin, industry.[116] Manufacturing of swords is mentioned in the *Agni Purāṇa*,[117] along with the distinctive qualities of the products. The centres of this industry were : Khatikhattara and Ṛṣika (unidentified), Sūrpāraka (Sopārā), Vaṅga (East Bengal), and Aṅga (Monghyr and Bhagalpur districts). Ibn Haukal[118] mentions the city of Debal in Sindh as famous for the manufacture of swords.

VARIETIES OF METALS

There were craftsmen proficient in melting metals. The traditional experience of craftsmen in this art served as the basis for advances in metallurgy during our

---

110. *RT*, IV, 161, 615, 617.
111. *Śukra*, 11, vol.; Cf. B.K. Sirkar, *Hindu Sociology*, 11, Ch. ii, p. 84; Monier-Williams, op. cit., p. 336.
112. Monier-Williams, op. cit., p. 336.
113. Pāṇini, 111, 1,145.
114. Ibid., 111.2.184; *Manu* (see Monier-Williams, p. 336); *Rāmāyaṇa*, L. 40. 27.
115. R.S. Tripathi, *History of Kannauj*, p. 343.
116. *Ab Ratna*, 11, 15f.
117. CCXLV, 21f.
118. *HIED*, 1, 37.

period. Hindu alchemists could extract zinc from calamine.[119] *Kāṁsya* was made by melting together eight parts of copper and two parts of tin. *Vartaloham* was produced from *kāṁsya*, copper, brass, iron and lead. *Rasaratnasamuccaya* describes the method of preparing alloys like bell-metal and *vartaloham*.[120] The Bhatera Copper-plate of Govindakeśava mentions the name of one Govinda, who used to make bell-metal.[121]

The use of gold and mercury for medical purposes has been known to the Indians since ancient times. The *Śukranītisāra*[122] and the *Śaiva Tantra* have the term *Dhātuvāda*, signifying the science of combination and purification of metals.[123] It appears from *Rasārṇava*[124] that chloride of mercury was used at that time. According to P.C. Ray,[125] the chlorides of mercury has been used medicinally since the twelfth century. The Tantras and the Nātha *yogīs* knew and popularised the use of mercury. Although, preparation of mercury was an intricate process, yet it was made by some workers for special purposes. The famous physician Cakrapāṇi of the eleventh century CE knew the use of black sulphide of mercury for curing certain disease.[126]

Other metals like sulphur, alum, silver, tin and lead could also be utilised after purification.[127] Three varieties of mica, viz. *piṇākam*, *nāga mandukam*, and *vajram*, are mentioned in *Rasaratnasamuccaya*.[128] Sulphide of mercury constitutes the main ingredient of another preparation called *Rasāmṛta Cūrṇa*. For this, one part of sulphur and half its weight of mercury are to be rubbed together.[129]

119. *Rasaratnasamuccaya*, V, 205 and 212-16, quoted in P.C. Ray, *History of Hindu Chemistry from the Earliest Times to the Middle of the 16th Century* CE, vol. 11, pp. 17, 18, 22.

120. Ibid., 1, p. 114.

121. B.P. Mazumdar, op. cit., p. 202.

122. *Śukra*, IV, 111, 145-49, fn. 3.

123. Monier-Williams, p. 336.

124. *Rasārṇava*, XI, 24.

125. P.C. Ray, 1, p. 250.

126. B.P. Mazumdar, p. 203.

127. *Rasarantnasmuccya*, III. 13-15, 24-25, 59; V, 32-34, 154-56, 176-79; *Rasaprakāśasudhākara*, Chap. 10,

128. *Rasaratnasamuccaya*, II, 5, 14.

129. Ibid.

Cakrapāṇi speaks of some compounds of silver.[130] The various methods of preparing compounds used in our period clearly indicate that the metal workers of the time knew well how to purify metals and mix them.

PROCESS OF MELTING

Metal workers used crucibles (*jāmāya-yantrams*)[131] for smelting gold, silver, copper and other metals. *Rudrayāmala-tantra* contains a separate chapter on metallurgy (*Dhātumañjarī*).[132] According to *Rasaratnasamuccaya*, crucibles were used for manufacturing swords and water vessels from iron.[133] Regarding the ingredients required for crucibles Vāgbhaṭa recommends that "the earth which is heavy and of a pale colour, sugar or earth from an anthill or earth which has been mixed with burnt husks of paddy, fibres of hemp plant, charcoal and horse-dung pounded in an iron mortar, and rust of iron are to be recommended for preparing crucibles.[134] Different kinds of crucibles were used for different chemical operations. *Vṛntaka*[135] crucible, which was in the shape of a brinjal (*Solanum melongena*) and had attached to it a tabular shape expanding towards its mouth like the flower of *dhatūrā* (*Stramonium*) and either 12 or 8 digits in length, was used for extracting the essence of calamine and other readily fusible minerals. *Rasaratnasamuccya* elaborately describes the ingredients for the respective crucibles which were used for the preparation of metals, salts, oils, alkalies, fats, urines, acids, and poisons.

IRON: ITS UTILITY AND IMPORTANCE

The process of purifying iron is elaborately discussed in contemporary literature. The Kashmir manuscript of C. Vrinda (*c.* CE 900) prescribes that iron be first lighted, and then "macerated in the juice of the *Emblic myrobalan* and *Trewia nudiflora* and exposed to the sun, and again macerated in the juice of certain

---

130. Ibid., p. 111.
131. *Rasāraṇava*, IV, 7.
132. See P.C. Ray, op. cit., 11, p. 126.
133. *Rasaratnasamuccya*, X, 5, 6.
134. *Vāgabhaṭa*. See P.C. Ray, op. cit., p. 191. See B.P. Mazumdar, op. cit., p. 198.
135. P.C. Ray, op. cit., p. 191.

other plants and then rubbed in a mortar." Cakrapāṇi mentions a better method of purifying iron. He suggests after a bar of iron is rubbed with the impalpable powder and the iron be heated to the fusion point and plunged into a decoction of *Myrobalans*, and roasted repeatedly in a crucible.[136] P.C. Ray thoroughly discussed the process of purifying iron.[137] The author of the *Rasaratnasamuccaya*,[138] prescribes his own method of purifying iron. According to him, a piece of iron should be rubbed with cinnabar weighing 1/20th of the weight of that iron, lemon juice and sour gruel, and roasted in a covered crucible forty times. It is curious to note that probably the greatest achievement of the metal workers (*lohāras*) was to have set up the famous iron pillar at Dhāra, the capital of Paramāras. Though now broken into three pieces, the length of the original pillar at the time of its installation was only a little short of 50 ft, thus making it the tallest of its kind in world.[139]

It is interesting to note that during the period under survey iron was used in building temples. Indian engineers used iron beams for strengthening temple roofs. Utbi[140] mentions in his work that on both sides of the city of Mathurā there were a thousand houses to which ideal temples were attached, all strengthened from top to bottom by rivets of iron. Craftsmen also manufactured iron beams. About 240 beams ranging up to 17 ft long and up to 6" by 4" or 5" in their section were used in the Gundichabari temple at Purī.[141] Graves gives a detailed account of these beams. As many as 95 beams were fixed at the lintels of doors and 114 below the temple. Iron beams are also used in the Koṇārka temple. Stirling[142] counted 9 beams in 1824 and Graves 29 beams. Indian engineers manufactured these big iron beams by welding. Whole of groups metal workers were engaged

---

136. P.C. Ray, op. cit., pp. 62-63.
137. Ibid., pp. 59 and 60.
138. *Rasaratnasamuccaya*, V, 113-14.
139. Henry Cousens, "The Iron Pillar at Dhāra", *ASI*, 1902-03, pp. 205-12, pl. XXXI; *Progress Report of the Archaeology Survey Western Circle*, 1904, p. 19.
140. *HIED*, 11.44.
141. Graves in *Journal Iron and Steel Institute* (1912) LXXXV, no. 1, pp. 200-02; See B.P. Mazumdar, op. cit., p. 197.
142. *Asiatic Researches*, XV, p. 330.

in this profession. The largest beam found by Graves was 35 ft long and 7" to 7½" square, and weighing 6000 lbs.[143] About these long and heavy beams Percy Brown[144] remarks:

> The larger ones were evidently produced by welding together a number of "blooms" of wrought iron by means of a hammer. However, this process of forging of beams seems to have been known only to Orissa.

QUALITY OF IRON

It has been observed that iron implements were made from various qualities of iron. *Rasaratnasamuccaya*[145] describes the characteristics of each quality of iron. *Muṇḍa* (cast iron) has been classified like this : *mr̥du* (easily malleable but unbreakable and glossy); *kuṇṭha* (expanding very little after hammering); and *kadara* (breakable). Six varieties of *tīkṣṇa* (steel) were used: *khara, sara, hr̥nnāla, tarabhaṭṭa, vajira,* and *kālālauha*. White swords were manufactured from the best quality of steel. Bhoja puts the relative quality of the following grades of iron thus: *krauñca* iron twice better than *sāmānya* iron, *kaliṅga* eight times better than *krauñca, bhadrā* hundred times better than *kaliṅga, vajra* hundred times better than *bhadrā, pandi* a hundred times better than *vajra, niraṅga* ten times better than *pandi*, and lastly, *kaṇṭha* a million times better than *niraṅga*. These gradations of iron obviously refer to pig, cast and wrought iron. Since so many different varieties of iron were there, the cost and demand of an implement depended on its variety and the technology involved in its manufacture. Only skilled workmen used the best quality of iron or steel for manufacturing costly implements. Other varieties of iron were: *bhrāmaka* (iron which moved all other iron); *cumvaka* and *karṣaka* (magnetic iron); *drāvaka* (iron which easily melted); *romakāntā* (iron which when burnt shot hair-like flaments). Artisans and craftsmen used iron crucibles in producing iron objects. Literary sources largely agree that the manufacture of iron and steel had reached a high stage of development in northern India in our period.

---

143. B.P. Mazumdar, op. cit.

144. Parcy Brown, *Indian Architecture (Buddhist and Hindu)*, p. 127.

145. *Rasaratnasamuccaya*, V, verses 71-72.

Armoury

The history of ancient India is one of almost continuous warfare, broken by occasional periods of short-lived peace. The doctrine of Maṇḍala, which epitomises the ancient conception of inter-statal relations, is essentially a doctrine of strife and struggle. No wonder that dangerous weapons and implements were used on a large scale. Defensive weapons were used for two purposes: one, in pursuit of the human instinct of self-preservation, and the other, for self-expansion.

It is clear that armourers fashioned metal implements for defence purposes. Daṇḍin, elaborately describes the various kinds of weapons and armours. He broadly divided them into four categories, namely, *yantras*, mechanical weapons; *āyudhas*, the weapons proper; *āvaraṇas*, weapons of defence; and *upakaraṇas*, other accoutrements of war.[146] Metal was used in almost in all implements. Skilled workmen and artisans fashioned weapons through metal industry. Muslim historians of the early medieval times also mention weapons of war like arrow-heads and swords. Al-Beruni refers to the makers of arrows, spear-points, swords and knives in northern India.[147] The author of the *Śukranītisāra* represents those who could make light machines, arrows, cannon-balls, swords, and bags and quivers as useful servants of the king.[148] Contemporary literature and inscriptions of our period furnish abundant evidence to the effect that weapons industry was directly under the royal court.

It seems that there was a regular science of weapons, mastery in which must have been considered a great qualification for administrator as well as warriors. About this specific reference are available in the Koni Inscription of Pr̥thvīdeva II which speaks of the 36 sciences of weapons (*śatatriṁśa śāstravidyā*).[149] Worship of various types of weapons is described in the *Kāvyamīmāṁsā* of Rājaśekhara.[150] The author tells us that weapons were worshipped on the auspicious day of *Mahānavmī*. It may be assumed that the rulers were interested in manufacture of

146. D.K. Gupta, *Society and Culture in the time of Daṇḍin*, p. 188.
147. E.C. Sachau, *Al-Beruni's India*, 1, p. 61.
148. *Śukra*, 11, 196-97.
149. *CII*, Ins. no. 90, verse 9.
150. *Kāv*, p. 101.

various kinds of defence weapons in order to perpetuate their rule. *Yantras* installed in a fortress and used for throwing stones were used in medieval India.[151] Such was the efficiency of these catapults, that Bhoja remarked humorously that they could do everything that was possible to imagine, and could even make a person dance or take part in a drama.[152]

SWORDS

Some metal workers were involved only in manufacturing different kinds of swords in northern India during our period. They had their specialization in this occupation. Possibly, they worked for the kings and made swords for soldiers according to their demand. The sword was the most important among the weapons, and was known as *asi* or *śṛgarbha* (the source of royal fortune).[153]

A large number of inscriptions of the Kaḷacuris refer to the use of sword. The terms used for sword are *khaḍga*,[154] *kaukṣeya*,[155] *karavāla*,[156] *asidaṇḍa*,[157] *mistriṁśa*,[158] *kṛpāṇa*,[159] *maṇḍalāgra*[160] and *asi*.[161] The medieval writers thoroughly discuss the relative qualities of different kinds of swords. *Agni Purāṇa*[162] observes:

> Swords manufactured in Khaṭi or Khaṭṭara country are noted for their good appearance, those produced in Ṛṣika for their quickness in cutting things, those in Sūrpāraka for strength, those in Aṅga for sharpness, and those in Vaṅga for keenness and durability.

---

151. *Agni Purāṇa*, 241, 28; 249, 4; 252, 18; *RT*, VIII, 1677; *Samarāṅganasūtradhāra*, Chap. 31.
152. *Samarāṅganasūtradhāra*, vol. 1, p. 174.
153. The sword is also known as *asi* or *asilata; asi*: *ASK*, pp. 99, 101, 109, 207; *DKC*, pp. 90, 173, 206; *śrīgarbha*, *ASK*, p. 113.
154. *CII*, IV, Ins. nos. 45 verse 47; 56 verse 11; 67 verse 31; 88 verse 12.
155. Ibid., Ins. nos. 45, verse 60; 48, verse 25.
156. Ibid., Ins. nos. 45, verse 69; 60 verse 16; Appendix 3, verse 28.
157. Ibid., Ins. no. 46, verse 27.
158. Ibid., Ins. nos. 48, verse 20; 96 verse 11.
159. Ibid., Ins. nos. 96 verse 21; 107 verse 12.
160. Ibid., Ins. nos. 48 verse 23; Appendix 5, verse 23.
161. Ibid., Ins. nos. 48 verse 21, 24; Appendix 5 verse 25; 97 verse 11.
162. *Agni Purāṇa*, 245, 21-22.

The elaborate description of the manufacture of swords is given in *Śārṅgadharapaddhati*, according to which, light and sharp swords were made in Madhyamagrāma and Sahagrāma, and smooth sharp and faultless steel in the Cedi country.[163] The importance of white sword is given by Utbi.[164] He says that soldiers of Brāhmaṇapāla, son of Ānandapāla, used white swords. In the eleventh century Paramāra Bhoja[165] observes that the swords manufactured in Aṅga are dirty and blunt.[166] While those produced in Banāras and Saurāṣṭra are the best. Nizami, in his *Taj-ul-Maasir*,[167] gives a vivid picture of the Indian swords used by the soldiers of Gwalior. Apparently, the swords industries were located in different parts of northern India. Banāras, Magadha, Nepal, Saurāṣṭra, Kaliṅga, Aṅga, Vaṅga, Sūrapāraka, Videha, Khaṭi-Khaṭṭara, Ṛṣika, Madhyamagrāma, Cedideśa, Sahagrāma and Kāliñjar[168] were famous centres of manufacture of different qualities of swords. In this industry organized and occupational blacksmiths earned their livelihood, their proficiency in their craft being the result of long experience of generations. Among weapons, swords were predominantly used by soldiers, and that is why literature of the early medieval period, particularly that dealing with wars, extensively mentions this weapon.

Contemporary inscriptions frequently refer to the use of metal and metal industry. Elaborate descriptions of the processes of metallurgy are given by the Kaḷacuri inscriptions.[169] In the period under study metal workers manufactured various kinds of implements, though the inscriptions deal only with the weapons of war. Kaḷacuri inscriptions refer to arrows,[170] swords,[171] spears,[172] battle-axes,[173]

---

163. *Śārṅgadharapaddhati*, verses 4677-78.
164. *HIED*, 11, p. 33.
165. *Yuktikalpataru*, p. 170.
166. Ibid.
167. HIED, p. 227.
168. *Śārṅgadharapaddhati*, verses 4672-79.
169. *CII*, IV, Ins. no. 50.
170. Ibid., Ins. nos. 67, 74 and 88.
171. Ibid., Ins. nos. 45, 67 and 88.
172. Ibid., Ins. nos. 60 and 67.
173. Ibid., Ins. no. 74.

discus,[174] noose,[175] and goad.[176] All of these tools were made of iron. Artisans and skilled workmen fashioned these metallic weapons, and a large amount of money was invested for their production.

Blacksmiths in the Village

The blacksmith was one of the most important and indispensable artisan belonging to the rural population. Making implements by heating iron in fire was one of the major processes followed by the smiths, and so they were often said to be "earning their livelihood by fire." Blacksmiths showed their skill in making agricultural implements of iron, namely spade, hoe, sickle, axe, ploughshare, chains, etc.[177] They also made iron rims and placed them on the wooden wheels of the bullock-carts. *Harṣacarita* refers to the blacksmiths (*vyokāras*) of a forest village who burned piles of wood for getting charcoal.[178] A Gāhaḍavāla land grant refers to already used charcoal in furnace for heating iron in the villages.[179] Village smiths also manufactured instruments for carpenters, gardeners and sculptors, and domestic articles for daily uses in the rural economy.[180]

UTENSILS

The metal workers manufactured utensils for domestic purposes on a large scale. Metal workers used different types of metals for making vessels of different shapes. A long list of vessels used in the period is furnished by Varāhamihira, mentioning the kind of metal of which each was made. Varāhamihira also refers to vessels[181]

---

174. Ibid., Ins. nos. 96 and 114.
175. Ibid., Ins. no. 67.
176. Ibid., ins. no. 65.
177. *BS*, V, 35; V, 28; X, 4; VI, 1; XVII, 13; LXXV, 29; V, 69; XCIV, 21; VIII, 3; V, 53; XVI, 12; See A.M. Shastri, op. cit., p. 307.
178. *Hcar*, pp. 212, 227; KP, VV, 109, 117, 118; *Sad*, 2, 173, 5.
179. *Hcar*, 228.
180. Quoted by A.K. Choudhary, *Early Medieval Village in North-Eastern India*, p. 197.
181. Many names are given to vessels (*bhājana* in LXXX, 26; *bhāṇḍa* in XXVIII. 5; XLI, 8; X, 10; LXXXVIII, 1; *pātra* in LII, 92; LXXVI, 2; XCII, 8; L, 18.

made of gold,[182] silver,[183] crystal,[184] earthenware,[185] iron,[186] and horns,[187] which were decorated with multi-coloured patterns (*citra-bhāṇḍa*).[188] Copper-vessels, being considered sacred[189] were used very commonly in Hindu religious ceremonies. It is supported by the archaeological finds at different places that copper bowls were used by Hindu monks.[190] The Edilpur Plate of Keśavasena mentions water-vessels of iron, possibly used by the poor people.[191] Vessels of precious metals like gold and silver were manufactured for the kings and nobles.[192] Thus, metal workers (*ayaskāra*s, *tāmrakāra*s, *kāṁsyakāra*s, and *suvarṇakāra*s) were proficient in the craft of making vessels, whereby they earned their livelihood.

Copper Workers

The mining of copper and other metals has already been discussed. There are scattered references to import of copper from other countries. The author of the *Rasaratnasamuccaya* tells us that superior quality of copper was brought from Nepal, and from the mines in Mleccha countries. During Marco Polo's time (*c.* 1293) Thānā port used to import copper.[193] It is difficult to say whether all copper was imported, but it may safely be assumed that the superior quality was imported. Copper was extracted from materials like blue vitriol and borax, as is made out in *Rasaratnasamuccaya*.[194] In this text the process of making copper is described and *mākṣika* has been identified with pyrites and *vimala*.[195] This process is also described

182. *BY*, XVII, 10.
183. Ibid., LXXX, 26.
184. *BS*, LXVII, 89; *YY*, V, 36.
185. Ibid., LII, 92; *BY*, XVII.
186. Ibid., XLI, 11; LXXVI, 12.
187. *BY*, IV, 22; *YY*, VII, 12.
188. *BS*, X, 10.
189. *Journal of Indian Art*, 111, no. 29, p. 29.
190. Sushil Malti Devi, op. cit., p. 112.
191. *IB*, 111, 123 and 118.
192. *RT*, VII, 265; *HIED*, 11, pp. 309ff.
193. *Marco Polo*, 11, 395.
194. *Rasaratnasamuccaya*, 11, 133-36.
195. P.C. Ray, op. cit., pp. 70, 84.

in *Rasaratnākara.*[196] The golden pyrite was available in Kannauj.[197] Sulphide and sulphate are two compounds of copper. The sulphide of copper could be prepared artificially by a process described thus: "Sulphur, copper and the pyrites are to be pounded together with mercury and subjected to roasting in a closed crucible, and the product thus obtained is to be administered with honey."[198] Cakrapāṇi also gives us the method of preparing powder of copper-compound.[199] The literary texts reveal that in northern India in our period different compounds of copper were prepared for special purposes. Specialized artisans sometimes extracted copper from other minerals.

Copper was used for making royal charters and coins. The business of engraving letters or royal orders on copper plates was a very highly technical one.[200] Most of the available land grants and royal orders of our period are issued on copper plates. The names of engravers or coppersmiths with their genealogy and professional achievements were mentioned on these plates. The importance of coppersmiths vis-à-vis blacksmith and goldsmith is made clear in *Amarakośa.*[201]

Metal Sculptors

It seems that some metal workers were sculptors or artists, and that they manufactured the sculptures of gold, silver, bronze and other metals. These images were valuable, usually portable, and consequently easily carried to far-off places. For this reason, they were more popular than massive sculptures of stone, clay, wood, etc. Metal sculptors made various types of sculptures based on mythology and folklore, according to the demand of people. These icons was mainly used for worship. The early medieval period texts like *Śukranītisāra* and *Mānasāra* describe in detail the technique and process of making sculptures in metal.

Varāhamihira mentions the material from which the images were fashioned, and furnishes examples of *sauvarṇī* (golden), *rajatamayī* (silver), *tāmramayī* (copper)

196. *Rasaratnākara,* 11, 35-36.
197. P.C. Ray, op. cit., *Sanskrit Texts,* p. 26.
198. P.C. Ray, op. cit., 1. 58.
199. Ibid., 1, p. 62.
200. *Supra,* Chap. Two.
201. *Amara,* 10, 8, p. 227.

sculptures.[202] According to Hieun Tsang, a golden sculpture of human size was established by Harṣa at Kannauj,[203] Golden images were made by some master-craftsmen for royal personages.

A Tibetan historian, Tāranāth, refers to "School of Ancient West" in his *History of Indian Buddhism*.[204] According to him, in the time of the King Śīla there lived an especially skilful delineator of gods in gold, *Śṛṅgadhara*. Born in Mārwāṛ, he left behind him paintings and master-pieces of sculpture.[205]

Tāranāth mentions two artists named Dhīmān and Viṭpāla, father and son respectively, who lived in Varendra (North Bengal) or Nalendra (Nālandā) during the time of Dharmapāla and Devapāla. Both these artists are stated to have produced many works in cast metal, as well as sculptures and paintings which resembled the works of the Nāgas. The father and son gave rise to a distinct school. Since the son lived in Bengal, the cast images of gods produced by his followers were called gods of the Eastern style, whatever may have been the birthplace of their actual designers.

A superior sculptor of eighth century CE, named Guggā, is mentioned in the inscription of a beautiful brass image of Gaṇeśa, recovered from Cambā in Himachal Pradesh.[206] There are three enshrined brass sculptures at the same site, two of which bear inscriptions similar to that on the Gaṇeśa. One represents the bull of Śiva and the other the goddess Lakṣmī Devī. Both were created by the artist Guggā. It is interesting to note that all the corpus of the four metal sculptures

---

202. *BS*, LIX, 4-5; A.M. Shastri, op. cit., p. 410.

203. Quoted by D.C. Bhattacharya and Devendra Handa (ed.), *Prācī Prabhā*, pp. 277-78.

204. Tāranāth, *History of Indian Buddhism*, written in CE 1608.

205. *Indian Antiquary*, vol. IV, 1875, p. 102.

206. J. Ph. Vogel, *Antiquities of Chamba State*, Part I, p. 143. See Pratapaditya Pal, "Munificent Monarch and a Superior Sculptor" (Eighth-Century Chamba), *Mārg*, XXXIX, no. 2, pp. 9-24. The dedicatory inscription on the base of the brass image of Gaṇeśa in essence reads thus:

"Oṁ, Adoration to Gaṇapati. Born in the lineage of Mushunasva and belonging to the Solar race, the great-grandson of Śrī Ādityavarmadeva, the grandson of Śrī Balavarmadeva, the son of Śrī Divākara-Varmadeva, the great king Śrī Meruvarman has caused this image of the god to be made by the workman Guggā."

bears the signature of a single artist (Guggā).[207] Clearly the master-sculptor Guggā was highly skilled in modelling animals and the human body on brass, and that is why he was patronized by the royal court.

There was an accidental discovery of a hoard of more than one hundred metal images from the old site of Aṅkoṭṭaka (the mound at Akoṭā village) on the other side of the Baroda railway line. The excavation has furnished an uncontroverted proof of the existence and prevalence of the "School of Ancient West" as described by Tāranāth. A few of these bronzes specifically refer to a Jaina monastery at Akoṭā (inscription on the image of Ādinātha). Probably these bronzes were kept in the Jaina temples at Akoṭā for veneration. Big bronzes of the Jaina *tīrthaṁkaras* have been discovered from Vasantagaṛh near Piṇḍwāṛā, and cast by the artist Śivanāga in Saṁvat year 744, i.e. CE 686. This affinity implied in the finds of the aforementioned two sites is continued by the artist up to *c.* eighth century CE. Three bronzes of standing *tīrthaṁkaras* are assignable to the same time.[208] In some images, serene and pleasant smile on the face is bewitching. It is surmised that the two sculptures belong to different styles, represented by the skill of different artists. For example, the Koṭyarka image is earlier and is executed by a superior artist,[209] and the other bronzes do not belong to the same style, and lack artistic beauty.[210]

The archaeological finds of numerous bronze and copper images of the Pāla period discovered in Bihar eloquently support the fine workmanship in metal sculpture. These images are of the Buddhist, the Brāhmaṇical and the Jaina divine personages found from Nālandā,[211] Kurkihāra,[212] and Candankeyārī,[213] along

207. Pratapaditya Pal, op. cit., pp. 9-24. The four brass sculptures are Gaṇeśa, Narasiṁha, Śakti Devī and Bull at Bharmaur, and bear technical similarities for all of them are sculptured by the same artist (Guggā).

208. U.P. Shah, *Bronze Hoard from Vasantgaṛh* (*Rajasthan*); *Lalit Kalā*, nos. 1-2, 1957), (Pl. LIV-b).

209. U.P. Shah, *JOI*, vol. 1, p. 72.

210. *Bulletin Museums Association*, vol. 1, no. 1, pl. LII.

211. *Catalogue of the Buddhist Sculptures in the Patna Museum*, pp. ii, 6lff.

212. Ibid., pp. ii, 37ff; *Patna Museum Guide*, pp. 35ff.

213. B.P. Sinha, *Bhāratīya Kalā ko Bihar kī Den*, pp. 28ff.

with furnaces and ovens. The metal images are also found containing inscriptions on their pedestals. The inscriptions are important in revealing the history of the images that is details regarding the person who set them up, the name of the sculptor, and that date of the inception of the image. The bronze image of Buddha in *dhyāna-mudrā*, on a double lotus pedestal, belonging to the ninth century CE and containing inscriptions on its back, has been preserved in the Nalanda Museum.[214] Another image of Buddha of the same period, containing an inscription has been preserved in the Kurkihar Museum.[215] The eequal account of bronzes Hindu divinities images are available in south India particularly during the period of colas. The dancing Śiva Nataraja image from Tamil Nadu of bronze, is a major attaraction of eleventh century and even today it has become a symbol of worship for music devotees. It is the rare example of the highness of the then wordwide famous craftsmanship of India art. The finest example of metal workers of eleventh century in which Kṛṣṇa subduring the nāga demon Kāliyā by dancing on its serpent hoods, moreover, in a metal sculpture the four-armed god Śiva appears together with Parvati is still being worshipped in the temples of south India.[216]

CASTING OF IMAGES

The glory of the metal workers of the period under review is recorded by contemporary commentators. The *Mānasāra* (a *śilpa* text) elaborately describes the method of casting images. In this text the role of sculptors in the process of casting of idols in wax (*madhucchiṣṭa-kriyā*) is described fully.[217] These artists are competent for all kinds of artistic work. In the bright or dark fortnight of all months, on an auspicious moment, or *lagna* meeting of *nakṣatra*s (planets) and *yoga* (conjunction), both the chief architect (*sthapati*) and the chief assistant (*sthāpaka*) should make the pit (for casting the image) with the usual incantations (*mantra*s). Then the artist (in this case, the sculptor) should besmear wax (over

214. No. 8445. See Bimal Bandayopadhyay, *Metal Sculptures of Eastern India*, p. 88.

215. No. 9632. See ibid., p. 93.

216. For detail of Michell, George, *Hindu Art and Architecture*, pp. 129-132.

217. Prof. P.K. Acharya has compiled and translated the *Mānasāra* text and the following extract will reveal the process as described in the 68th Chapter of the *Mānasāra*, entitled Madhūcchiṣṭavi-dhānam, or "The Lost Wax Method."

the idol) according to the rules of the science. The sculptor (*vardhakī*), at the command of the chief architect (*sthapati*), should think over (lit. meditate on) the correct image, and purify with the five powders (*pañca varras*) the idol to be cast in wax. The eyes (of the idol should be furnished with crystal and covered with the spider's net, the hands (arms) of the idol should be covered with a copper-leaf, and the ornaments should be fixed with a peg. Adorned with all ornaments the idol should be taken round the village and should be shown to the prospective worshippers. Then (i.e. if the idol is approved of) it should be taken into the studies of the artists, and the best artist should measure it along the length, height and width. However, if the master or the sculptor himself is not quite satisfied the measurement should be made again.

The twelfth-century work *Abhilāṣitārthacintāmaṇi* is a classical commentary on the subject of the artists or sculptors, and describes in detail the process of casting images in metal.[218] It describes the preparation of the model and its drying up, preparation of the crucible for the melting of the metal, melting of different metals, pouring in of the molten metal into the mould, the latter's removal, etc. Further, it lays down how the expert (artist) should prepare the image (i.e. the model), complete it with all the limbs, yellowish in colour, beautiful to look at, and with the weapons and arms as prescribed. After placing the wax tubes of the length of a *dhatūrā* flower on the back, on the neck or on the crown (of the image), (the artist) should besmear the image with refined clay. It is interesting that Al-Beruni[219] also refers to the images of gold, silver, and bronze. Thus, we can conclude that the art of preparing sculptures of metals was veritably a religious ritual for the metal workers or sculptors. The laws of the priest were imposed on them, and their role in the ritual activities was prescribed. C. Sivaramamurti observes:

> In the early period metal images were very carefully fashioned with all the details present in the wax model itself, and these were naturally imprinted in metal, and there was little finishing work after the casting. But in later times, as also in the present day, the image as cast was usually a rough one. The

---

218. S.K. Sarasvatī, "An Ancient Text on the Casting of Metal Images," *JISOA*, vol. IV, no. 2, pp. 140-44.

219. Sachau, *Al-Beruni's India*, pp. 120-21.

> final finishing touches were added at the end of the process, which involved so much of chiselling work that the result was almost a carved image rather than a cast one.[220]

In the foregoing pages a brief survey has been made of the highly technical skill and significant role of the metal workers during the early medieval period. They used various qualities of metals for preparing different kinds of implements for productive purposes. The sources of the period indicate that the metal workers collected the raw material from various places in north India. Then the workers in the industrial centres used different kinds of crucibles for smelting different metals like gold, silver, copper and iron. Then the process of purifying the metal was carried out in the laboratories. Iron workers used various qualities of iron, and were proficient in making different varieties of implements for use in cities and villages. Master-craftsmen used iron beams for strengthening temples on large scale. Some iron workers or armourers fashioned implements for defensive purposes on a large scale for maintenance and expansion of the rule of the king, by whom they were patronized or in whose state they lived. The armoury not only gave work to the metal workers on a massive scale, but also made them important in the eyes of the society. Some workers who sculptured on gold produced some very useful implements for domestic purposes. The copper workers of the period also had a marvellous mastery of their craft, and they fulfilled the demands of people. Some specialized artisans extracted copper from certain minerals in the laboratories. Some metal workers fashioned very artistic sculptures for religious purposes, and for other purposes. Thus, it is seen that the metal workers during the early medieval period were actively engaged in satisfying the needs and urges of people by producing implements scientifically and on a very massive scale. Their creative constituted a whole heritage to be bequeathed to the coming generations. Some books were also written during the period to enlighten the apprentices and the metal workers about the principles and methods to be followed in smelting metals and purifying them in order to produce precious sculptures and implements.

220. C. Sivaramamurti, *South Indian Bronzes*, p. 17.

4

Weavers

NEXT to food, the most required thing for human beings is cloth. Costume, whatever might have been its origin, provides a visible index of the homogeneity and the unity of a people. Ghurye opines, "Costume, and that too cut and sewn, appears in the history of culture much earlier than a house or any other attested item of higher culture."[1] It may be noted that people of the Indus Valley used different types of garments.[2] Archaeological remains of this culture vividly show that people used cotton.[3] In a few centuries the profession came to flourish on a large scale. During the Vedic period weaving was mostly done with wool, which was obtained from the Gāndhāran sheep,[4] though cotton was also used by these people. The *Yajurveda* refers to certain techniques of spinning and weaving.[5] Obviously, the craft of weaving was transmitted from father to son or from master-craftsman to his apprentices.

We notice that during the Mauryan period weavers made a considerable progress in their work. Bengal, Kāmarūpa, Magadha, Madurā, Aparānta, Kāśī, Kaliṅga, Vatsa and Mahiṣa were the main centres of textile industry, where people of the weaving profession worked collectively.[6] As mentioned in *Arthaśāstra*, the superintendent of weaving was called *sūtrādhyakṣa* and his job was to look after the weaving industry.[7] Both the literary and archaeological sources of the Kuṣāṇa

---

1. G.S. Ghurye, *Indian Costume*, p. 23.
2. For details see J. Marshall, *Mohenjo-daro and the Indus Civilization*, II, pp. 585-86.
3. R.S. Sharma, *Perspectives in Social and Economic History of Early India*, p. 112.
4. *Ṛ̥V*, I, 123, 7.
5. *YV*, 20, 43; *AV*, 6, 12, 2; 10, 7, 42.
6. *Kauṭilya*, II, 2.
7. See R.S. Sharma, op. cit., p. 130.

period in India indicate that weaving was a flourishing profession, and that Indian cloth had become a coveted article in international trade. At that time Vārāṇasī was an important centre of textile industry and dyeing, tailoring and washing were also done thereby a number of artisans and craftsmen,[8] who formed guilds.[9] The spindles excavated from some Kuṣāṇa sites such as Saikhan Ḍherī,[10] Taxila[11] and Hastināpur[12] indicate that the weavers used cotton, linen and jute.[13] In the Gupta period, weavers also manufactured silk garments on a large scale. Some of the weavers produced fine silk,[14] and then bleached[15] it. Some weavers specialized in producing warm clothes from wool and fur.[16] According to *Bṛhatsaṁhitā*, garments were made of various fabrics, such as *kārpāśika*[17] (cotton cloth), *aurṇika*[18] (cloth made from wool), *kṣauma*[19] (linen made from yarn of flax), and *dukūla*[20] (cloth made from fibres of the *dukūla* plant). Dyers dyed these clothes in different colours, and their profession was called *rāgayukti*.[21]

A convenient classification of work relating to fabrics can be made on the following basis: (a) skilled work of professional weavers and dyers who usually

---

8. Jātakas, I, 38, 80; IV, 453; VI, 542-43; *Milindapañho*, I, 2, p. 3; I, 33, p. 27; 4, p. 210.
9. *Nasik Inscription*, Luder's List, no. 1133.
10. *Ancient Pakistan*, p. 128.
11. J. Marshall, *Taxila*, II, p. 502.
12. *Ancient India*, nos. 10-11, p. 89.
13. G.L. Adhya, *Early Indian Economics*, p. 75; Kameshwar Prasad, *Cities, Crafts and Commerce under the Kuṣāṇas*, pp. 109-10.
14. *Amara*, 6, 113, p. 157.
15. Ibid., 3, 180, p. 313; 6, 113, p. 157.
16. Ibid., 6, 111, p. 157; 8, 55, p. 186. Various kinds of blankets were made of hair, *Amara*, 10, 107, p. 224; 6, 116, p. 158.
17. *BS*, XLVII, 72; XCIV, 15.
18. Ibid., XVI, 29; LXXXVI, 12; CIII, 12, 61; *BY*, XVIII, 9-10. Among woollen articles, blankets (*kambalas*) were manufactured on large scale *BS*, XLI, 8; XLVII, 50.
19. *BS*, XXVI, 6; XLVII, 50; LIII, 108; CIII, 61; *BY*, XVII, 8.
20. Ibid., XXVI, 6; XLVII, 50; LIII, 108; CIII, 61; According to V.S. Agarwal (NPP, no. 4, p. 313) the word *kula* marketed probably denoted cloth in folk language, and as it was in two folds it was called *dukūla*.
21. *BS*, XVI, 17.

worked close to large market towns; (b) work to produce articles of luxury made under court patronage or in the court tradition (c) folk embroidering; and (d) fabric used by the aboriginal tribes.[22] It is clear that textile industry provided occupation to various classes of craftsmen and artisans. The art of fine weaving, the complex process of bleaching and dyeing, and the arts of hand and loom embroidery, all these required highly skilled craftsmanship. The qualities of a skilled weaver were developed through apprenticeship, devotion to work and cooperative effort. It was because of the experience of many generations of the weavers that textile industry flourished in India and bore international reputation.

The Implements of the Weavers

The process of weaving cloth in the period under study was more or less similar to that which is followed these days in the handloom industry. In the villages and cities clearing and carding of cotton was done with the help of an instrument called *piñjana*.[23] "Spinning was done by spindles called *tarku* (*takalī*).[24] Weaving shuttles and looms were used for winding threads and weaving. *Trasara*[25] and *sūtraveṣṭana* are the terms used for shuttle. Among the weaver's instruments loom was the most important one. It was variously known as *tanta*,[26] *vemana*,[27] *vāṇī vāndaṇḍa*,[28] *vemā*[29] and *avapana*.[30] *Abhidhānacintāmaṇi* elaborately describes the workmanship of the weaver. According to it dampers stood for spinning and weaving as *prasevaka* (*āvapana*) did for the loom.[31] It uses the term *tantravāya* for the weaver.[32] The acts of weaving and interweaving are denoted by terms like

22. John Irwin, "Textile in Historical Perspective," *The Indian Experience*, ed. Ken Barrett and S. Sharma, pp. 178-79.
23. *Ab Chin*, III, 576.
24. Ibid., Ill, 575.
25. *Bālarāmāyaṇa*, III, 85.
26. *Jātaka*, I, 356.
27. *Vāj Saṁ*, XIX. 83; *Maitrāyaṇī Saṁhitā*, III.11.
28. *Ab Chin*, III, 577.
29. Ibid., III, 577.
30. Ibid., III, 576.
31. *Ab Chin*, III, 577.
32. Ibid., III, 576.

vyūti,[33] *vyūta*[34] and *syūta*.[35]

In some inscriptions also the Sanskrit term *tantravāya* has been used for the weaver,[36] and *dukūla* for garments.[37] In *Harivaṁśa*, a weaver and his wife have been denoted by the term *vemaka*.[38] There are words in *Uktivyaktiprakaraṇa* for carding, ginning,[39] and warping.[40] It would appear, however, that there was no marked development in weaving-implements from later Vedic period to the period under review.[41] There is no reference to *carkhā* or *cakra*, the spinning wheel of the modern days used in the villages.

Village Weavers

The peasants of early medieval period supplied abundant of cotton to weavers located in the cities and villages. It has been observed that during the period villagers used different types of clothes[42] and weaving was carried on in the villages by professional workers. Weaving was not possible without spinning, and in the villages the work of spinning was done by both men and women. Medhātithi tells us that wives left unprovided for by their husbands should live by such unobjectionable occupations as *kartana* (spinning) and *jālikakaraṇa* (lace-making), and widows forced to live by their own labour should subsist by these occupations.[43] Some references to carding of cotton also testify to spinning being pursued by the village artisans.[44] According to *Mānasāra* the houses of weavers

33. Ibid., III, 577.
34. Ibid.
35. Ibid., III, 576.
36. *EI*, XXV, pp. 160ff.
37. *CII*, IV, p. 189, V, 12.
38. Monier-Williams, *A Sanskrit–English Dictionary*, p. 1013, col. 2.
39. *Utkivyaktiprakarana*, 39, 8; 45. 9.
40. Ibid., 40, 16.
41. See Devi Sushil Malti, *Economic Condition of Ancient India*, p. 87.
42. A.K. Choudhary, *Early Medieval Village in North Eastern India*, pp. 206-307.
43. On *Manu*, IX, 75.
44. *Ārya*, Chap. VI, "Cotton."

were to be between south and south-west[45] — near the tailors and washermen — in the village plan.[46] The Śubhaṅkarapātaka grant of Dharmapāla also speaks of the weavers living in villages.

Varieties of Clothes

According to the literary and epigraphic sources, during the period under review cotton cultivation was done on a large scale in north India. Among the textiles cotton cloth was the main article of consumption. Cotton plants were grown not only in fertile land,[47] but also in the forest villages. Bāṇa refers to cotton quilts, which certainly implies that cotton was cultivated in several parts of north India,[48] *Kṛṣiparāśara,* mentions the *karapāsaśodhana*[49] (carding of cotton). The word *karpāsa*[50] is used for cotton in *Paryāyaratnamālā.* The *caryāpada, sabarapada* and *śāntipada* also refer to *karpāsa.*[51] Cotton cultivation is described in *Kālikā Purāṇa,*[52] and some inscriptions also refer to it.[53] Thus, various accounts show that the commercial crop of cotton was grown in many parts of north India, and the peasants supplied it to the textile industries.

A number of centres of textile industry developed in north India in the early medieval period. Most of the centres were situated on the trade-routes and near the cities, depending upon availability of raw material and centres of consumption for the products.

Āvika or *ūrṇa* variety of cloth was manufactured for use in winter. This variety was prepared from the hair of animals. Wool was collected from goats and sheep, which were domestic animals.[54] During the period under review, villagers must

45. *Mānasāra,* V, 63-81.
46. Ibid., V, 82-158.
47. Watters, *On Yuan Chwang's Travels in India,* I, p. 301.
48. *Hcar,* p. 228
49. *KP,* V, 90.
50. *Prm,* 1, 590
51. B.P. Majumdar, *Socio-Economic History of Northern India,* p. 179.
52. *Kālikā Purāṇa,* 73, 1, 9; 89, 130.
53. Deopārā Inscription of Vijayasena, *EI,* I, 21, *Daśakumāracarita.*
54. Before our period these animals were domesticated. *DKC,* p. 157; *ASK,* p. 18. Nārada also mentions that wool was collected from the hair of mountain goats: I, 63.

have domesticated sheep and goats for commercial purposes. The existence of this industry is also witnessed in Kaḷacuri inscriptions.[55]

Kṣauma was a linen garment, which was made of the fibre of *kṣauma* or *atsī*. It was available in the form of barks, and was an agricultural product. *Āryasaptaśati* describes the rows of hemp plants (*śaṇaśreṇī*) with yellow flowers standing in a field or fields near a small village (*pallī*)[56] in Bengal. *Harṣacarita*[57] and *Kālikā Purāṇa*[58] also refer to cultivation of hemp. The preparation of wool was a household vocation. After necessary carding and cleaning of wool and fur, proficient weavers prepared warm clothes.

Some weavers obtained the material for textiles from worms and insects. This material, called *kauśeya*, was possibly collected in the forests.

There are also references in our sources to cultivation of silk-cotton tree (*śālmalī*). *Harṣacarita* refers to its production.[59] *Paryāyaratnamālā*,[60] *Āryasaptaśati*[61] and *Kṛṣiparāśara*[62] also mention cultivation of silk-cotton tree on a large scale.

As stated above, for textile industry the raw material was available from different sources. Weavers collected it according to the variety of cloth they had to produce. On the basis of the nature of cloth, the raw material may be divided into four categories : (a) agriculural products, such as cotton (*karpāsa*); (b) the barks from which the *kṣauma* variety of cloth was prepared; (c) the texture called *kauśeya*, obtained from the worms and insects; and (d) the hair (*romaja*) of animals.[63]

---

55. *CII*, IV, Ins. no. 74, verse 19.
56. *Arya*, V, 476.
57. *Hcar*, p. 217.
58. *Kālikā Purāṇa*, 63, 15.
59. *Hcar*, p. 230.
60. *Paryāyaratnamālā*, I, 336.
61. *Ārya*, V, 541 .
62. *KP*, V, 216.
63. *Ab Chin*, III. pp. 332-33. Hiuen-Tsang describes the different kinds of clothing material used in north India, such as *kauśeya, kṣauma, kambala* (woollen textiles); S. Beal, *Life of Hiuen-Tsang*, I, p. 148.

Different varieties of cloth were made by the weavers on a large scale. From our sources we know that both men and women were very fond of cloths. For different varieties of clothes terms like *patrorṇa, dhauta-kauśeya, dukūla* and *kuṭapa* were used. In the lexicons, *patrorṇa* is equated with *dhauta-kauśeya*.[64] While *Amarakośa* and *Abhidhānacintāmaṇi* speak of *patrorṇa* being produced from a worm reared on the leaves of *lakuca* and *vaṭa*,[65] and *dhauta-kauśeya* was obtained from bleached or white *kauśeya*.[66] We find the same characteristics of *patrorṇā* in *Nāmaliṅgānuśāsana* as in *Amarakośa*, which equates it with *dhauta-kauśeya*.[67] There is ambiguity in the terms used for different varieties of cloth. It is observed[68] that *kauśeya* indicates silken threads of any colour made from any variety of silk-worm. *Dhauta-kauśeya* was of white colour, and was obtained from a particular variety of insects living on the leaves of *lakuca, vaṭa,* etc. Silk worms were reared on the leaves of other kinds of trees as well. It is possible that the *kauśeya* variety of silken threads were differentiated from those prepared from the *kusuma* and *śālamali* flowers. *Naiṣadhīyacarita* refers to clothes dyed red in flowers.[69] The variety *patrorṇa* is equated with white *kauśeya* (*dhauta-kauśeya*) in *Abhidhānaratnamālā*.[70]

Kuṭapa was a woollen product of the hair of mountain goats, and blankets were made of it, as described by Devala,[71] Devaṇa Bhaṭṭa[72] and Vijñāneśvara.[73] The lexicons always allude to *dukūla* as a synonym of *kṣauma*,[74] while according to commentators *dukūla* is finer than *kṣauma*.[75] Haradatta suggests that *kṣauma*

64. *Ab Chin,* 111, 331; See *Ab Ratna,* 11, 394.
65. *Ab Chin,* 331 (1), See also *Amara.*
66. Ibid., 331(2).
67. *Nāmaliṅgānuśāsana,* See B.P. Majumdar, op. cit., p. 194; Sushil Malti Devi, op. cit., p. 79.
68. Sushil Malti Devi, op. cit., p. 79.
69. *Naiṣadh,* XX, 11, 10.
70. *Ab Ratna,* II, 394.
71. Devala quoted in *Smṛti Candrikā; Amarakośa,* II, VI, 3, 14.
72. *Smṛticandrikā,* Ahṇikaṇḍa, II.
73. *Amara,* II, VI, 3, 14.
74. *Ab Ratna,* II, 394; *Ab Chin,* III, 333.
75. Bhaṭṭasvāmī on *Arthaśāstra of Kauṭilya,* II, xi, p. 82; fn. 15.

was a white garment.[76] (Kauṭilya also refers to *dukūla* as a soft white fabric.)[77] Clearly colour did not determine the appellation of a particular variety of clothes, for they could be dyed fancifully.

Hence, from the accounts of contemporary digest writers and commentators it seems that different varieties of clothes were worn by the north Indian people. Some varieties like *kṣauma* and the *dukūla* were manufactured only for the richer people in the society. According to *Mānasollāsa,* expensive clothes were used by the kings.[78] *Kalpadrumkośa* of Keśava refers to a very costly garment called *prāvārī. Ākhyānakamaṇikośa* specially mentions white *paṭṭula,*[79] white *dugulla* (*dukūla*), *rayaṇakambala* (*ratnakambala*), from *Nepāla-viṣaya*[80] *navaraṅganivasanu* (garment of nine colours) worn by ladies, the *jalavatta-suvasaniya,*[81] *paṭṭāṁśuka, jaddara, devaṅga*[82] *niraṅgī* (a sort of cover for the head, *śirovastra*) used by ladies[83] and sometimes made of *kosambhavastra* (cloth of saffron colour), and *kambīyā* (a small blanket). The author of the same text also mentions *kaṇṭhā* (garment of patched rags or pieces of cloth)[84] and *kośeyapītavattha,* yellow *kauśeya* (silken garment).[85] Some people used very costly clothes, which were imported from other countries. *Upamitibhavaprapañcakathā* refers to several fine clothes like *cināṁśuka, devāṁśuka* and *paṭṭāṁśuka.*[86] *Cināṁśuka,* according to this source, was silk imported from China. *Paṭṭāṁśuka* was a very beautiful dress, and was used by the heroine of *Karpūramañjarī.*

---

76 Haradatta on *Āpastamba,* I, i, 2, 41.

77. *Arthaśāstra,* II, xi, p. 82.

78. *Mānasollāsa,* III, 1017-20.

79. *Amk,* 47, 27.

80. Ibid., 183, 10.

81. Ibid., 214, 611.

82. Ibid., 257, 394.

83. Ibid., 64, 106.

84. Ibid., 148, 17, 19.

85. Ibid., 319, 263; See B.N. Sharma, *Social and Cultural History of Northern India,* p. 138.

86. *Upamitibhavaprapañcakathā,* p. 154.

Centres of Textile Industry

In this regard Bāṇa mentions that Puṇḍravardhana Bhukti (North Bengal) was an important centre where *dukūla* was manufactured.[87] Weavers of Bengal continued this occupation in later centuries too, and their achievements in the field have been appreciated by Muslim writers. Sulaiman in the ninth century CE remarks that in the kingdom of Rahmi (Bengal), there was "a stuff not to be found elsewhere." According to him, so fine and delicate was this material that a dress made of it would be passed through a signet ring.[88] This shows the efficiency of the Bengal weavers of the period. This fact of these craftsmen was supported by Khurdādbeh of the tenth century CE.[89] According to the Chinese work *Chau Ju-Kua*, Bengal was famous for *tou-lo* cotton.[90] It may be concluded that Bengal remained a very rich centre of textile industry for quite a long period.

Besides Bengal, there were some other famous centres of textile industry. About Gujarat, *Chau Ju-kua* tells us that its chief products were cotton and indigo.[91] It also says that Malwa was also a great centre of textile products.[92] About the importance of Malwa's clothes Wassif states that fine linens (*kirbas*) were among the precious articles carried off by the victorious people.[93] That the Malwa region was a great centre of weaving industry is also borne out by *Prabandhacintāmaṇi*.[94] Moreover, in the Candella records, *karpāsa*, *kṣauma* and *saṇa* are frequently mentioned, which proves their predominant use in the textile industry. Perhaps they had monopolized the textile industry, and no private unlincensed industrialists were allowed to carry on the business.[95]

---

87. *Harṣacarita — Eka, Sāṁskṛtika Adhyayana*, p. 77; Huien-Tsang mentions the textile industry located in Kāmarūpa (Assam); *Kālikā Purāṇa*, p. 69.
88. *HIED*, I, p. 361.
89. Ibid., I, 14.
90. *Chau-Ju-kua*, p. 97.
91. Ibid., p. 92.
92. Ibid., p. 93; *HIED*, III, p. 31.
93. *HIED*, Ill, p. 31.
94. *Prabandhacintāmaṇi*, II, 66.
95. Sushil Malti Devi, op. cit., p. 84.

Varanasi was also an important centre for manufacturing textile goods.[96] The plunder of drappers from the whole markets of the city by Ahmad Nialtgin as described by Abul-Fazl-Al-Baikaki, attests this fact.[97] *Kālikā Purāṇa* mentions Kāmarūpa as an important centre of textile industry where clothes were prepared from *karpāsa* (cotton), *kambala* (wool), *balka* (bark) and *kośala* (silk from cocoons).[98] In the thirteenth century CE Marco Polo mentions Paiṭhan as a famous centre of textile industry.[99] He says that "the quality of the products of this centre were delicate buckrams of the highest price and that they looked like the tissue of the spider's web. There could have been no king or queen in the world but might be glad to wear them."[100] Evidently the weavers maintained their skill in producing finest clothes even in the later centuries of our period.

In Kashmir, Śaṅkarapura was a popular centre of woollen clothes during the time of Śaṅkaravarman, who founded the city.[101] In the same region shawls and several kinds of blankets were manufactured on a large scale. The chief centre of woollen manufacture was Paṭṭan, where there was also a market for the sale of sheep and cattle.[102] Kṣemendra's *Narmamālā* and *Samayamātṛkā* also mention blankets. Possibly wool was one of the essential commodities of trade in Kashmir, and the weavers had a busy time. This is evident from a passage in *Rājataraṅgiṇī* where Kalhaṇa mentions the fact of high prices of certain goods during the famine under Harṣa. These goods included rice, the staple food of Kashmir, and wool.[103] Besides woollen articles, cotton clothes, hemp-made garments and silk goods were also produced in the valley of Kashmir as stated by *Rājataraṅgiṇī*.[104]

A short list of textile centres is also given in *Mānasollāsa*.[105] It includes

96. *Uktivyaktiprakaraṇa* of Dāmodara, p. 84.
97. *HIED*, II, pp. 124ff.
98. *Kālikā Purāṇa*, p. 69/2.
99. *Marco Polo*, II, 391.
100. Ibid.
101. P.N.K. Bamzai, *A History of Kashmir*, p. 172.
102. Ibid., p. 210.
103. *RT*, VII, 1221.
104. Ibid., IV, 349; V, 162; VIII, 857
105. *Bodhisattvāvadānakalpalatā*, pp. 113-14.

Poḍḍalāpura (Paiṭhan), Cirapalli (Trichinapalli), Nāgapaṭṭana (Nāgapaṭṭiṇam), Coḷamaṇḍala, Allikākula (Chicakole), Siṁhala (Sri Lanka), Anahilavāḍa (Anahilapaṭṭan), Mūlasthāna (Multān), Toṇḍideśa (Touḍimaṇḍala), Pañcapaṭṭana (perhaps Pañcamahal in Gujarat), Mahā Cīna (China), Kaliṅgadeśa (Orissa and Bengal).

Export Variety of Clothes

Indian weavers were very proficient in the craft of weaving various kinds of clothes. Therefore, their goods had a great demand in international market. The accounts of the Arab writers are of great value here, for they not only throw considerable light on the degree of perfection the textile industry had reached during the period, but also make a mention of export of Indian clothes to other countries. The *Hudūd-e-Ālam* (CE 982-83) informs us that Arabia imported muslin and turbans from Kannauj.[106] Sulaiman, in the ninth century CE, writing about the famous muslin of India, remarks: "The finest muslins woven there are so thin that the whole role could be passed through a ring. Muslin is a cotton textile, and I have myself seen it."[107] It seems that printed calicos from India were exported to Egypt. Many examples of such printed calicos have been found from Fostat in Egypt.[108] Fine white flowered (or dotted) cotton garments of Gujarat[109] and cotton (*tou-lo*) of Bengal[110] are also appreciated by *Chau-Ju-Kua* which informs us that every year 2,000 oxen or more laden with cotton stuffs were sent to other countries for barter.[111] *Rājataraṅgiṇī* tells us that manufactured woollen goods were the principle articles of trade and commerce.[112] We are also told by this source that the clothes prepared on a large scale by a large organized body of skilled craftsmen, and meant for trading purposes, were of the best quality.

106. V. Minorsky, *Hudūd-ul-Ālam*, London, 1937, p. 86ff.

107. *HIED*, p. 361.

108. R. Pfister, *Tes Toiles Imprimees de Fostat et l' Hindustan*, Paris, 1938; Motichandra, *Trade and Trade Routes in Ancient India*, p. 204.

109. *Chau-Ju-Kua*, Eng. tr. F. Hirth and W.W. Rockhill, p. 98.

110. Ibid., p. 97.

111. Ibid., p. 93.

112. *RT*, VII, 122.

Evidence is available about the plundering of costly clothes from India by foreign invaders during the period. The point worthy of our notice is that Indian cotton and woollen clothes were considered precious by foreigners. Wassaf's testimony is that fine linens (*kirbas*) were among the precious articles carried off by foreign victorious invaders.[113] He furnishes a vivid account of the plunder by the Muslim invaders of Cambay who fell for silk and cotton goods, stamped, embroidered and coloured.[114] Similarly, another work, *Mulfujat-i-Timuri*, although a late one, also mentions the booty collected by the invaders in the form of brocades and silk of great value in the course of the sack of Delhi.[115]

It is clear that textile manufacturers gave occupation to different types of artisans. They were engaged in washing and dyeing of clothes, tailoring and embroidering. These workers augmented the value of clothes with their work. The demand of their profession was according to the taste of the people.

Dyers

In the period under review, people were fond of dyed clothes. Most probably, dyed clothes were used on marriage occasions and in religious performances and fairs. The high demand of coloured clothes gave incentives to the dyeing industry. Although not many direct references in this context are available, contemporary digest writers and commentators do refer to garments prepared to meet the taste of people. According to the *Bṛhatsaṁhitā*, the fondness for coloured clothes led to the growth of dyeing profession.[116] The same text makes a mention of garments of various colours and their weavers.[117] Brides and the women attending marriage festivities dressed themselves in clothes coloured in *kusumbha* (*Carthalus tinctorius*) flowers,[118] blue,[119] and red,[120] so popular during the time. Huien Tsang tells us

113. *HIED*, III, p. 31.
114. Ibid., III, p. 43.
115. Ibid., III, p. 446.
116. *BS*, XVI, 17.
117. Ibid., LXXXVI, 15, 40; C, 8.
118. *Vāmana Purāṇa*, 10, 12.
119. *BS*, XXIV, 18; LVII, 32; LXXXVI, 25.
120. *BS*, LXXXV, 79.

that people were fond of different colours.[121] While Bāṇa of the same period speaks of five primary colours (*pañcaraṅgāḥ*),[122] he mentions a number of different mixed tints, prepared by mixing the primary colours.[123] We also know about the variegated and multi-coloured cotton and silken clothes from the same text.[124]

Gauḍavaho of Vākpati also refers to the dyed clothes worn by village women on festive days.[125] *Kṛṣiparāśara* mentions the decoration of the chief bull by cowherds with multi-coloured cloth on the day of the cow-festival.[126] Elsewhere,[127] it is stated that a yellow piece of cloth was worn by the daughter of the village chief on this occasion. The fondness of the villagers for dyed clothes certainly reveals that in the villages some artisans were definitely engaged in dyeing clothes.

The story in *Bṛhadkathākośa* by Hariṣena also bears out the practice of dyeing clothes in the period.[128] The story says that a Persian brought a girl and fed her well for six months. Later on he extracted her blood by means of leeches. From the germs produced by this blood was obtained carmine, which was used for dyeing woollen clothes. Thus on the basis of this story we may surmise that *kermes*, which was later known as *kiramdānā*, was imported from Persia for colour, though it seems that the Persian traders invented many fenciful stories about its origin to impress its preciousness upon Indian merchants,[129] Āśādhara, commenting on 567th Gāthā of *Bhagavatī Ārādhanā* also observes that in *Carmaraṅga Viṣaya* (Samarkand) the *mleccha*s got human blood through leeches, gathered it in a pot and with the germs produced dyed blankets.[130]

---

121. Watters, op. cit., Art. I, p. 148.
122. *Hcar*, p. 47.
123. *JORM*, VII, 1933.
124. *Hcar*, p. 125; Also see LXXXVI, 19 and *YY*, II, 1.
125. *Gauḍavaho*, V, 598.
126. *KP*, V, 101.
127. *Ārya*, V, 476.
128. *Bṛhatkathākośa*, ed. A.N. Upadhye, pp. 80-82.
129. Moticandra, op. cit., p. 209.
130. "Prastāvanā," *Bṛhatkathākośa*, p. 88.

Dyers are also found referred to in *Abhidhānaratnamālā*.[131] According to Aparārka, different kinds of clothes were dyed by the professional dyers.[132] Red-dye (*mañjiṣṭhā*),[133] *kausumbha*,[134] *lac*[135] and *nīlarāga*[136] (blue dye) were the products from which the dyers dyed clothes. According to the Arthuna inscription, *mañjiṣṭhā* was a dyieng reagent.[137] Sometimes dyers imported dye objects from abroad.[138]

Embroider

Embroidery was done by some artisans on textile commodities with silver and gold threads. These dresses were worn by the kings, queens and rich people of the society. During Harṣa's time, artisans produced on a large scale silken garments embroidered with gems. Huien Tsang says that kings assembled in the Kannauj assembly of Harṣa wore such type of clothes.[139] Damodar Gupta tells us that Cintāmaṇi, the son of a government official used to wear a yellow-coloured gold-embroidered cloth.[140] Similarly rich people used *kṣauma* and *cīnāṁśuka* (gold-embroidered clothes). The same text speaks of a prostitute to whom a pair of *cīnāṁśuka*s was given by her admirers.[141] Rājaśekhara, in his *Kāvyamīmāṁsā*, refers to embroidered white *kauśeya* clothes.[142] Wassaf, a Muslim writer, also refers to stamped and embroidered clothes which were plundered by invaders.[143] Proficient workers connected with this profession worked for royal courts and rich people. Thus, in addition to weaving, embroidery of cloth with gold and silver thread

131. *Ab Ratna*, II, 433.
132. On, *Yājñ*, II, 289-90.
133. *Ab Ratna*, 4, 48.
134. *Naiṣadh*, XXII, sl. 10.
135. *Prabandhacintāmaṇi*, III, 97; RT, VIII, 3303.
136. *Ab Ratna*, 2, 219.
137. *EI*, XIV, pp. 295ff.
138. *Prabandhacintāmaṇi*, III, 110.
139. S. Beal, *Life of Yuan Chwang*, I, p. 219.
140. *Kuṭṭanīmatam*, ed. T. Ray, verse 66, p. 12.
141. Ibid., verse 344, p. 62.
142. *Kāv*, chap. 5, p. 57.
143. *HIED*, III, p. 43.

was a well-known and respectable craft entitling its practitioner to be known after it.[144]

Tailoring

After the cloth is made, it goes into the hands of other artisans, including the tailor, before dress is made out of it. However, cloth was also used without sewing to cover some parts of the body. The sewing of clothes was done through a sharp needle.[145] In the villages sewing was done by the villagers themselves or by the members of their family. However, in course of time some people adopted sewing of clothes in villages and cities as a profession. The job of the tailor fulfils the aesthetic need of people. Although direct references to tailors are not available in the literature of the period, we find mention of costumes and dresses, which indicates the existence of expert tailors.

It seems that people were very fond of wearing the different kinds of tailored clothes. Bāṇa[146] mentions trousers of three kinds, viz. *savasthāna, piṅgā* and *satulā;* coats of four types, viz. *kañcuka, cinacolaka, vārabāṇa* and *kūrpāśaka.* Apparently, these types of garments were used by kings and nobles.

In different parts of north India different types of costumes were worn by people. In Kashmir poor people wore miserable *bhaṅga* (hemp-made garments).[147] Prisoners were also given such clothes in jails.[148] They had to satisfy themselves only with cotton clothes and sometimes even with clothes made of hemp.

In *Kāvyamīmāṁsā,* the author describes the *nepathya* — costume (*attri*) of ladies in the east, north-west, west and south in accordance with the natural surroundings, costumes and manners of people.[149] Besides the *sāṛī,* he mentions in detail the ornaments and toiletry of the ladies. *Karpūramañjarī* and *Viddhaśālabhañjikā* also refer to women's dress. Rājaśekhara divides ladies costume

---

144. G.S. Ghrye, *Indian Costumes,* p. 64.
145. Patañjali mentions this instrument, *tikṣṇaya sūcya sivyan, Māhabhāṣya,* II, 1, 2, p. 373.
146. *Hcar,* pp. 150-53 and 202.
147. *RT,* VII, 300.
148. Ibid., VIII, 93.
149. *Kāv,* p. 8.

into three items, viz. *dukūla*[150] (mantle), *colaka*[151] (bodice), sometimes *nīlcolaka*[152] (blue in colour), also called *kañculikā*[153] and *nīvī*[154] (known as skirt). During the period bathing garments were called *snānavastra*.[155] The ladies of rich families used to wear *nīlama-paṭāśuka* (blue silk) in an attractive form.[156] An over-garment was called *uttarīyam*.[157] Among men's garments the poet refers to the loin-cloth, which was used universally.[158] There are references to *uṣṇīṣa* (headdress)[159] for males and to *tuṣa* (blanket).[160] The Amgachi grant of Vigrahapāla III also mentions a kind of silk cloth in which Jayadeva's Śrī Kṛṣṇa is described to have worn a *dukūla*.[161] An inscription of the Kaḷacuris refers to silk cloth, and clearly indicates that it was in use.[162] Tailoring (*darjunī*) is also mentioned in the songs of *Sarahapada*.[163]

The secular and religious sculptures of the period show different kinds of garments. The costumes which are referred to in literature can be identified in the sculpture of this period. The female garments, including *sāṛī, cunarī* and *colī* are shown in the Khajurāho sculptures. Generally men are shown in *dhotī*. The soldiers, hunters, musicians and elephant-riders wear knickers in these sculptures.[164] Different kinds of blouses and upper garments of males and females in these sculptures may be taken as an evidence of the existence of proficient tailors.[165]

150. *Viddh*, I, 18.
151. Ibid., I, 34.
152. Ibid.
153. *Karpūr*, I, 24.
154. *Viddh*, I, 34.
155. *Karpūr*, II, 24.
156. Ibid., II, 14.
157. Ibid., I, 32.
158. B.N. Puri, *The History of Gurjara Pratihāras*, p. 123.
159. B.P. Majumdar, op. cit., p. 195.
160. *Samayamātṛkā*, p. 124.
161. *Gītagovinda*, I, 44; II, 12.
162. *CII*, IV, Ins. no. 90, verse 12; 107, verse 12.
163. *Dohākośa*, II, 3, V, 42.
164. For details see Urmila Agarwal, *Khajuraho Sculptures and Their Significance*, pp. 128ff.
165. See B.N. Sharma, *Social and Cultural History of Northern India*, p. 138.

5

Miscellaneous Artisans and Craftsmen

Potters

CERAMIC is one of the most important products ever made by man. It is thought that the potter's wheel originated in Elam.[1] It was a round piece of wood with a piv.ot-hole. The early high craftsmanship of the potter is attested by the pre-Haṛappan and Haṛappan pottery. The quality and variety in shape and fabric of the earthenware of the period clearly indicate that a separate class of potters had already emerged in the society, and that its members had gained a high degree of proficiency in their work. Both plain and painted pottery, in the form of beakers, jars, vases, bowls, goblets, dishes, basins, pans, dishes-on-stand, handled cups, lids, etc. has been discovered from Moheṅjo-Dāṛo[2] and other sites[3] of the Haṛappan civilization. It is interesting to note that this pottery is painted in different colours and also has various designs carved or painted on it.

The work of the potters is mentioned in the Vedic texts, and its continuity is attested by the literary and archaeological sources. *Vājasaneyī Saṁhitā* refers to the occupation of the potters (*kaulālas*).[4] Patañjali mentions that potters made different kinds of pots out of lumps of clay.[5] They were known as *kumbhakāras* or in the case of having a bigger establishment, *mahākumbhakāras*.[6] Pots available in

---

1. *Cambridge Ancient History*, vol. I, p. 579.
2. J. Marshall, *Moheṅjo-Dāṛo and the Indus Civilization*, Chap. XVII.
3. M.S. Vats, *Excavation at Harappā*, Chap. IX.
4. *Vāj Saṁ*, XXX.
5. *Mahābhāṣya*, 1, 1, 1, p. 7, 1. 13. Also ibid., VI, 1, 84, 57, t. 2 (*piṇḍākṛtim upamṛdya ghaṭikā kriyante anayo mṛtpiṇḍayor ghaṭaṁ kurvīti*).
6. Ibid., 111, 1, 92, p. 75, 11. 13, 22.

the house were called *kumbhakārakulas* (*ghaṭena kāryaṁ kṛṣyan kumbhakārakulam gatvā*).[7] The potters manufactured not only pottery but also human and animal figurines, toycarts, toys, bricks, tiles, and a number of miscellaneous household objects. This is evident from the excavations of Taxila, Mathurā, Śrāvastī, Kauśāmbī, Rājghāṭ, Vaiśālī, Kumrahār and various other sites.[8] It appears that there was ample difference between the rural and urban pottery, which shows that the potters working in the towns, were more proficient in comparison to those who lived in the rural areas.

The skill and efficiency of the potters during the Gupta period is attested by the way they moulded, coloured and burnt the pottery. The most distinctive class of pottery of this period is what the archaeologists have called "red ware."[9] Excavated pottery and terracotta objects at Rājghāṭ, Ahicchatra, Bhītā, Basārh and other sites of Gupta period reveal the achievements of the potters in the society of the period.[10] Sometimes these vessels were decorated with multi-coloured patterns like rosettes, geometrical figures, bands of lotuses alternating with conches, a running boar, and elephant designs. Possibly, this was done to cater to the taste of the buyers.

Comparing the work of a potter[11] with that of an oil miller, Varāhamihira observes that both the craftsmen worked with the wheel and were consequently known as *cākrikas* or *cakracaras*. Among the clay objects (*mṛṇmayas*) manufactured by them were a variety of vessels, burnt bricks and figurines. The vessels were particularly prepared to fulfil the common household needs. Among the earthenware, Varāhamihira refers to *kalaśa*,[12] a small pitcher with unburnt bottom (*akāla-mūla*), which was regarded as specially sacred; *kumbha* (a large pitcher fashioned from clay); *kamaṇḍalu* (a ground or water-vessel made of clay); *kusūla*[13]

7. Ibid., 1, 1, 1, p. 7, 1. 28; See B.N. Puri, *India in the Time of Patañjali*, p. 103.
8. Kameshwar Prasad, *Urban Occupations and Crafts in the Kuṣāṇa Period, PIHC* (Thirty-eighth Session Calcutta, 1977), pp. 107-17.
9. R.S. Sharma, *Perspectives in Social and Economic History of Early India*, p. 174.
10. *AI*, vol. 1, 1946, pp. 46ff, 1. *ASI* (*AR*), 1911-12, p. 84, pl. XXX, nos. 70ff; *ASI* (*AR*), 1903-04, p. 93.
11. *BS*, *ghaṭākāra*, XVI, 1; *vivāhapaṭala*, 9; *ghaṭakṛt*, XVI, 28.
12. Ibid., XXIV, 7; XLII, 20; XLVII, 37; LV, 26; LXVII, 46.
13. Ibid., XCVI, 6; *BY*, XXX, 13.

(a large earthen pot for storing grain). Evidently, the writer mentions not only the common earthenware of daily use, but also special types of vessels which were used in rituals.

The hereditary occupation of the potter continued throughout the period under study. It is clear that the potters fulfilled the needs of the villages as well as of the towns. The rich people generally used metal vessels for their household needs, but for religious and ceremonial purposes, the earthenware was used. The villagers commonly used earthen pots. *Subhāṣitaratnakoṣa* mentions earthen vessels used in the villages.[14] *Āryasaptaśati* refers to churning of milk and curd in earthen pots.[15] This leads us to believe that there was a large-scale demand of earthenware, and that the potter enjoyed a good deal of importance, particularly in the villages.

Naiṣadhacarita describes the process used for making earthen pots. It tells us that the craftsmanship of a potter was dependent on his apparatus, i.e. on the wheel for moulding pots.[16] The lump of clay was put on the wheel, which was then rotated, and the potter moulded the clay into various shapes. Glazed clay was collected from particular places for making vessels. The durability of the pot depended on the quality of clay and its firing. The earthenware was heated on a particular temperature in the hearth. The technique of firing the pots in kilns is given in the *Prabandhacintāmaṇi*.[17] Al-Beruni also refers to the potter and his wheel.[18]

POTTERS' GUILDS

Since ancient times potters (*kumbhakāra*s) have formed guilds, as have many other categories of artisans and craftsmen. A clay sealing, acquired from Ahicchatra, bears the legend *kumbhakāra seṇiyai* in Brāhmī characters.[19] The Sanskrit rendering of the Brāhmī legend would be *kumbhakāra śeṇyai,* and its translation "(seal of)

14. *Subhāṣitaratnakoṣa*, V, 1312; *Saduktikarṇāmṛta*, 2, 84, 1.
15. *Arya*, VV, 104 and 344.
16. *Naiṣadha*, 11, 32.
17. Ibid., IV, 7; *Prabandhacintāmaṇi*, 111, 127.
18. Sachau, *Al-Beruni's India*, 1, p. 239.
19. S.P. Shukla, "Ahicchatra Sealing of the Kumbhakāra Guild," *Journal of the Epigraphical Society of India*, vol. XII, 1986. The sealing is now in the collection of the Gurukul Museum, Jhajjar (Haryana).

the potter's guild." The impression is that of the seal of the potters of Ahicchatra, who had organized themselves into a guild or corporate body. On the palaeographic grounds the seal may be assigned to the first century CE.[20] The Buddhist text *Mahāvastu* also refers to the potters guild, and includes the *kumbhakāras* in the list of eleven artisans.[21] It is interesting to note that the potters' guild also served as a bank. From the Nasik Inscription we learn that one thousand *kārṣāpaṇas* were deposited with the *kulirika* (*kumbhakāra*) *śreṇī* as a permanent endowment, so that from its interest medical facilities could be provided to the Buddhist *saṁgha* situated in the Triraśmi mountain.[22]

The inscriptions of the early medieval period also refer to the potters and their guilds. The uniformity in the shapes and designs of pottery on a large scale indicates that the potters must have had some kind of a corporate body. In this context the Kāman Stone Inscription[23] and the Śiyadoṇī Inscription[24] give important information about the guilds of potters, and attests their prosperity. *Amarakośa*[25] names different guilds, and includes the *kumbhakāra śreṇī* among them.[26]

HOUSES OF THE POTTERS

Vāstuśāstra makes provision for the residence of the potters,[27] which clearly indicates the importance of the potters in the society of the period. *Mayamata* mentions that the houses of the potters should be in the east or the north of the village.[28] An inscription of Someśvaradeva refers to a number of professional colonies including *kumbhāravāḍā*,[29] (potters' locality). Similarly, the Kamauli Grant

20. Ibid.
21. *Mahāvastu*, 11, pp. 463-78.
22. *EI*, VII, p. 89; Luder's List No. 1137.
23. *EI*, XXIV, p. 329ff.
24. Ibid., 1, p. I62ff.
25. *Amara*, 11, 10, 6.
26. Ibid.
27. *Maya*, 9, 88-96; *Mānasāra*, 9, 72-78 and 116-27.
28. *Maya*, VV, 88-91.
29. *EI*, X, No. 4, 1.27; Kurushpala Stone Inscription,

of Vaidyadeva refers to a *kumbhakārabhogyavahin*.[30] Thus, we find that potters lived in a particular area in the village. They made kilns, where they prepared pots for people. The Nidhanpur Copper Plate of Bhāskaravarman refers to the potters' ditch (*kumbhakāragartta*),[31] where potters lived so that they might collect clay and heat pots in kilns, and also sell their ware.

Although, the pottery of the early medieval period, cannot be compared favourably in refinement and smoothness with the deluxe potteries of the earlier periods, yet there is no doubt that the potters of the period under review enjoyed very busy hours. The archaeological excavations at Pahārpur Mahāsthān (Bogra), Sabhar, (Dacca) and other places have yielded numerous specimens of the pottery of the period in the form of storage jars (*loṭās*), cooking utensils, dishes, saucers, inkpots and lamp stands, besides terracotta plaques.[32] Huge quantities of this pottery have been recovered from the excavations of many sites of north India related to our period.

The potters made different kinds of vessels. *Harṣacarita* mentions several kinds of water-pots, such as *karkarīs*, *sikatilakalaśīs*, *aliñjara*, *udkumbha*,[33] *śarāva* (a type of plate), was used at *prapās*, drinking inns in some villages of north India. Some potters manufactured special water jars, which were used by the village elders in honour of the king marching with his army through the countryside.[34] Hiuen-Tsang noted with interest that vessels used in households were mostly earthenware, and a few of brass.[35]

Leather-Workers

The use of leather by man is very ancient. In the Vedic period, the profession of leather-worker was known as *carmamna*.[36] The leather worker of that time

---

30. *Gauḍalekhamālā*, 1; Kamauli Grant, 1, 60.
31. *EI*, XII, no. 13, last plate, p. 46; *Kāmarūpa Śāsanāvalī*, p. 1ff, 131.
32. R.C. Majumdar, *The History of Bengal*, vol. I, pp. 656-57.
33. *Hcar*, p. 228.
34. Ibid., p. 212.
35. T. Watters, *On Yuan Chwang's Travels in India*, 1, p. 178.
36. *R̥V*, 1, 85, 5; 110, 8; 161, 7; 3, 60, 2; 4, 13, 4; *AV*, 5, 8, 13; 10, 9, 2; 11, 1, 9; *Taittirīya Brāhmaṇa*, 2, 7, 2, 2.

prepared bags and pots,[37] bridles,[38] whips,[39] traps,[40] strings of bows,[41] etc. The art of making shoes of leather by tanners is referred to in *Taittirīya Saṁhitā*,[42] *Gobhila Gṛhyasūtra*[43] and *Mahābhārata*.[44] A cobbler is mentioned as making shoes, and leather jerkins, big sacks, ropes and straps are also mentioned in the Jātakas.[45] Leather was also used in making musical instruments.[46]

It is recorded in the inscriptions that in the Gupta period some of the leather workers had attained a sound economic position. It would appear that they (*carmakāras*) even paid taxes to the king. The Charter of Viṣṇusena (*Saṁ.*, 649) mentions a shoe-maker (*padakāra*) as paying taxes to the state. Shoe-makers[47] with some of their tools and leather products, such as knife,[48] shoes,[49] leather fan,[50] and leather bottle for oil,[51] are referred to in *Amarakośa*. Nārada[52] forbids a brāhmaṇa to sell skins, even in the time of distress. Chakraborti observes that leather (*carma*) was the monopoly of the state, and even after bequeathing lands to individuals or collectivities, the state reserved its right to hides (*carma*).[53]

---

37. *The Vedic Age*, Chap. XXIII, XXVII, pp. 449-67 and 506-26; Bandyopadhyaya, *Economic Life and Progress in Ancient India*, pp. 506-26.
38. *AV*, 6, 46, 18.
39. Ibid., 6, 53, 9.
40. Ibid., 1, 121, 9.
41. *ṚV*, 6, 75, 11; 27, 22; *AV*, 1, 2, 3.
42. *Taittirīya Saṁhitā*, V, 44; VI, 6, 6, 1.
43. *Gobhila Gṛhyasūtra*, 111, 1, 6.
44. *Mbh*, Anuśāsana Parva, Chap. 95.
45. Jātakas, 111, 324, 336; V, 514 and VI, 538.
46. *Urban Occupations and Crafts in the Kushana Period*, Kameswar Prasad; *PIHC*, 38th session (Calcutta, 1977), pp. 107-17.
47. *EI*, XXIV, pp. 296ff.
48. *Amara*, 10, 7, p. 226.
49. *Amara*, 10, 35, p. 233.
50. Ibid., 10, 30-31, p. 232.
51. Ibid., 7, 23, p. 167.
52. *Nāradasmṛti*, 1, pp. 60-63.
53. *EI*, 1, XV, p. 42, 1, 17; *JASB* (N.S.), XX, p. 59, 1, 19; H.P. Chakraborti, *Crafts and Industries as Reflected in the Gupta Period*, *PIHC*, thirty-first session (Calcutta, 1974), pp. 77 to 80.

In the early medieval period we have a number of references to leather workers from which we learn about their socio-economic position in the society of the period. The leather workers belonged to a particular caste. In our sources the terms used for them are *mocī*,[54] *mocīvāḍā*,[55] *carmāvāḍā*[56] and *carmakāra*.[57] Kalhaṇa mentions the tenders as belonging to a particular profession.[58]

Although leather workers belonged to a lower caste, generally regarded as untouchables in the society, yet sometimes they participated in religious performances.[59] Some leather workers enjoyed a fairly good economic position. The Charter of Viṣṇusena of the Kaḷacuri dynasty refers to a tax on *khalla* (leather).[60] It is noteworthy, however, that if the material was required for a religious purpose, a concession was made, and the measure was only 1¼ silver coins. Presumably, both in north and south India, the leather workers supplied articles like straps for making drums, strings (guts) for lutes of various types, and bezoar for the worship of the deities.[61] Elsewhere,[62] we find that a *mocī* (shoemaker) named Devapāla was a religious-minded and rich person, and got erected a temple in honour of god Nārāyaṇa at Khalvāṭika, modern Khalari in the Raipur district of Madhya Pradesh.

ARTICLES OF LEATHER

Carmakāras collected hides from the particular places near villages and cities to which the dead bodies of cattle were consigned. Despite our records being silent on this point, we may assume that the economic condition of the tanners was largely dependent on the quantum of the raw material they could avail of. The *carmakāras* carried the dead animals to particular places, where their skins were

54. *CII*, IV, p. 169.
55. *EI*, X, pp. 30-31, 11, 27-28.
56. Ibid.
57. *Prāyaścitta Prakaraṇa*, *HBR*, 1, p. 577.
58. *RT*, IV, 55.
59. B.N. Sharma, *Social and Cultural History of Northern India*, p. 38.
60. *EI*, XXX, I63ff.
61. K.A. Nilakanta Sastri, *The Cholas*, p. 569.
62. *CII*, IV, p. CIXIX (169).

cast off. The skins were then transported to the tanning establishments, the skeletons being left to be used for other purposes.[63]

The shoe-makers (*mocī*) were particularly valued in the society of the time for their art of making shoes, which were a common necessity of people. From the accounts of Hiuen-Tsang, we learn that leather worker prepared shoes to be used by people.[64] Kṣemendra also refers to leather shoes.[65] The Khalāri Stone Inscription of Haribrahmadeva speaks of a shoe-maker.[66] The high craftsmanship of leather workers is indicated by the "peacock-shoes," which were used by rich and fashionable women in region of the present-day Jammu & Kashmir.[67] Possibly there were some important centres of tannery where quality shoes were produced. This is attested by an Arab writer, who speaks of Cambay as one of the more important centres of manufacture of sandals.[68]

A cultural study of the sculptures of the period under review reveals that leather articles were in common use. Images of soldiers and the Sun god are shown with high boots.[69] Sculptural representations from Bengal, Bihar and other places also show the use of boots by Sūrya[70] and Revanta.[71] Hence, making of shoes was a thriving profession of leather workers. They not only manufactured new shoes but also repaired the used ones.[72]

Besides shoes, other household goods of leather were also manufactured by the leather-workers. Leathern thing and a vessel called *dṛti*, which was a large leather bag for storage of water, are described in *Bṛhatsaṁhitā*.[73] Drums were much in use in north India, and according to the *Harṣacarita*, the leather workers

63. A.K. Choudhary, *Early Medieval Village in North-Eastern India*, p. 207.
64. T. Watters, *On Yuan Chwang's Travels in India*, 1, p. 151.
65. *Narmamālā*, 1, 109, 204.
66. *CII*, IV, Ins. no. 108, Verse 9.
67. P.N.K. Bamzai, op. cit., 221.
68. Masudi (ed. Ferand), p. 95.
69. Urmila Agarwal, *Khajuraho Sculptures and Their Significance*, p. 186.
70. *National Museum*, New Delhi, 50, 178; *Ajmer Museum*, 1, (54), 370.
71. *Ajmer Museum*, 1, (65), 373/3; R.C. Majumdar, *History of Bengal*, 1, pp. 457-58.
72. *RT*, VIII, p. 137.
73. *YY*, 1, 4.

themselves were the drummers.[74] It shows that making of drums by leather workers was also a common profession. According to Bāṇa, leather workers also prepared leathern bags and sacks for carrying goods by army when on march. These bags and sacks must obviously have been lighter and more durable than many other kinds of containers for the purpose of transporting merchandise. Kṣemendra speaks of leather water bags used by the people,[75] and leathern bottles were manufactured for keeping oils.[76] A surgeon carrying a bag[77] of quite a modern design with a long strap with which to hang it on the shoulder and a button to keep the lid in place has been shown in a Khajurāho sculpture. We also learn that leather workers manufactured leathern cushioned seats used in the theatres.[78] Literary evidence also shows that leather puppets flourished in the present-day Andhra Pradesh in the twelfth century CE.[79]

Leather-workers also produced defensive weapons like shields for battle-fields. These leather shields (*carmans*) mentioned in the inscriptions, were used in battles.[80] Hence, some leather workers worked under the royal patronage and produced leathern goods for their defence needs. *Śukranītisāra* refers to leather artisans as deserving of the attention of the king.[81]

EXPORT OF LEATHER ARTICLES

As mentioned above leather and leathern goods were produced on a large scale in north India during our period. Marco Polo observes that leather was exported in large quantities from Thānā.[82] Again he tells us that dressed hide was exported to Arabia and the Persian Gulf.[83] Cambay was an important centre of leather,

---

74. *Hcar*, p. 142.
75. *Narmamālā*, 1, 109, 124.
76. *Deśīnāmamālā*, 111, 21; V, 22.
77. Back Inner Pradakṣinā, the Lakṣmaṇa Temple.
78. P.N.K. Bamzai, op. cit., p. 260.
79. M.V. Ramanamurthy, *The Art and Tradition of Shadow Leather Puppet Show in India, BITC*, pt. 2, 1965, pp. 260-62; *PT.*, vol. IV, p. 46.
80. Rājim Stone Inscription of Pṛthvīdeva, II, *CII*, Ins. no. 90.
81. *Śukra*, 11, 202.
82. H. Yule and H. Cordier, *Travels of Marco Polo*, 11, 395.
83. Ibid., 11, 393.

and there hundreds of workers worked in this industry. The craftsmanship of these workers was so famous that in foreign countries the sandals produced by them were known as "sandals of Cambay."[84] According to the foreign writers, the superior craftsmanship of the leather workers of the early medieval period was widely recognized, and their goods were in great demand in foreign countries.

Wood Workers

Wood, because of its easy availability from forests was accepted as a useful material by the artisans. In the pre-historic period, wooden articles were used, along with those made of bones and stones, for daily use. Wood remained the central structural element in the Neolithic technology, in mud or mud-brick houses with wooden roofs.[85] Haṛappan wood workers manufactured household furniture and other objects on a large scale. The highly developed craftsmanship of the wood workers of this period may be seen in the granaries of Haṛappā and Moheṅjo-Dāṛo, in which wood was used in roofs, floors and pillars.[86] Wheeler observes that Haṛappans used wooden pestles to pound grain on a large scale.[87] Representations of boats and ships on the seals and other objects discovered testify to the importance of the Haṛappan wood worker.[88]

The artisans and craftsmen who worked in wood were called *takṣaṇa*, *vardhakīs*, *rathakāras*, etc. in the Vedic literature. The Ṛgvedic *takṣaṇas*[89] (carpenters) produced all kinds of articles for domestic purposes. The *rathakāras* were specialized in the art of manufacturing chariots. It is said that the Bhṛgus (probably a class of carpenters) had specialized in the art of chariot making.[90] The *rathakāras* were held in high esteem in the society because of their art of manufacturing chariots, which were particularly useful in warfare. Ship-building

84. A. Sprenger, *Al-Masudi's Historical Encyclopaedia* (tr. from the Arabic work), p. 95.
85. David E. Hunter and Phillip Whitten, *Readings in Physical Anthropology and Archaeology*, p. 227.
86. See J.R. Fairservis and A. Walter, *The Roots of Ancient India*, p. 252.
87. M. Wheeler, *Harappa: The Indus Civilization*, p. 252.
88. Bridget Allchin and Raymond Allchin, op. cit., pp. 188-89.
89. *ṚV*, 1, 57, 3; IX, 65, 6.
90. Ibid., 1, 61, 4; P.C. Jain, *Labour in Ancient India*, p. 101.

and boat-making was also an important occupation of the Vedic wood workers.[91]

Because of their skill some carpenters were patronized by the king and were not allowed to entertain any private work.[92] The wood workers of the Mauryan period had busy hours in ship-building,[93] which, according to Megasthenes and Strabo,[94] was a monopoly of the state. A large number of skilled wood workers were engaged by the state to construct a wooden defence-wall with holes for the discharge of arrows around the city of Pāṭaliputra.[95] The same source also tells us that all the cities situated on the banks of the rivers or on the sea-coast were made of wood instead of brick.[96] The royal palace of Candragupta was chiefly made of wood.[97] Evidently, wood workers were in great demand in the Mauryan period.

During the Kuṣāṇa period wood workers continued to manufacture different kinds of wooden objects like boats, bullock-carts, and household furniture.[98] Possibly for the first time wood workers formed their guilds.[99] Some of them were employed by the state, and they worked under a superintendent (*dārukādhikārika*),[100] who supervised their work. It is on record that wood workers had a high status in the society,[101] and some of them even made donations.

In the Gupta period, the work of the carpenter was considered an act of art. Vātsyāyana includes the art of wood-carving in his list of 64 arts.[102] In the

---

91. *R̥V*, 1, 116, 5; X, 143, 5.
92. *Patañjali*, 11, 2, 1.
93. Kauṭilya refers to ships of various sizes sailing on the ocean mouths of rivers, lakes (natural or artificial), and rivers in the vicinity of fortified cities; *Arthaśāstra*, 11, 27.
94. J.W. McCrindle, *Ancient India as Described by Magasthanes and Arrian,* Book 11; P.C. Jain, op. cit., p. 151.
95. J.W. McCrindle, *Ancient India as Described in Classical Literature,* Book 11, Frag. XX, p. 65.
96. Ibid., p. 67.
97. B.K. Das, *The Economic History of Ancient India*, p. 149.
98. See Motichandra, *Introduction to Angavijjā*, pp. 35ff.
99. *Mahāvastu*, XVI-XVIII. 179.
100. Motichandra, op. cit., p. 47.
101. *EI*, IX, no. 2, p. 239. In this context an inscription of Kaniṣka's 12th regional year records a dedication by a lady who belonged to the carpenter (*vaddhakin*) class.
102. *Kāmasūtra*, 1, 3 (*takṣaṇam*).

description of a *nāgarakas* house he prescribes a separate room on a solitary side to be exclusively reserved for wood-carving.[103] *Amarakośa* mentions two kinds of wood-carvers. One, those who were hired by the villages, and the other; those who carried on their industry independently,[104] *sthapatis*, supervised the work of the first kind.[105] The same text also mentions the implements used by the wood workers, such as the chisel, the saw,[106] and the workbench.[107]

WOOD WORKERS IN THE EARLY MEDIEVAL PERIOD

In the early medieval period different kinds of wooden articles were manufactured by the professional class of wood workers. It appears that by this time the wood artisans and craftsmen organized themselves into a caste. Rājaśekhara mentions the caste of *vardhakīs*[108] as being connected with the professional work of carpenters. An inscription of King Kethanadeva, dated VS 1221 (CE 1164), refers to the *rathakāras* who were settled in Rajasthan.[109] There are references to proficient carpenters in a contemporary text.[110]

WOOD USED BY WOOD WORKERS

Different kinds of wood was used for making tools, furnitures, boats, ships, carts, etc. *Bṛhatsaṁhitā* mentions the following varieties of wood as used by *vardhakīs*: *asana* (*Pentaptera tomentosa*), *spandana* or *syandana* (*Dalbergia* or *Geinensis*), *candana* (*Petrocarpus santalinus*), *haridra* (*Mesua ferrea*), *suradāru* (*Pinus deodaru*), *tindukī* (*Niosperos glutinosa*), *śāla* (*Shorea robusta*), *kāśmarī* (*Gambhar, gmelina arborea*) *añjana* (*Micheelea champaka*), *padmaka* (a Nepalese timber tree yielding a red wood); *śaka* (teak, *Techtona grandis*), and *siṁśapā* (*Dalbergea sisu*).[111] Although Someśvara does not mention the names of the trees yet he states that trees Jāti One, Jāti Two and

---

103. Ibid., 1, 4., p. 101.
104. *Amara*, X, 9, p. 227.
105. Ibid., 111, 61, p. 284; 111, 4.
106. Ibid., X, 34 and 35, p. 233.
107. Ibid., 11, 35, p. 267.
108. See B.N. Puri, *The History of Gurjara Pratihāras*, p. 132.
109. *EI*, XI, p. 41.
110. *Naishadh*, XV, 34; XIX, 54; XXI, 18, 79.
111. *BS*, LXXVIII, 2; See *Viśvakarmā Prakāśa*.

Jāti Three[112] should be selected for building purposes.[113] The recommended timber of particular trees to be used for certain specified purposes. For instance, *Mānasollāsa* lays down that the trees *nīpa, bibhītaka, nīmba, ślesmāntaka,* and those having dry branches should always be avoided for construction purposes.[114] Someśvara suggests that wood should be cut in on an auspicious day. He recommends the wood of particular trees for construction purposes. *Yuktikalpataru* says that wood like *gambhārī, panasa, candana* and *bakula* should be used for making bedsteads and *pīṭhas*.[115] *Mānasāra*[116] approves *neem* for agricultural implements and couches.[117] Wood-cutters cut down trees on a large scale, and transported the wood to the wood worker. Instruments of wood cutters and the expertise of two carpenter brothers are mentioned in *Kathāsaritsāgara*.[118] The saw, the work bench, the chisel, etc. were the implements used by wood workers.[119]

VILLAGE CARPENTERS

The wood workers fulfilled the needs of the people in the villages. These workers produced and repaired wooden objects of household use. *Bṛhatsaṁhitā* mentions cots, different kinds of wooden vessels, boxes, chairs, tables, palanquins, pestles, combs, ladles, pastry-boards and numerous other articles which were used in the period under review.[120] The village carpenters produced the mortars and pestles,[121] oil-presses,[122] and wooden frames (*kāṣṭhamañcikas*)[123] for keeping water jars at the inns. *Adahaka,* (a wooden vessel), was also used by the villagers for measuring

112. X, 50. The word *jāti* denotes the quality or the variety of a tree.
113. *Mānasollāsa*, 3, 1, 21.
114. Ibid., 3, 1, 17-20.
115. See B.P. Majumdar, op. cit., p. 207.
116. *Mānasāra,* Chap. V, VV, 56-57.
117. Ibid., XLIV, 72-77.
118. *Kss*, 111, p. 282.
119. Ibid.
120. Varāhamihira also refers to *kamaṇḍalu*, a gourd or water-vessel which was made of wood: *BS*, LVII, 39, 41.
121. *KP*, V, 91; *Sad*, 2, 84; 2, 73, 2, 5; 1, 3; *Subhāṣitaratnakośa*, V, 1178.
122. *Ārya*, V, 592; *Subhāṣitaratnakośa*, V, 1365.
123. *Hcar*, p. 228.

paddy.[124] The village carpenter was also engaged in making implements for peasants. Two most important implements that he manufactured for the villagers were the plough and the harrow.[125] Some agricultural implements were made of *neem* wood.[126] In some implements wood and metal were jointly used, such as in oil-presses, sugar-presses, spades, sickles, *rahaṭa*s (machines for drawing water from wells for irrigating fields), and implements for cutting grass and wood.[127] Thus it seems that in our period the role of the village carpenter was highly conspicuous in the economy of north Indian villages during the period under review.

WOOD WORKERS IN CITIES AND TOWNS

Literary works of the early medieval period indicate that there were a large number of wood workers both in cities and towns in the various regions of north India. The wood workers who worked to fulfil the requirements of the urban people probably earned more money. They manufactured all kinds of vehicles, household objects, tools for various purposes, houses, temples and numerous artistic objects.

CARTS AND CHARIOTS

Contemporary literature and epigraphs refer to various kinds of wooden vehicles which were manufactured by skilled wood workers. The sculptures of the period frequently display the cart and the chariot.[128] *Harṣacarita* refers to the wooden bullock cart.[129] The wood workers made these vehicles for transporting agricultural products and people from one place to another. The chariot, which has always been an important vehicle since the ancient times, was very much in vogue in the early medieval period too. We find mention of the *Rathakāra* (chariot maker) in our sources.[130] It is attested by the *Rathayātrā* (car-festive) ceremony of the gods

---

124. *KP*, VV, 112ff.
125. Ibid.
126. *Mānasāra*, Ch. V, VV, 56-57.
127. A.K. Choudhary, op. cit., p. 197.
128. Urmila Agrawal, op. cit., li. VII.
129. *Hcar*, p. 229; See *Sad*, 2, 84.2, *EI*, XI, p. 41.
130. *EI*, XI, p. 41.

of both the Hindus and the Jainas.[131] The Banāras Plates of Karṇa[132] and the Jabalpur Stone Inscription of Jayasiṁha[133] describe the construction of chariot, which was the specialization of some wood workers of the time of Kaḷacuris. According to certain epigraphical sources, some wood workers specialized in preparing chariots, and some others in making carts.[134]

BOATS AND SHIPS

Some wood workers prepared different kinds of boats on a large scale. This was a very specialized work. The extensive use of boat in our period made this profession a prominent one. Boats were used in transporting goods and people,[135] carrying armies across rivers,[136] military expeditions,[137] journeys,[138] and forming boat-bridges.[139] Big boats and ships were also used for internal and external trade. In some parts of north India, mainly in Kashmir boats were used on a massive scale.

In *Yuktikalpataru*[140] there is a detailed description of the various kinds of boats and of the method of building boats. The author classifies boats on the basis of the wood used in them. According to him, the kind of wood distinguished the four classification as follows :

(i) light, soft and pieceable wood used in boats belonging to the "brāhmaṇa" class;

(ii) light and yet strong and not easily pieceable wood used in boats belonging to the "kṣatriya" class,

(iii) soft and heavy wood used in boats belonging to the "vaiśya" class.

(iv) strong and heavy wood used in boats belonging to the "śūdra" class.

---

131. Ibid.
132. *CII*, IV, Ins. 48, verse 20.
133. Ibid., Ins. 64, verse 23.
134. *EI*, XI, p. 47.
135. Traders and Boatmen used boats for trade. *EI*, II, p. 345.
136. *Rāmacarita*, 11, 10.
137. *EI*, I, pp. 307f.
138. *Naiṣadha*, XX, 71; *EI*, XIX, pp. 279f.
139. *RT*, VIII, 1502.
140. *Yuktikalpataru*, Chap. 120-21, pp. 224f.

The work mentions ten types of boats, and the classification was based on the size and shape of the boats. These are *kṣudra, madhyamā, bhīmā, capalā, pāṭālā bhayā, dīrghā, patraputā, garbharā* and *mantharā*. Evidently, the boat industry was fully developed in the period. The great advancement in boat-making may be inferred from the advice of the writer that the wooden parts of the oceangoing vessels were not to be joined together with iron, as the magnetic iron in the sea could lead to capsize of the vessels.[141]

In the period under review, ships could be with or without cabins. Ships with cabins were known as *agramandirā, madhyamandirā*, and *sarvamandirā* depending on whether the cabins were in front, in the rear or situated all over it. The third type was used by the kings and queens, the second one by the sovereign during rainy season, and the first one for military expeditions.

The sources of the period also show the value of boats in wars. Some wood workers supplied boats to the king for carrying defensive weapons and soldiers over rivers. Boats were used by the Pāla army to cross rivers in a naval engagement.[142] The Deopārā inscription says that boats were used in a military expeditions by Vijaysena.[143] The importance of boats in war is also testified by Sultān Mahmūd of Ghazni, who won victory over the powerful Jāṭs in CE 1207 by the use of 1400 war boats.[144] The Madanpur Plate of Śrīcandra also refers to *nauvāṭaka* and *ardhanauvāṭaka*, which mean a fleet of boats and half a division of fleet of boats.[145]

The geographical features of Kashmir called for construction of boat-bridges over rivers. *Rājataraṅgiṇī* tells us that Sujji was able to win the battle of Gambhīrā by erecting a boat-bridge.[146] During the period of Pravarasena II boat-bridges were made on the Vitastā River.[147] The source also makes frequent references to

---

141. See B.P. Majumdar, op. cit., p. 205.
142. Commentary on *Rāmacarita* by R.C. Majumdar; R.G. Basak and N.G. Banerji, II, 10.
143. Deopara Inscription, verse 22.
144. *HIED*, II, p. 478; See B.N. Sharma, op. cit., p. 145.
145. *EI*, XXVIII, 55-56.
146. *RT*, VIII, 1502.
147. Ibid., III, 354.

river journeys, and thereby implies that boats were a common means of travel in the Kashmir Valley.[148]

HOUSEHOLD OBJECTS

Tilakamañjarī and *Śrinagaramañjarīkathā* refer to wooden furniture like chairs, couches and bedsteads.[149] *Yuktikalpataru* of Bhoja acquaints us with the household commodities of our period, such as chairs, couches and bedsteads. He also describes the varieties of wood used for making furniture. The *pīṭha*s (seats) called *subhāsaṅgaka*s, *jaya*s, *sukha*s and *jaraka*s were used during the royal coronation.[150] Wood workers manufactured eight types of bedsteads, viz. *maṅgalā, vijayā, puṣṭi, kṣamā, tuṣṭi, sukhāsana, prachaṇḍā* and *sarvatobhadrā*.[151] *Mānasāra* mentions nine varieties of *paryaṅka* each of them being distinguished on the basis of its width, which ranged from 21 to 37 *aṅgula*s with successive increase of 2 *aṅgula*s each.[152] Cotton-padded couches are referred to by *Rājataraṅgiṇī*.[153] Proper care was taken to see that every part of bedsteads and seats was without any weak spot. It seems that manufacturing of furniture was a popular occupation of wood workers.

HOUSES AND TEMPLES

Some wood workers worked only for the king or the palace. The king and the rich people lived in highly decorated mansions, with very precious household furniture. The doors and windows of their houses were decorated and painted by proficient women. Ivory was also used for decoration.[154] According to Kalhaṇa, wood workers constructed wooden houses in Kashmir.[155] These buildings were very large — four or five storeys high and very durable.[156] Timber was available profusely in the state, and could also be imported from the nearby Himalayan regions.

148. Ibid., V, 84; VII, 347; 714, 1628.
149. Quoted by B.N. Sharma, op. cit., p. 145.
150. *Yuktikalpataru*, pp. 57-59.
151. See B.P. Majumdar, op. cit., p. 207.
152. P.K. Acharya, *Indian Architecture*, p. 62.
153. *RT*, VIII, 2145.
154. See *BS*, LXXVIII, 19; *Raghu*, XVII, 21; See *Viśvakarmā Prakāśa*, X, 71.
155. *RT*, VIII, 2390.
156. *HIED*, III, p. 476.

One of the most distinctive specimens of the wood work of the early medieval period can be seen in the wooden temples of Cambā (Himachal Pradesh). Judging by the surviving Lakṣaṇā Devī temple at Chatrahī, which includes parts of the original structure, one can surmise that Śiva and Gaṇeśa temples were largely made of wood. Goetz[157] believes that the carved wooden columns and façades of goddess temples survive from Meruvarman's time[158] (though for the Chatarhi wooden structures, a somewhat later date is fixed). An idea of the excellent wood carving of the period can be formed from a balcony window of the Markulā (*kālī*) temple at Markulā-Udaipur in the Cambā district.[159] Thus, making wooden temples and houses in the hilly regions was a regular practice of the wood workers. A high degree of craftsmanship in wood was executed by the workers in the famous Somanātha temple in Saurāṣṭra, which was erected on 56 pillars of teak wood covered with lead.[160] In the Kharoḍ Inscription of Ratnadeva III (*Sam.* 933) mentions the Gaṅgādhara Maṭha, which was made of well-seasoned wood (*kaṭhorakāṣṭha*).[161] Lastly, it is worth noting that the roofs of the houses were generally covered with wooden planks.

Thus, it appears from a scrutiny of the literary and the epigraphical sources of the early medieval period that wood-carving (*takṣaṇam*) was well developed during the period under survey. In ancient times it was one of the 64 arts. The wood workers also fashioned different kinds of wooden implements for domestic and other purposes both in the villages and the cities on a very large scale. Implements like the chisel, the saw and the work-bench were commonly prepared by the wood workers. Some wood workers worked only for the rich people, and some others were patronized by the king. These workers also manufactured articles like couches, bedsteads, chairs, and boats and ships. The high degree of wood craftsmanship may be seen in the excellent wooden buildings, houses and carvings of the period. All this indicates that the wood workers were in great demand, and at least some of them enjoyed high prestige in the society of the time.

---

157. H. Goetz, *The Early Wooden Temples of Chamba.*

158. M. Postel; A. Neven and K. Mankodi, *Antiquities of Himachal* (Bombay, 1985), p. 47.

159. H. Goetz, op. cit., pp. 93-95, p. LVII.

160. *HIED*, 1, pp. 98ff.

161. *EI*, XXI, V. 31.

Ivory Workers

The term *dantakāra* in our literary and archaeological sources denotes "ivory workers." Articles of ivory have been used for domestic purposes since ancient times. Some of the important bone objects were combs, hairpins, bangles, dice, handles of mirror, furniture, decorative pieces, small boxes, and some small weapons. The Neolithic people used the bones of antlers and other animals for making weapons, tools, etc. Articles like carved combs, hairpins surmounted by shapes of birds and animals, dice, etc. discovered in excavations show that the use of ivory was quite extensive in the Haṛappan times.[162] Highly conventionalized anthropomorphic Mother goddess figures fashioned by the ivory workers of the early historic period have been discovered from Taxila, Nāgadā and Ujjain.[163] Numerous references to bone and ivory workers are preserved in the Jātakas.[164] The ivory workers of Vidiśā are also mentioned in an inscription of Sāñcī.[165] Ivory is a precious material gained from the tusk of the elephant. Kauṭilya, while describing the duties of the superintendent of forest produce, refers to skins, bones and teeth of elephants.[166] Four ivory dice are known to have been found in the course of the excavations at Kumrahāra.[167] Many objects of ivory, shell and bone have been discovered from the Kuṣāṇa sites.[168]

Kālidāsa describes seals made of ivory.[169] A Large number of ivory seals discovered from Bhītā (fourth or fifth century CE) throw light on the products of ivory workers and their manufacture. The beautifully inscribed surface of the seal surrounded by a headed line and a crawling tortoise is a good specimen of

---

162. Vinod P. Dwivedi, "Life Depicted in Ancient Indian Ivory Carvings", *Journal of Indian History*, Trivandrum, LI, pt. 3, 1973, pp. 463-70.

163. Ibid.

164. Jātakas, 1, 60, 72; 221, etc.; See *Milinda,* V, 4, p. 210; *Mahāvastu*, 11, p. 473; *Divyāvadana*, p. 410; *Buddhacarita*, 1, 86; *Kāmasūtra*, 111, 16; *Aṅgavijjā*, pp. 15, 112, I36ff; *Manu*, V, 121; *Viṣṇu*, XXXIII, 34; See Kameshwar Prasad, op. cit., p. 119.

165. *EI*, II, p. 92.

166. *Arthaśāstra*, II, xvii.

167. *Kumrahara Excavation Report*, p. 136.

168. See Kameshwar Prasad, op. cit., pp. 119-20.

169. *Raghu*, XVII, 21.

the exquisite ivory work of the Gupta period.[170] The art of manufacturing ornaments from ivory is one of the 64 arts prescribed by Vātsyāyana to be mastered by a *nāgaraka*.[171] Besides ornaments, ivory carvers also manufactured pegs for hanging articles on.[172]

MATERIAL FOR IVORY WORKERS

It seems that during the period under review the artistic products of ivory were in great demand. The ivory workers gained their raw material from the forests where elephants were to be found. Their main task was to get tusks of elephants. Kaḷacuri Inscriptions[173] give us valuable information about the raw material for ivory carvers. The fourfold unit of army caught the elephants from the forests and ivory was gained from tusks after the death of elephants. The ivory workers also used the horns of buffaloes and other animals. Bose[174] traces the origin of the name of the town Dantapura, once the capital of Kaliṅga, to the ivory industry. The raw material for the ivory industry was obtained from the surroundings of this town. The ivory industry of this area, thriving much before our period, continued into it. A copper-plate inscription from Orissa, referring to a gift of some land apparently situated in a forest, records that the privileges of the brāhmaṇa donee include, in addition to other things, his right to the ivory (*hasti-danta*) obtained in the forest.[175]

ARTICLES OF IVORY

Ivory is a precious material and difficult to carve on, but in the early medieval time, the Indian craftsmen had mastered this art. Some goldsmiths also used ivory as a filling in gold ornaments. The craftsmanship of the ivory workers is described in the contemporary records, and specimens of it are discovered from

---

170. J. Marshall, *ASI* (1911-12), p. 48. Such ivory seals have been found in a large number.
171. *Kāmasūtra*, 1, 3, p. 84.
172. Ibid., 1, 4, p. 101.
173. *CII*, IV, Ins. 84, verse 11.
174. A.N. Bose, *Social and Rural Economy of Northern India*, p. 212.
175. *EI*, XXVIII, pp. 324ff.

various parts of the country. Rajavigā, an ivory-worker,[176] is mentioned in the Bhatera Plate of Govinda Keśava.

The ivory carvers manufactured various kinds of ornaments. *Naiṣadhīyacarita*[177] refers to ivory bracelets (resembling the orb of the moon), while anklets of well-polished ivory are described in *Mānasollāsa*.[178] We learn from the same text that ivory sandals were also prepared,[179] and *āsana*s were decorated with ivory (*dantidantasucitritam*).[180] *Mānasāra* also provides the same information.[181]

Vāmaṇa Purāṇa mentions that the residence of Śiva, built by Viśvakarmā, had an arched gateway of ivory with ledges (*danta-toraṇa nirvyūha*).[182] Balconies made of ivory (*dantavaḍabhī*) are mentioned in *Mānasollāsa*[183] and in *Śṛṅgāramañjarīkathā* of Bhoja.[184] The Edilpur plate of Keśavasena refers to palanquins supported by staffs made of elephant tusks.[185] Such palanquins are also described in contemporary literature. The king's seat, called *sukhāsana*, is said to have been covered with lion's skin and studded with gold. The ivory poles, fixed under it, enabled the four bearers to carry it.[186] The legs of cots were also made of ivory.[187] People used ivory cages (*nāga dantikā*) for housing sparrows.[188] Kṣemendra speaks of the figures made of dirty ivory (*danteṣu malpūraṇeṣu*).[189] Thus the ivory carvers produced several articles of daily use, and also luxury items for the rich people.

---

176. Ibid., XIX, p. 286; The ivory worker (*dantakāra*) is also described by another inscription of Bhatera, *EI*, IX, 1, 51.
177. *Naiṣadha*, XI, 108.
178. *Mānasollāsa*, I, 956.
179. Ibid., I, 121.
180. Ibid., III, 9, v, 44.
181. *Mānasāra*, XLVI, v, 51.
182. *Vāmana Purāṇa*, 54, 2-3.
183. *Mānasollāsa*, II, 126.
184. *Śṛṅgāramañjarīkathā*, p. 46.
185. *IB*, III, pp.127ff.
186. *Mānasollāsa*, III, 16, 1943-44.
187. Ibid., 18, 1670-71.
188. *Naishadh*, XVIII, 15.
189. *Deśopadeśa*, II, 30.

CENTRES OF IVORY WORK

Mentions may be made of some important centres of ivory industry. In these centres groups of craftsmen worked together and produced ivory articles on a large scale. Ivory pieces of great artistic beauty were made in Orissa. A throne leg of the period, depicting an elephant-faced animal with the body of a lion (*gajavyāla*), is published by Stella Kramrisch.[190] Orissa ivories, belonging to the mid-thirteenth century CE, are preserved in the Freer Gallery of Art, Washington and in the Philadelphia Museum of Art.[191] An inscription engraved on the Jagannātha temple at Purī, recording the gift of eight ivory thrones also bears out the existence of expert Orissan ivory workers.[192]

The ivory workers of Kashmir achieved considerable fame in ivory carvings. A fragmentary ivory *dampati* plaque found in Khoṭan by Stein[193] has been assigned by Lohuizen-de Leeuw to Kashmir.[194] It shows a beardless male figure with short and wavy hair, dressed in a single robe with tight sleeves. After observing this figure carefully Douglas Barrett has confirmed its Kashmiri origin, and has assigned it to early eighth century CE,[195] and may be of early period. The artisans of Kashmir especially fashioned ivory sculptures. The ivory workers were extremely well-versed in their handicraft, and carved diverse shapes out of ivory. Articles like bangles, trinklets, ornaments, handles for mirrors, and inlay of royal chariots were made of ivory. Making of ivory ornaments was a common occupation of ornament-makers anywhere, but Kashmir was traditionally famous for manufacture of ivory images. Among the ivory articles discovered is a diptych

---

190. *Philadelphia Museum of Art Bulletin*, LIV (no. 261, Spring 1959), pp. 55-56.

191. J.E. van Lohuizen-de Leeuw, *Arts Asiatiques*, VI, 3 (1959), pp. 198-216, figs. 1-8 and 13-14.

192. R. Mitra, *The Antiquities of Orissa*, 11, pp. 165.

193. M. Aurel Stein, *Ancient Khotan*, vol. 1, p. 222 and vol. 11, Pl. XLVIII, No. Kh. 008; See V.P. Dwivedi, *The Kashmir Ivories*, Reprint from the *Chhavi* Bharat Kala Bhavan Golden Jubilee Volume, Varanasi, 1972, p. 322.

194. J.E. van Lohuizen-de Leeuw, "Indian Ivories with Special Reference to Medieval Throne Leg from Orissa", *Arts Asiatique*, Tomb VI (1959), pp. 195-217. D. Barret, "A Note on Ivories", *Lalit Kalā*, no. 10, New Delhi, 1962, p. 56.

195. D. Barret, "A Note on Ivories", *Lalit Kalā*, no. 10, 1962, p. 56.

now in Kansu Province of China.[196] Although this diptych became more popular in later Christian art, it seems to have originated with the Buddhist artists.[197] One of the most outstanding creations in ivory, a figure of the Buddha with the attendants carved in deep relief, is in the Prince of Wales Museum, Bombay.[198] This image, with a most graceful outlook, is a Kashmir product of the exquisite ivory craftsmanship of the eighth century CE.[199] Among other Buddhist ivory sculptures, one is a Buddha, now in the Museum of Fine Arts, Boston,[200] seated in *padmāsana*, and another is a small plaque showing the Buddha in the standing[201] posture. A similar standing figure of the Buddha exists in the Cleveland Museum of Art, Cleveland.[202] In addition, there is an excellent carving in ivory of Avalokiteśvara in his Lokanātha aspect.[203]

The versatility and genius of the Kashmir ivory carvers is clear from their masterly folding of ivory tusk in the course of their preparation of images. It is interesting to note that these ivory images are ornamented, painted and fashioned in different model.[204] We can safely assume that ivory workers were deft in shaping the ivory tusk into different forms as ornaments, sculptures and so on.

THE EXPORT QUALITY OF IVORY PRODUCTS

In the early medieval period, there was a great demand of Indian ivory objects in the foreign countries. This implies a high degree of craftsmanship of ivory workers in carving artistic goods. From Orissa it was exported to the Arab countries in substantial quantities.[205] The Muslim travellers speak of the presence of ivory-

196. D. Barret, "An Ivory Diptych", *Lalit Kalā*, no. 13, 1967, pp. 11-14.
197. Ibid., p. 13.
198. Motichandra, "Ancient Indian Ivories," *Bulletin of the Prince of Wales Museum of Western India*, no. 6, p. 38, pl. 6.
199. Ibid., p. 42.
200. Milo Beach, "Two Indian Ivories: Newly Acquired", *Bulletin of the Museum of Fine Arts*, vol. LXII, no. 329 (1964) pp. 95-101, pl. 1.
201. Ibid., p. 99 pls. 5 and 6.
202. Ibid., Pl. 7.
203. Motichandra, op. cit., p. 47, Pl. 106.
204. For detail see V.P. Dwivedi, *The Kashmir Ivories*. Ibid., pp. 322-26.
205. V. Minorsky, *Hudud-e-Alam*, p. 86.

dealers in Multan, and refer to a row of shops near the Sun temple.[206] King of Pirañj is said to have been well provided with elephant teeth.[207] Coḷamaṇḍala as Cauju-Kuā of tenth century CE vouchsafes that ivory was exported from Coḷamaṇḍala.[208]

Ivory, a very precious material, was gained from the tusk of the elephant. Ivory workers fashioned various objects of daily use and luxury items for the rich people. There were some famous centres of ivory work in north India during the period under study. The superior skill of the ivory workers in their craft is attested by the literary and archaeological sources. Some ivory carvers fashioned highly conventionalized anthropomorphic figures of various gods for religious purposes. Their products were in great demand in the society of the period. Different kinds of ornaments were also prepared by the ivory workers. The masterly craftsmanship of the ivory workers is easily indicated by the substantial demand of their ware in foreign countries.

Glass Makers

No true glass has yet been found from Indus Civilization,[209] says Marshal. However, authentic evidence of the process of glass-making has been described by Kauṭilya.[210] He has made a mention of glass (*kāñca*) beads in connection with some ornamental work in gold (*kṣepaṇa*). Glass-makers seem to have achieved a prominent place during the first-third centuries CE.[211] The contemporary literature of the Kuṣāṇa period refers to terms like *śīsapiccatākara*[212] (lead sheets) and *śīsākara*.[213] The articles made of glass, such as beads, bangles, rings, vessels, etc. have been excavated from the Kuṣāṇa sites.[214] In addition, the fine colour of the

206. *HIED*, I, p. 28 and 35.

207. S.H. Hodivala, *Studies in Indo Muslim History*, p. 7.

208. F. Hirth and W.W. Rockhill, *Chau-ju-Kua*, pp. 92-93.

209. J. Marshal, *Mohenjo-Dāṛo and the Indus Civilization*, II, p. 578.

210. P.C. Ray, *History of Chemistry in Ancient and Medieval India*, pp. 73-76.

211. Kameshwar Prasad, *Cities, Crafts and Commerce under the Kuṣāṇas*, p. 117.

212. *Mahāvastu*, III, pp. 112, 444.

213. *Milindapañho*, V, 4, p. 210.

214. Dheri Saikhan, *Ancient Pakistan*, 11, pp. 121-22; J. Marshall, Taxila, pp. 650-742; See *IAR*, 1970-71, p. 62; 1971-72, p. 42; 1964-65, p. 43; *ASI*, 1911-12, pp. 29-94. See Kameshwar Prasad, op. cit., pp.117-18,

glass used in these articles and its low specific gravity shows that the glass craftsmen had a good knowledge of the chemical aspect of glass technology.

References to glass by terms like *kāca*,[215] *kācakūpī*[216] and *kācapātra*[217] are furnished by some literary sources of our period. From them it seems that the glass-makers prepared various kinds of vessels for domestic purposes. The use of different kinds of glass vessels is also suggested by *Rasaratnākara* of Nityanātha Siddha.[218] Another text speaks of the different types of glass articles of domestic use in the early medieval period.[219] Apparently, the profession of glass-making assumed considerable importance in the society of the period. In fact, glass became an article of inter-national trade. An Arab writer named Ibn Khurdādbeh, who died in CE 912 tells us that glass was obtained from Gujarat.[220]

The author of *Rasaratnasamuccaya* describes precisely the characteristics of glass.[221] P.C. Ray observes that purification of glass was well known to the glass-makers of the period.[222] The original text mentions an apparatus of glass known as *Valukāyantram*, which is described as follows : "A glass flask with a long neck containing mercurials is wrapped with several folds of cloth smeared with clay and then dried in the sun." Glass workers used this apparatus for chemical purposes and prepared several kinds of glass articles.

It seems that Kashmir was also fairly advanced in glass technology. According to Kalhaṇa, large glass jars were regularly despatched to the King Bhoja of Mālwā by a merchant named Padmarāja.[223] Moreover, a quantity of ancient glass fragments was found strewn on the road leading from the village of Kother to

---

215. Dohākośa, p. 229; *Mānasollāsa*, 11. *Vimśati* 3.128.
216. *Pb, Chin.*, V. 224.
217. *Dohākośa*, 341, 117.
218. Bhartīya *Vidyā*, VII, pp. 148-60.
219. *Rasaprakāśasudhākara*, quoted in *Bharatiya Vidya*, VII, pp. 148-60.
220. Motichandra, *Trade and Trade Routes in Ancient India*, p. 203.
221. *Rasaratnasamuccaya*, IX. 34-36.
222. P.C. Ray, *History of Hindu Chemistry from the Earliest Times to the Middle of the 16th century* CE, 1, pp. 123ff.
223. Bamzai, *A History of Kashmir*, pp. 210-11.

the spring of Papasudana.[224] It seems appropriate to conclude that this area was an important centre of glass manufacture in the early medieval times in India.

Mirror Makers

The mirror, an important article of toilet, has been made by some artisans since the ancient times. References in this context are very few, and it has been simplicistically assumed that glass was not used for this purpose. Possibly metals were polished and used as mirrors. Gopinath Rao contends that metallic mirrors were used in ancient India.[225] The art of making mirrors was prevalent in Indus culture. An oval copper mirror was noticed during the excavations at Haṛappā.[226] It may be believed that since the time of Indus Valley Civilization the mirror manufacturers have fulfilled the demand of the people by producing metallic mirrors.

Examples of mirrors are delineated in the Gandhāra reliefs. A woman is shown arranging her coiffure with the help of a mirror.[227] Mirrors have also been found from the excavations at Taxila, Basārh, Ahicchatra, Brahmapurī and Raish.[228] All these mirrors are of the Śuṅga–Kuṣāṇa periods. This indicates that the art of metallurgy was well known, and mirrors were made of both copper and bronze. A Taxila specimen had an ivory handle intact, and its sides framed for preservation.

In *Raghuvaṁśa* there is a reference to a mirror made of gold.[229] Artisans made this type of mirror for the royal houses and the rich people. A cultural study of the Ajantā frescos has been carried out by Codrington.[230] He notices depiction of metal articles as having a mirror surface. Codrington makes the following

224. Ibid.

225. T.A. Gopinath Rao, *Hindu Iconography*, vol. I, Part I, p. 12; See B.S. Upadhyaya, *Kalidāsa Kā Bhārata*, vol. I, p. 323.

226. M.S. Vats, *Excavations at Harappā*, vol. I, p. 391, pl. CXXIV.

227. K. Krishna murthy, *The Domestic Art Delineated in the Gandhara Reliefs, Purātattva,* no. 7, 1974, pp. 96-102.

228. C. Margabandhu, "A Note on Some Ancient Mirrors", *Puratattva,* no. 7, 1974, pp. 94-95.

229. *Raghu*; XVII, 26.

230. S.K. Maity, *Economic Life in Northern India*, p. 140.

observations : the metallic mirrors are circular and have a central knob behind, pierced to take a ring or a cord. This form can be associated with China, tanged or handled mirrors being common all over the east — in bronze, brass and steel in the Muhammadan times, and in bronze in Java at a period closely succeeding that of Ajantā. In India, mirrors of any kind are rarely found during excavations. In spite of the archaeological rareness of mirrors in India in general, modern Newārī-made copper and brass mirrors were common in Tibetan rural use. This observation also shows that metal plates were used in the form of mirrors.[231] Professional workers made metallic mirrors for household use, and they were in vogue up to the early medieval period, and even up to later times.

Literary sources of our period refer to the mirror as a domestic object which was most probably used in every household. But most of the references are to metallic mirrors. Probably Indian craftsmen did not know the method of making looking-glasses. Indian craftsmen were highly skilled and proficient in the field of science and technology. How can their ignorance about looking-glass technology be explained? However, literary evidence abounds with descriptions of mirrors in use in those days. Sometimes, more than one mirror was used.[232] Not only women but men also used mirrors.[233] Sometimes mirrors were manufactured for special purposes. From *Ākhyānakamaṇikośa* we learn about the halls of mirrors (*darpaṇagṛhas*), which were specially designed to give reflection of the king from all the sides.[234]

The songs of *Sarahapada* mention mirrors and inform us that they were made of metal.[235] A close study of *Yuktikalpataru* reveals that mirrors were manufactured from *suvarṇa*, *rajata*, *trapu*, and *lohā*.[236] The best mirrors were made from *aṣṭadhātus*.[237] Another quality of mirror, according to *Dohākośa,* was *riddhidarpaṇa,*

231. *IA*, 1930, p. 172.
232. *Naisadh*, XV, 50-52.
233. Ibid., XV, 70.
234. *Āmk*, 347, 8-11 .
235. *Dohākośa*, p. 337, V. 106.
236. *Yuktikalpataru*, p. 80, V. 5.
237. Ibid., p. 81, V. 10.

which was bright and clear on both the sides.[238] *Yuktikalpataru* tells us that mercury was also one of the ingredients used in making mirrors. The author of the same text classified the mirrors as *bhavya,* which was one *vitasti* in length; *vijaya,* which was four *aṅgula*s long and broad, and *pauruṣa,* on which fell the full length of a person. Thus it would appear that making of mirrors was a fairly popular profession.

From the above description it seems that the profession of mirror-making had its own importance in the society of the early medieval period. The mirror-makers earned their livelihood by producing mirrors of different shapes. A text asserts that mirrors should be circular, and have a decorated rim with the edge a little raised.[239] The craft of making metallic mirrors prevalent earlier continued into our period.[240]

From several sculptures appearing on the temples of Khajurāho and Bhubaneswar, it is evident that mirrors were widely used during the period under review. In the sculptures on the bas-reliefs of these temples, mirrors are shown mostly used by women.[241] For instance, in a scene a woman is shown looking into a mirror, admiring her personal beauty. In another scene, a lady is shown arranging her hair with her right hand while she holds the *ārasī* near her face in the other hand.[242] In most of such scenes women are shown adjusting their ornaments, applying toiletry articles and admiring beauty. Mirror is used in its different shapes and for reflecting different parts of the body. It is curious to note that in a scene the mirror is held by a woman so as to reflect the back of her body to advantage.[243] The woman holding the mirror is shown in the sculptures as standing in various attitudes, sometimes folding her hands above her shoulders,[244]

---

238. *Dohākośa,* p. 335, v. 102.

239. *Mānasāra,* Also see B.S. Upadhyaya, *Kālidāsa kā Bharata,* vol. 1, p. 323.

240. *Bhāratīya Vidyā,* VII, p. 159. However, around CE 1550 India began to import foreign European glasses.

241. O. Takata and T. Uneo, *The Art of India,* 1, pls. 209 and 210; Urmila Agarwal, *Khajuraho Sculptures and Their Significance,* pp. 143ff, fig. 94.

242. Left outside Vāmana temple.

243. Left outside Kandarīya, Right outside Caturbhuja Temples.

244. Back outside Vāmana Temple.

resting them on her hips[245] or thighs,[246] and sometimes supporting her breasts and admiring them in the mirror,[247] and sometimes again she is represented in a dance pose.[248]

The depiction of mirrors found at Khajurāho, mostly in the hands of ladies are of convex surface, which shows that metallic mirrors were in vogue. The looking-glass was an indispensable accessory of toilet, and in its absence polished metal was used as a mirror. Whenever a woman was to apply powder or rouge to her cheeks, the *tilaka* mark on her forehead, unguent to her eyes or vermillion in the middle parting of her hair, she had to do so with the help of a mirror. No wonder that mirrors were very popular in the early medieval period, and the mirror-makers met the requirement of the age competently.

Makers of Musical Instruments

The Sanskrit term *saṅgīta*[249] means more than what is ordinarily denoted by the English word music[250] in its sense of a cultivated discipline. Man started playing on instruments of music with the very dawn of civilization.[251] The various musical instruments found in the excavations of Haṛappā and Moheṅjo-Dāṛo include a flute with seven keys, denoting the seven notes of music; a stringed musical instrument resembling the *vīṇā*; and several other percussion instruments.[252]

---

245. Left outside Citragupta temple, Right outside Caturbhuja and Vśvanātha, Right inner Pradakṣinā, Kandarīya Temples.

246. Left outside Kandarīya Temple.

247. Left outside Bharata Citragupta and Kandarīya Temples.

248. Left and right outside of the Viśvanātha Temple.

249. *samyak rupeṇa gīyate iti sanītam*: Jagdish Narayan Pathak, *Saṅgīta Nibandha Mālā* (Hindi edn.), p. 1.

250. *gītam vādyam ca nṛtyam trayaṁ saṅgīta mucyate*: Sarangadev Pandit, *Saṅgīta Ratnākara* (Hindi edn.), Chap. 1, verse 2.

251. The history of the earliest musical instruments goes back up to 20,000 years in the village of Mezin, near Chernigov in Ukraine, and it has been brought to light by the remains of musical instruments that were made from the bones of mammoths: Gergei N. Bibikov, *Astone Age orchestra,* David E. Hunter and Phillip Whitten, *Readings in Anthropology and Archaeology,* p. 59.

252. D. Goswami, *The Story of Indian Music,* p. 293.

Possibly, the Vedic hymns were sung with the help of musical instruments. References to the *vīṇā* and the *mṛdaṅga* are recorded in the Saṁhitās.[253] A number of musical instruments like the drum, the conch, the lute, the tabours, the tambour, and different kinds of cymbals, gongs and tambourines are mentioned in the Jātakas.[254] The depiction of the *vīṇā* in the sculptures of Bharhut, Besnagar, Amarāvatī, and the Buddhist caves, and on the coins of Samudragupta and Kumāragupta I provides sufficient evidence of the importance and popularity of the musical instruments and their evolution.[255] The great demand of music instruments in the early medieval times afforded a source of income to some artisans.

Bṛhatsaṁhitā refers to several kinds of musical instruments prepared by artisans and craftsmen. The author of the text contends that the sounds produced by singing and those by musical instruments are contrasted.[256] In his work he mentions the *vīṇā, vallakī* (lute); the *veṇu* (flute), the *paṇava,* the *tūrya* (trumpet); the *mṛdaṅga, muraja* (tabor); the *śaṅkha* (conch-shell); the *ghaṇṭā* (gong); *paṭāha, bherī* and *dundubhi.* The tradition of making instruments continued from the earliest times. Vātsyāyana includes music among his 64 arts. According to Daṇḍin, the lute,[257] the drum[258] the clarionet, flute and conch[259] were generally used.

Musicologists classify the fine art of music of the early medieval period into three broad categories: *gīta* (vocal music), *vādya* (instrumental music) and *nṛtya* (dance). Although there is consonance among the three, and all the three are theoretically music, yet singing with musical instruments is most charming and expressive of the three. In the period under review, we find four types of musical instruments : (i) *tāta* (stringed instruments), such as the *vīnā,* (ii) *suśira* (wind instruments), such as the *veṇu* (made of ivory, wood, brass, gold or silver), (iii)

253. *Taittirīya Saṁhitā,* VI, 1, 4, 1; *Kāṭhaka Saṁhitā,* XXXIV, 5; *Maitrāyaṇī Saṁhitā,* 111, 6, 8.

254. *Jātaka,* I, 59, 60; 11, 327; VI, 544.

255. Mukund, Lath, "Reflections on the Vīṇā in Gupta Coinage", *Journal of Numismatic Society of India, Varanasi,* XXXIX, pts. 2-2, 1977, pp. 114-23.

256. *BS,* XXXIII, 23; XLV, 60; LXXXV, 22, 39.

257. *DKC,* p. 149; *ASK,* pp. 7, 9, 162; *RA,* III, 21.

258. *ASK,* pp. 76, 89, 231; *ASK,* VI, 113, *ASK,* 105, 162.

259. *ASK,* pp. 162-63.

ayanaddha (percussion instruments), such as the *mṛdaṅga*, and (iv) *ghana* (instruments made of brass or bronze) such as *karatāla*, and *mañjīrā*.[260] King Someśvara, who was also an eminent musicologist, in his *Mānasollāsa*,[261] refers to four types of musical instruments:

(i) *pṛthak vādya* (an instrument by itself);

(ii) *gīta-saṅgata* (an instrument accompanying *gīta*),

(iii) *nṛttānuga* (an instrument accompanying dance),

(iv) *gītanṛttānuga* (an instrument accompanying *gīta* and dance).

Though the author does not mention the names of instruments, yet, it seems that by his time artisans had specialized themselves in making and supplying particular musical instruments.

It also appears that different musical instruments were used for different purposes. According to Kalhaṇa, some instruments like drums, conches, bells, lutes, flutes and bagpipers (*huddukas*) were used in temples for religious purposes in Kashmir.[262] Some musical instruments were made to be used on festivals and marriage occasions.

Some of the musical instruments were manufactured only for military purposes. This enhanced the importance of musical instrument-makers and their profession. Instruments like drums, flutes and lutes were used for stimulating the army or making terror prevail in the battlefield. War music was performed by special musicians and instrument-players. Among them drummers were very important. *Bṛhatsaṁhitā*[263] mentions a band of musical instrument-players accompanying a military march. The description of the musicians of army is also given by Bāṇa. "At the close of the third watch," further says Bāṇa, "When all creatures slept and all was still, the marching drum was beaten with a boom deep as the gaping roar of the sky elephants . . . and straightaway the drums rattled, the *nandī*s rang out joyously, the trumpets brayed, the *kahala*s hummed

---

260. Devendra N. Dixit, "Indian Musical Instruments," *Bhavan's Journal*, XVII, no. 7 (November 1970), pp. 209-18.

261. *Mānasollāsa*, 2470.

262. Bamzai, *The History of Kashmir*, pp. 259 and 261.

263. *BS*, XLIII, 23; *YY*, XIII, 4.

the horns blared, the noise of the camp gradually increased."[264] Musical instruments used in the battlefield have been described by Hiuen-Tsang.[265] According to him Harṣa was always accompanied in his marches by several hundred persons with golden drums called "music pace drums," beating one stroke at each step. Someśvara describes the importance of music in war in the period under study.[266]

We learn from *Rājataraṅgiṇī* that in Kashmir kettle-drums were beaten between the night watches in a fort or camp, and that a surprise attack was often announced by the blare of trumpets and drums.[267] A particular number of musical instruments were preserved for the battlefield. Kalhaṇa tells us that musical instruments were used for loud announcement and for many other purposes.[268] Elsewhere we read about commencement of wars with great noise of drums.[269]

Contemporary epigraphic records also throw light on the use of musical instruments in the battlefield. The Kurram Plates of the Pallava king Parameśvaravarman I speak of the "thunder-like sound" of kettle-drums and conch-shells inspiring terror in the battlefield.[270] The kettle-drums, "loud *jharjharas*," and "shrill *ḍamarūs*" are talked of as means of giving signals in the Nagpur Stone Inscription of CE 1104-05.[271] Similarly, *paṭaha* and *ḍhakkā* drums are mentioned in an inscription as instruments of war music.[272] We find from the contemporary records that the drums were generally used in the battlefield, and that they were manufactured by leather workers on a large scale.

Various types of musical instruments with their players have been depicted in sculptures on the bas-reliefs of temples in north India. The *ḍamarū*, the *mṛdaṅga*, the harp and the clarionet are shown along with musicians on Viśvanātha Temple

---

264. *Hcar*, pp. 199-211.
265. Samuel Beal, *The Life of Huien-Tsang*, p. 173.
266. *Mānasollāsa*, p. 137, V, 1209.
267. *RT*, VIII, 2563.
268. *RT*, VIII, 1080-81.
269. Ibid., VIII, 1879, 2942.
270. *EI*, XVII, 343.
271. *EI*, 11, 192.
272. Ibid., IV, 348.

at Khajurāho. A beautiful scene on the Javari Temple depicts a party of men and a women playing on various musical instruments, such as the flute, the cymbals, the conch-shell, the *vīṇā*, and the bell.[273] Khajurāho sculptors depict a number of scenes of women playing on musical instruments,[274] which suggests that in the tenth and eleventh centuries women were free to choose the particular art in which they were most interested, and that the society put no bar on their natural inclination. Their personal interest in music also attracted musicians and dancers to accompany them by playing on musical instruments.

It is evident that artisans and craftsmen manufactured musical instruments on a massive scale. There were professional workers — those who earned their livelihood by supplying musical instruments. Some artisans or leather-workers manufactured only drums of many varieties.[275] The flute (*bāṅsurī*) had its many varieties.[276] It seems that some workers prepared only flutes of different shapes. We find that musicians played on instruments at festivals, fairs, marriages, religious ceremonies or in the battlefields. Groups of people purchased these instruments from professional musical instrument-makers.

Umbrella Makers

Umbrella (*chātā*) protects one from the rain and the sun. Since ancient times it has been used by the common man and in the royal courts alike. However, when it is used in the royal court, it is also a symbol of the power of the king or a person when it is used on his head on special occasions. In our period, as in any other, its utility and demand gave employment to many artisans who manufactured umbrellas. Some umbrella-makers worked only for the royal court, and they manufactured the best qualities of umbrellas of different sizes and colours.

---

273. Archamandap Javari Temple, both left and right sides.

274. R.C. Majumdar, *The Age of Imperial Kanauj*, Chap. XII, p. 367.

275. *HIED*, 11, 215. The drum itself was of many varieties, such as Dundubhī, Bherī, Paṭāha, Puṣkara, Ānaka or Mahānaka, Pesī, Jharjhara, Ḍamarū, Diṇḍima, Dhakka, Pratidhakka, Kāhalā, Konikā, and Ālambara or Aḍambara; Paṭāha, Kāhalā and Konikā are also mentioned in *Harṣacarita* (VII) Paṭāha, Jharjharu and Ḍamarū are described in the Nagpur Stone Inscription (*EI*, XI, 192).

276. M.N. Rao, Padma, "Bānsurī" the long flute in Hindustāni Music, *Journal of the Music academy*, Madras, XLIII, Pts. 1-4, 1972, pp. 84-87.

Among the sculptures represented on the western gate of the Sāñcī *stūpa* there is shown an attendant holding an umbrella.[277] Here umbrella represents the power or identity of the person on whose head it is held. The tradition continued into our period from the earlier epoch. Pāla sculptures also show the umbrella.[278] Many Hindu gods and goddesses like Revanta,[279] Gaṅgā[280] and Yamunā[281] are shown in sculptures with an umbrella held over their heads. There are numerous example of the Jain sculptures of *tīrthaṁkara*s shown shaded by a canopy of a tripple umbrella.[282]

The expertise of the umbrella-manufacturers and the importance of umbrella are elaborately discussed by Bhoja in his *Yuktikalpataru*.[283] Different kinds of umbrellas are recommended in this text for the kings, princes and the ordinary people. Some artisans prepared umbrellas only for the kings. The *viśeṣa,* a special type used by the rulers, had two categories: *nirdaṇḍa* (which could not be folded), and *sadaṇḍa,* which could be folded. Good material was used in these umbrellas and special colours were lent to them according to the taste of the kings. For instance, in the *Naiṣadhacarita* Nala is described as using a white umbrella.[284] Again *Yuktikalpataru* mentions that the stick of the royal umbrella was made of the finest (say, sandal) wood, and the thread and cloth were either scarlet or pure white. A miniature golden cone adorned the top. A different variety of umbrella was prepared for the princes. Its height was to be one fourth less than the length of the umbrella of the king. This variety was called *pratāpa*. It had bluish cloth, and its stick was decorated with a golden cone at the top. Another variety of umbrella, called *navadaṇḍa,* was used during the marriage ceremony.

There was a considerable difference between the umbrellas used by the common men and by the rich people. The stick of the common man's umbrella

---

277. F.C. Maisey, *Sāñchi and Its Remains,* p. 59.
278. S. Kramrisch, *Pāla and Sena Sculptures,* Figures 29 and 51.
279. *Ajmer Museum,* 1 (66) 299.
280. *National Museum,* New Delhi, p. 238.
281. Ibid., 64, 379.
282. Ibid., 59, 202.
283. *Yuktikalpataru,* Chap. XXXVI, pp. 62f.
284. B.P. Majumdar, op. cit., p. 195.

was half in length to that of a crown prince, and was made of ordinary timber. The artisans used the timber of *panasa, śāla, campaka, śrīphala,* sandal, *neem, vakula,* and *varjarvarṇa* for this purpose.[285] The umbrellas were not only used by the kings and the common men but also by the ascetics. *Ākhyānakamaṇikośa* describes a *parivrājaka* entering the *samavasaraṇa* of Mahāvīra carrying a *tridaṇḍa* (three staves tied together), a rosary and an open umbrella.[286]

It is interesting to note that sometimes the umbrella-makers prepared a special quality of umbrella for rituals. In this context an inscription[287] of our period refers to the dedication of an umbrella to the deity Somanātha by Vatsarāja, the father of Trilocanapāla.

We learn from various references in our sources that umbrellas were also used for military purposes, say, for concealing the army march. The rows of umbrellas were unfurled, and held close to one another, so that the daylight was hidden and darkness ensued.[288] Big umbrellas on a large scale were used for this purpose. This is attested by the early medieval writers.[289] The craft of manufacturing umbrellas on a large scale was necessitated and satisfied a real need in the society of the early medieval period in India.

Perfume Makers and Cosmetics Makers

From the ancient times men and women have used many scented pastes and perfumes to make themselves appear attractive. Some artisans and workers used their technical skill to prepare perfumes from flowers, roots and herbs to cater to the requirements of people. The workers engaged in this occupation prepared perfumes, cosmetics and unguents. The *Rāmāyaṇa* mentions dealers in scents (*gandhopajīvīs*).[290] Perfumers (*gandhikas*) of the Śuṅga and Sātavāhana period produced the luxury article of scent.[291] It seems that perfumes and cosmetics

285. *Yuktikalpataru*, pp. 62f.
286. *Āmk*, 96, 12.
287. Copper Plate of Trilochanapāla Cāḷukya of Lāṭadeśa, dated CE 1050, *IA*, XII, pp. 201ff.
288. *Kaliṅgattu Purāṇa*, X, 33-34.
289. See P.C. Chakravarti, *The Art of War in Ancient India*, pp. 103ff.
290. II, 82, 13; See P.C. Jain, *Labour in Ancient India*, p. 158.
291. K. Gopalachari, *Comprehensive History of India*, vol. II, p. 306.

were very much in demand among the *nāgarakas* during the Kuṣāṇa period. The Jātakas refer to the process of making perfumes, and mention a perfumer's shop.[292] *Aṅgavijjā* mentions the cosmetics-makers (*prasādhakas*) and the perfumers (*gandhikas*).[293] Some epigraphs from Mathurā[294] record a gift made by the *gandhikas*, which indicates their prosperous condition. The references to perfumes and perfumers are also found in the works of Manu[295] and Viṣṇu,[296] which bears out the importance of the perfume industry.

The perfume-makers of the Gupta period manufactured a large variety of fragrant powders, scented hair oils, incenses, collyriums, ointments, pastes and lac dyes for the feet. The chief cosmetics were *kaleyaka*,[297] *kālāguru*[298] (black *agaru*), *śuklāguru*[299] (white *agaru*), *haricandana*[300] (a kind of yellow pigment looking like sandal paste), *manaḥśīla*[301] (realgar), *haritāla*[302] (orpilment), *lodhra* dust,[303] *dhūpa*[304] *kumkuma*,[305] *gorocana*[306] and *ālaktaka*[307] (lac-dye for reddening the lips and the feet). Sandal paste was commonly used.[308] Sometimes it was rubbed into a paste or oil. Both the paste and the oil were popularly used in toilet and on all ceremonial

292. Jātakas, III, 408; IV, 454, 481; VI, 538.
293. Motichandra, op. cit., p. 47.
294. *EI*, I, no. 7, p. 385; no. 16, p. 202; *IA*, XXXIII, no. 21, p. 107 and no. 23, p. 23.
295. *Manu*, II, 177; X. 85-89
296. *Viṣṇu*, III. 25; LII, 13. 18; LXXXVI. 18.
297. *Kum*, VII, 9; *Ṛtu*, Sec. IV, 5.
298. *Ṛtu*, Sec. II, 21; IV.5; V. 5; 12; VI. 13; *Raghu*, XIV, 12.
299. *Kum*, VII, 15.
300. *Ragh*, VI, 60.
301. *Kum*, VII, 23.
302. Ibid., 33.
303. *Kum*, VII, 9, 17.
304. *Ṛtu*, Sec. IV, 5; V.5; VI-13; *Kum* VII-14; *Ragh*, XVI, 50.
305. *Ṛtu*, Sec. IV, 2; V-9.
306. *Kum*, VII-15, 17.
307. *Mal*, 111, p. 1045; *Kum*, V, 34; *Ṛtu*, Sec. I, 5; VI, 13.
308. *Rītu*, Sec. I, 2, 4, 6; II, 21; III, 20; V, 3; VI, 6, 12; *Ragh*, XVII, 21.

occasions. After taking notice of the importance of perfumery, Vātsyāyana includes it among his 64 subsidiary arts connected with erotics.[309]

The author of the *Bṛhatsaṁhitā* presents a very interesting picture of the citizens who used perfumes, ointments and other cosmetics with great care. Different methods of preparing the perfume articles are elaborately discussed, in a chapter under the title "Gandhayukti."[310] The word *gandhayukti*, according to the text, stands for the science of cosmetics and perfumes. It literally means "a combination of perfumes."[311] Perfume-makers used chemical processes for manufacturing perfumes. Mention is made of decoction (*pakva*), heating (*tapta*), mixing (*saṁyuta*), fumigation (*pradhūpa, dhūpya, dhūpayitavya*), sprinkling (*sikta*), and combination of one powder with another (*bodha, prabodha, udbodha, bodhita*). Various kinds of perfumes are described in *Bṛhatsaṁhitā*, which indicates a widespread use of perfumes, and the resultant prosperity of the perfume-makers.[312]

Evidently perfumes and cosmetics were used to maintain and enhance physical beauty and charm. That the people were very much fond of scented unguents, such as sandal and saffron, is attested by some works of the seventh century CE. The description of Hiuen-Tsang, *Harṣacarita*, and *Kādambarī* bear out an extensive interest of people in perfumes and cosmetics.[313]

Viddhaśālabhañjikā, a work of Rājaśekhara, speaks of methods of applying cosmetics and perfumes in particular seasons. It refers to an ambrosial unguent of the eyes (*ayanamṛta vṛṣṭi*).[314] Collyrium purified with oil (*tailamārjitakajala*),[315] was applied with a small pencil called *kajjalaśalākā*.[316] The poet forbids wax on

---

309. *Kāmasūtra*, I, 3, 16.

310. *BS*, Chap. LXXVI.

311. Śūdraka takes *gandhayukti* to denote a cosmetic preparation made by combining certain fragrant substances, and meant to disseminate perfume : *Mṛcchakaṭika*, VIII, 13; See A.M. Shastri, *India as Seen in the Bṛhatsaṁhitā of Varāhamihira*, p. 236.

312. *BS*, LXXVI, 12, 16, 26, 27. For details, see : A.M. Shastri, op. cit., pp. 237ff.

313. Watters, vol. I, p. 152; *HCCTH*, p. 17; *Kādambarī* (tr. Ridding), p. 84; *Nag*, III, 9.

314. p. 38.

315. Ibid.

316. *Karpūr*, L, 21.

the lips.[317] It was not to be used in spring; nor was fragrant oil needed in arranging braids.[318] Thick saffron,[319] and thick sandal paste and camphor powder were rubbed over the bosom. According to the poet, Marāṭhā girls rubbed their cheeks with saffron paste.[320]

According to the Mahaban Inscription there was a class of the perfumers called *gandhavaṇika*[321] who used *yantras*[322] (machines) for extracting liquids from flowers and other fragrant materials. The phrases (*yantreyantre-yalī* and *puṣpamālākārata*) suggest that machines were utilized for preparing scents. Another phrase *rasādika* also points to the same direction.[323] In the *Uktivyaktiprakaraṇa*, oilmen are described to have manufacture fragrant oil from fragrant sesamum.[324] *Śukranītisāra* mentions oil-seeds, the materials from which oil was extracted, as the phrase *tila māṁsadi* would suggest.[325] In *Līlāvatī*, perfumes are said to have been prepared out of a mixture of comphor, sandal-wood and also wood.[326] Similar methods of preparing various kinds of perfumes are mentioned in *Kālikā Purāṇa*.[327]

P.K. Gode, in his article "Indian Science of Cosmetics and Perfumery" refers to two Sanskrit treatises on the subject, believed to have been composed some time between CE 1000-1200.[328]

Some other people were also connected with the work of perfumes and cosmetics. The merchant class carried these products to far-off places, and set commercial value upon them in the national and international markets. The Ahār

---

317. Ibid., L, 13.
318. Ibid.
319. Ibid., I, 14.
320. Ibid., I, 16.
321. *Bṛhaddharma Purāṇa*, Chaps. XIII-XIV.
322. Sushil Malti Devi, op. cit., p. 74.
323. *EI*, II, p. 279, II, 25-27.
324. *Uktivyakiprakaraṇa*, XVIII, 6.
325. *Śukra*, IV, iii, 185.
326. Līlavatī, Chap. IV, Sec. III, Ex. 98.
327. The two treatises are Gaṅgādhara's *Gandhasāra* and an anonymous author *Gandhavāḍā*; See P.C. Ray, *History of Chemistry in Ancient and Medieval India*, pp. 236-38.
328. *Kālikā Purāṇa*, Chap. 69, VV, 37-55.

Inscription refers to a merchant Mādhava, son of Devanāga, who belonged to the Māthura caste and was a seller of perfumes (*gandhika māthura jātīya-vaṇika*).[329]

Some epigraphs of our period refer to cosmetics and perfume industry. Manufacturing saffron-paste,[330] scents,[331] collyrium,[332] sandal-paste,[333] vermillion[334] and powdered-camphor[335] was a common occupation of artisans and perfume-makers. According to Kalhaṇa, some of these preparations were prepared in Kashmir.[336] It seems that during the period under review the perfume industry was mostly carried on by private workers, individually or on a corporate basis. Nowhere does the state appear to have undertaken manufacturing of perfumes, though, in the Nadlai Stone Inscription of Rāyapāla (VS 1189), the king is mentioned as realizing the taxes.[337] The workers produced the material for the traders, who supplied it to the users. *Mayamata*[338] and *Mānasāra*[339] specially mention the residences of perfume dealers. *Ākhyānakamaṇikośa*[340] and an inscription[341] also refer to the sellers of perfume. Thus we can say that making and selling of perfumes and cosmetics were important occupations in the society of the period under review, and that various varieties of perfumes and cosmetics were produced on a large scale. The credit for the popularity of such items greatly goes to the skill of the artisans engaged in the profession of making perfumes and cosmetics.

---

329. *EI*, XIX, p. 60.
330. *CII*, IV, Ins. no. 67, verse 40.
331. Ibid., Ins. no. 42, verse 14.
332. Ibid., Ins. no. 51, verse 21; 96, verse 2.
333. Ibid., Ins. no. 50, verse 9; 89, verse 13.
334. Ibid., Ins. no. 84, verse 19; 93, verse 2.
335. Ibid., Ins. no. 87, verse 12.
336. *RT*, V. 380; VII, 928-31; VIII, 2835.
337. *EI*, XI, pp. 35-36, no. 4, 13.
338. P. Niyogi, *The Economic History of Northern India*, pp. 251-252; See Sushil Malti Devi, op. cit., p. 75.
339. P. Acharya, *Architecture of Mānasāra*, pp. 63-92.
340. *Āmk*, 81, 2.
341. *EI*, XIX, p. 60.

Oil Makers

Oil manufacturers were considered *śilpin* in the ancient Indian society. They got their livelihood by extracting oils from seeds. A small industry of oil manufacturing was established in various villages and cities. Oil was used for cooking food, for burning lamps at night, and for a number of other purposes of daily life. Oil-pressing was a regular business, which was particularly in great demand during the days of festivals and religious ceremonies.

In the inscriptions and literary sources of the period under study the oil-millers were generally known as *tailikas*.[342] These artisans worked with the wheel and were, therefore, also called *cākrikas*[343] or *cakracaras*.[344] The oil mill was called *ghrāṇaka*.[345] The preparation of oil required a very simple process, and the oil-men used it to produce oil from mustard seeds,[346] both black[347] and white,[348] sesamum (*tila*),[349] and linseed[350] during the Gupta and later periods. The use of ingudi oil for lighting lamps,[351] curing boils[352] and rubbing in hair[353] is referred to by Kālidāsa. Varāhamihira[354] mentions the lamp (*dīpa*), with its wick (*vartti*) and oil.

There were guilds of oil-millers in the Gupta period. Their economic position was very sound, and sometimes they made donations to the temples. During the reign of Skandagupta, in the city of Indrapura (Indore) there was a famous guild

342. *BS*, X, 5; XVI, 31.
343. Ibid., X, 9.
344. Ibid., X. 12.
345. *CII*, IV, 45; See B.N. Puri, *The History of Gurjara-Pratihāras*, p. 132.
346. *Amara*, 9, 17, p. 203; *BS*, XXIX, 5.
347. Ibid., 9, 19, p. 204.
348. Ibid., 3, 189, p. 316.
349. Ibid., 9, 19, p. 204; 4, 76, p. 99; *BS*, V, XXV, 2.
350. Ibid., 9, 20, p. 204.
351. *Ragh*, XIV, 81.
352. *Abhijñānaśākuntalam*, IV, p. 903.
353. Ibid., 11, p. 848.
354. *BS*, LXXXIII, 1, 2.

of oil-men headed by Jīvanta.[355] We find a mention of the *Tailika Śreṇī* in the Gwalior Inscription of the Pratihāras.[356] The chiefs of the oil-millers (*tailika-mahattaras*), who were the inhabitants of Śrīsarve-svarapura, Śrīvatsasvāmīpura, Caccikahaṭṭikā and Nimbādityahaṭṭikā and other members of the whole *śreṇī* of oil-millers made a perpetual endowment to the temples of Viṣṇu and Navadurgā. They agreed to give one *palikā* of oil per *kolhuka* every month for the lamps of the temple. All this goes to show that oil-pressing was a very profitable occupation for both the producers and the sellers.

Oil-mills were directly dependent on agricultural products. *Harṣacarita* mentions numerous oil seeds. According to it, mustard was grown in the Sone (Sona) Valley of Bihar,[357] and also in parts of Śrīkaṇṭha Janapada[358] (Haryana and Uttar Pradesh). In *Harṣacarita* Bāṇa twice refers to sesame (*tila*) as an object of oblation to fire.[359] This points to cultivation of sesame. The same writer speaks of the linseed (*alasī*) crop.[360] Castor, another important oil-seed, was grown in house-gardens.[361]

Kṛṣiparāśara, a work on agriculture, mentions mustard[362] and sesame[363] cultivation. A few verses of *Saduktikarṇāmṛta* deal with mustard crops, and mention the maturing time of this crop.[364] *Abhidhānaratnamālā*,[365] *Varṇaratnakara*,[366] *Kālaviveka*.[367] *Rāmacarita* of Sandhyākaranandin,[368]

355. The Indore Plate of Skandagupta's Fleet, p. 70, 1, 8.
356. Gwalior Stone Inscription, *EI*, I, pp. 156ff.
357. *Hcar*, pp. 56-57.
358. Ibid., pp. 110 and 134.
359. Ibid., pp. 51 and 56.
360. Ibid., p. 228.
361. Ibid., pp. 229-30.
362. *KP*, V, 217.
363. Ibid., V, 167.
364. *Sad*, 2, 171, 2; 2, 177, 1, 2, 4.
365. *Abh*. Rat, 11, 425-29.
366. *Varṇaratnākara*, p. 43.
367. *Kālaviveka*, pp. 378-80.
368. *Rāmacarita*, 1, 14.

Brāhmaṇasarvasva,[369] *Kālikā Purāṇa*,[370] *Paryāyaratnamālā*[371] and *Āryasaptaśati*[372] furnish important references about cultivation of oil seeds in north India during the period under review.

The references, although few in number but spread over a long time span and a large area, clearly indicate that oil manufacturing was an important and regular business. Oil manufacturers were wealthy, and made religious endowments. In some cases, they had to pay taxes to the king. An inscription of the time of Allaṭa from Udaipur records the levy of one *pala* of oil from every oil mill.[373] Another inscription of Gurjara–Pratihāras refers to a levy on oil-millers.[374] It appears that sometimes oil-mills were asked to pay a religious cess in the form of their products.[375] Frequently, the oil-millers were also asked by the king to make donations to the temples.[376] It is clear that economically the oil-manufacturers were very sound. An inscription of the Paramāra dynasty speaks of a religious endowment where Tailakarāja Bhaiyāk gave oil (two *ghāṇīs*) to a temple for a perpetual lamp.[377]

Sometimes, the oil manufacturer made donations for social causes. In this context an inscription of Udayāditya of CE 1083 records that an oilmen Jannaka got a tank constructed.[378]

Salt Makers

Salt is a common necessity of human beings. Salt-makers were included among *śilpīs* in ancient India. Kauṭilya gives a vivid account of salt, its varieties and manufacturing. He mentions an officer, a *lavaṇādhyakṣa*[379] (superintendent of

369. *Brāhmaṇasarvasva*, pp. 32, 33, 34 and 35.
370. *Kālikā Purāṇa*, 74, 23.
371. *Prm*, II, 17-18.
372. *Ārya*, V, 149.
373. *EI*, III, p. 168; II, 22-23; Pāla is a measurement of oil.
374. Ibid.
375. *EI*, XIV, pp. 176ff; *IA*, XLI, pp. 85ff.
376. Ibid., I, p. 287; *JOHRS*, 1 and 7.
377. *EI*, XXIII, pp. 137, 141.
378. The Inscriptions of Imperial Paramāras, L.D. Series, 73, p. 38.
379. R.S. Sharma, *Perspectives in Social and Economic History of Early India*, p. 131.

salt), who looked after the salt industry. This indicates the monopoly of the state over salt-making. Kauṭilya distinguishes various types of salts, viz. *saindhava* (salt derived from the country of Sindhu); *samudra* (salt produced from sea-water), *yavakṣara* (literally "ashes of barley," *potash*), but often employed for making nitre; *sauvarcala* (salt derived from the country of Suvarcala) and *udbhedaja* (salt extracted from saline soil).[380] Evidently, there was a considerable advancement in people's knowledge about salt and its preparation.

Five kinds of salt[381] are described by Caraka: *sauvarcala* (nitre), *saindhava* (rock salt), *vit* (black salt), *audbhida* (vegetable salt), and *samudra* (sea salt).

Two varieties of salt are referred to in *Amarakośa*: One, salt obtained from the sea water,[382] and the other, salt procured from rock.[383] Apparently the first variety of salt was prepared in the Gujarat sea ports. Even today geographical location and climatic conditions are fit for the preparation of salt in this area. The second source for obtaining salt was from rocks, which suggests that it was got from the mines and rocks. There are reserves of rock-salt in Maṇḍī (Himachal Pradesh),[384] and across the Indus in Kohāṭ in Pakistan.

Salt is a mineral product, and the salt-makers engaged in this profession collected it from the salt pits, and then purified it. The contemporary inscriptions of Candellas,[385] Gāhaḍavālas,[386] and Kaḷacuris of Tripurī[387] and Rājpūtānā[388] speak of grant of salt-pits and the right of manufacturing salt to donees. Kṣemendra says that salt was imported to Kashmir. Probably salt was not produced in the Valley of Kashmir, and was imported from central India and the Arab countries.

---

380. P.C. Ray, *History of Chemistry in Ancient and Medieval India*, p. 56.
381. P.C. Ray, op. cit., p. 62.
382. *Amara*, 941, p. 208,
383. Ibid., 9. 42, p. 209.
384. Spate, *India and Pakistan*, p. 267.
385. *IA*, 16, 206.
386. *EI*, X, 99.
387. *HIED*, II, 44.
388. H.C. Ray, *Dynastic History of Northern India*, II, 1066.

Others

In the period under study, a number of artisans and craftsmen were engaged in several crafts of somewhat lower category in the villages and towns in north India. These artisans and craftsmen, however, had their own importance in the society. In this context, the basket-makers or shield makers are enumerated by Al-Beruni.[389] Various kinds of baskets were highly useful in agricultural economy. Baskets (*karaṇḍas*, or *piṭakas*) were used in carrying curd molasses, candied sugar and flowers.[390] Yogeśvara speaks of the winnowing fan (*sūrpa*) and the sieve (*titau*) in his verses in village life.[391] Mats were also made for several purposes. Closely-woven mats were used for constructing small huts at the drinking inns,[392] and sometimes were also used for drying heaps of *kāśmarya* plants in the villages.[393] These mats were naturally more lasting than those used as seats and beds. Some artisans prepared brooms for sweeping houses. These were made of grass, date-leaves and slender mid ribs of the palm.[394]

For making ropes, rope-makers used hemp, *muñja, kuśa, kāśa,* coconut-fruit fibres, and hair of cows.[395] *Mānasāra,* describes the bark of banyan, palmyra and *ketaka,* and cotton and *kiṁśuka* yarn as material for ropemaking.[396] Several types of strings were used in tying the bundle of reaped stalks.[397] In other words, ropes were commonly used for domestic purposes.

Liquor manufacturers prepared different varieties of wine from coconut juice (*nārikelarasāsava*),[398] *mahuā* flowers (*madhūkāsavamadya*)[399] and juice of grapes,

---

389. Sachau, *Al-Beruni's India,* I, p. 101.
390. Hcar, p. 212.
391. *Subhāṣitaratnakoṣa,* V, 1312; *Sad.,* 2, 84, 1.
392. *Hcar,* p. 228.
393. Ibid., p. 230.
394. See A.K. Choudhary, op. cit., pp. 202-03.
395. Vyasa quoted in *Mit. On Yājña* 3, 263 and 264, p. 1317 of Setlur's edition.
396. *Mānasāra,* 2, 35.
397. *KP,* V, 116.
398. *Sad,* 2, 173, 5.
399. *Hcar,* pp. 95 and 230.

dates, palmyras and sugar canes.[400] Contemporary literary texts like *Deśīnāmamālā*,[401] *Prāyaścittaprakarṇa*,[402] and *Gṛhastharatnākara*[403] mention the knowledge involved in the preparation of different kinds of liquors. Different kinds of liquors were produced according to the taste of the people. People used wine on a large scale. *Śukranītisāra* praises wine for developing talent, sharpening intelligence, increasing patience and making the mind steady.[404] The importance of liquor manufacturing is indicated by the inscriptions which mention it as an item of taxation.[405]

Conch-shell workers (*śaṅkhakāras*) prepared bracelets and other articles. *Dohākośa* contends that these conches were obtained from the ocean,[406] and were a source of income for the coastal people. Both the inscriptions[407] and the literary[408] sources refer to the conch-shell workers. Bracelets of conch-shell were used by women,[409] and sometimes toilet boxes were also made from conch-shells.[410] Moreover, cowrie-shells[411] and *ullaryams*[412] were also collected by the conch-shell workers.

The profession of the barber (*nāpita*) may be placed in the class of independent occupations. It means that the barber's work or business is individual; he need not depend on other craftsmen. His instruments like scissors, razor and sometimes mirror (a plate of brass or copper) were sufficient to enable him to earn his livelihood. The presence of the barber (*nāpita*) was necessary in ceremonies like

400. *Agni Purāṇa*, 173, 21.
401. *Deśīnāmamālā*, III, 41, 45; VIII, 4, 1, 46; II, 2; IV, 4; V, 34; VI, 35, 41, 50, 75 and VIII, 40.
402. *Prāyaścittaprakarṇa*, p. 40.
403. *Gṛhastharatnākara*, pp. 393-95.
404. *Śukra*, I, 116-17.
405. Jabalpur Plate of Jayasiṁha, *CII*, IV, Ins. no. 63, line 25ff.
406. *Siddhasarahapada*, p. 229.
407. *EI*, XXII, 139; XXIII, p. 141, no. 22; XXVIII, 244; XXIV, 329ff.
408. *Naiṣadha*, XII, 35; XV, 45.
409. *Sad*, 5, 1, 4; 5, 1, 3; 2, 118, 3 and 2, 173, 2.
410. *Naiṣadha*, XXI, 24.
411. *JNSI*, VII, pp. 82ff.
412. *Deśīnāmamālā*, I, 110; V, 1.

marriage. Patañjali includes the barber among artisans.[413] Varāhamihira also mentions the occupation of the barbers.[414] Some barbers were patronized by the rich people and some worked in the royal court. They earned more then those who worked for the common people. Their good economic position may be attested by the Villavatti Inscriptions of the Gupta period, where they are enumerated among craftsmen and among tax-payers.[415] *Mayamata,* a work on architecture makes provision for the residences of the barbers in the villages.[416] Barbers are also mentioned as a caste in the Charkhari Plate of VS 1346 (CE 1289).[417]

---

413. *Mahābhāṣya, (Pañcakārukī)*, 1, 1, 48, p. 118.
414. *BS, nāpita*, X, 9; XV, 1; L, 5; *nāpīti*, LXXVII, 9.
415. *EI*, XXIV, pp. 296ff.
416. *Maya*, vv. 88-91.
417. *EI*, XX, p. 136, 1, 10.

Part Two

6

Training of Artisans and Craftsmen

LEARNING in India through the ages has been prized and pursued not for its own sake, but for the sake, and as a part, of religion.[1] Education in ancient India must be understood to ultimately have been the outcome of the Indian theory of knowledge and a part of its corresponding scheme of life and values. The pursuit of objective knowledge in itself is thus not the chief concern of ancient Indian education.[2] The system of education outlined in the Dharmaśāstras and Nibandhas fails to convey an adequate idea of the institutions and methods for imparting education to students of different categories in the early medieval period. The works of the period under review confine their attention almost exclusively to the education of the brāhmaṇas.

It appears that there was no proper institutionalized provision for the education of artisans and craftsmen as there was that of "the upper classes of the society." Generally, the former adopted the occupation of their parents, and the hereditary skill was acquired, maintained and enhanced as it was transferred from father to son. However, we cannot ignore the fact that the highly skilled architects of huge temples, the sculptors of beautiful images, the jewellers of wonderful ornaments and other expert artisans and craftsmen who displayed superior technological expertise in the early medieval period must have had some sort of education.[3]

Śukranītisāra,[4] a text of the period under reference enumerates some technological subjects like construction of palaces and buildings, excavation of

---

1. Radha Kumud Mookerji, *Ancient Indian Education*, p. xxi.
2. Ibid., pp. xxii-xxiii.
3. B.P. Mazuradar, *Socio-Economic History of Northern India*, pp. 145-46.
4. Quoted by B.P. Mazumdar, op.cit., pp. 147-48.

tanks and canals, manufacture of clocks, watches and musical instruments, dyeing, testing of metals, preparation of artificial gems and metals, enameling, extraction and preparation of oils from seeds, glass work, work in iron foundries, testing of gems, rope-making, thread-spinning, weaving, polishing of earthen, wooden, stone, and metallic vessels, and drawing. We do not come by in any book the method of teaching these highly technical subjects in a period when there was neither any engineering college nor any technological institution. Haribhadra Sūri, in his *Samarādityakathā*, mentions technical subjects for higher studies. Among the important sciences he includes *pānavidhi* (preparation of drinks), *maṇiśikṣā* (training about jewels), *hiraṇyavāda* (science dealing with unminted gold), *maṇivāda* (science dealing with jewels), *prastara-chedya* (the art of cutting designs on stones), *kaṭaka-chedya* (the art of cutting designs on bracelets), *vāstuniveśa* (the technique of laying out a building), *sūtrakāra* (the art of imparting form to *sūtras*), *carmalakṣaṇa* (science of leather),[5] etc. Lakṣmīdhara refers to the gift of education in the agricultural science and the art of making images in his *Dānakanda*.[6] There is also an extensive literature on *vāstu-vidyā,* science dealing with principles of Indian architecture. The better class of śūdras, especially persons engaged in trade and industry may be presumed to have an elementary knowledge of reading, writing and arithmetic. In fact, the brāhmaṇa writers did not, as a rule, condescend to take any notice of the methods of education of artisans and craftsmen because the brāhmaṇas regarded all those who earned their livelihood by professing any of the fine arts as socially inferior. That is also the reason why the writers of the period seldom refer to technical education.[7]

In the existing literature there are mentioned a number of ways of giving training to the artisans and craftsmen, which may be classified as follows:

(a) Training by parents

(b) Training by guilds

(c) Training by individual masters

---

5. B.N. Sharma, *Social and Cultural History of Northern India*, p. 43.
6. pp. 208-09.
7. There are some scattered references in the literature, but these are not of much use. See, *The Age of Imperial Kanauj*, p. 367.

(d) Training by educational institutions

These different kinds of training may each be taken up in some detail.

Training by Parents

The home of the artisan functioned as the school for imparting instruction in particular crafts. Families of carpenters, metal- workers, potters, weavers, stone-workers, architects, oilmen, barbers, tanners, etc. trained their young members by initiating them into their ancestral crafts.[8] Thereby professional families maintained their mastery over their technical trades, which were bequeathed from father to son for generations. In other words, continuation of hereditary occupation proved a good way of schooling artisans and craftsmen, who learned their technical trades in their childhood, and earned their livelihood under conditions governed by the customs of their families.

Technical training was carried out in the families of artisans and craftsmen during the working hours. The young learners started learning the family arts and crafts by helping their parents as their assistants. Gradually, they became skilled in their profession. It may be noted here that the members of the families of artisans picked up the technical aspect of their respective trades, they did not but much know the art of writing or reading. They went without formal education due to the dominance of the brāhmaṇas.

A study of the genealogy of the *śilpī* class in our inscriptions gives us some information about the professions in which they were engaged over a long time. It is clearly indicated that the son learned his father's craft, and when he became skilled in his trade, he mentioned the names of his ancestors in inscriptions and on monuments. The Candella monuments mention a number of names of fathers and sons who had both adopted sculpture as their occupation. The most famous sculptors of this period were Śrī Sātana and his son Citanaka, both well-versed in their art.[9] The inscription of Vijayasena records the name of the great artist as śūlapāṇi, the chief of the guild *goṣṭhī* of the *śilpī*s of Vārendra, and also mentions his parentage. It gives the name of his father as Bṛhaspati, grandfather as

8. Cf. A.K. Choudhary, *Early Medieval Village in North-Eastern India*, p. 252.

9. *citrakāra śrī sātanastaya putraḥ sakalaśilpavidākuśalaḥ citnakas tasyeyam.* — C. Sivaramamurti, *Indian Sculpture*, p. 5.

Mānadāsa, and great-grandfather as Dharma. Such pride in their ancestory and craft in Bengal is coupled with the gusto with which their names are mentioned by several *śilpīs* like the *sūtradhāra* Viṣṇubhadra, the *śilpī* Mahīdhara, son of Vikramāditya, Karṇabhadra, Maṅkhadāsa son of Śubhadāsa.[10] Some sculptures on a temple were chiselled by Sūtradhāra Dāṇḍī's son Sūtradhāra Śīlaśrī. They clearly show the craft of this family to be paternal.[11]

A stone inscription of the tenth century CE from Garh (Rajasthan) refers to a family of architects the members of which were quite proficient in their craft.[12] Their art travelled from father to son, and this was the main reason of their superb skill. Ārdraṭa, who was an expert in carving sculptures in stone, trained in his art his son Deddulaka, whose son, Sarvadeva, in turn, mastered fine arts at the feet of his father. The same inscription also speaks of the architect Varaṅga, son of Sarvadeva, as being unusually skilled in his ancestral occupation.

Similarly the art of engraving inscriptions was passed on from father to son. For instance the inscription of Vijayāditya III (CE 844-88) was engraved by the foremost of the goldsmiths of the period, Kaṭṭaya, the son of Mādhava and the son's son of Īśāna.[13] The Khalīmpur plate of Dharmapāladeva was engraved by skilful Tataṭa, the son of Subhaṭa, and grandson of Bhogaṭa.[14] The art of engraving such inscriptions is easily seen to have been paternal.

Training by Guilds

In the early medieval times the artisans and craftsmen carried forward their *śreṇīs*. Most of the crafts had their own corporations, where the individual craftsman had a better scope to develop his skill and ingenuity. The most significant role of these guilds was to provide technical training to apprentices. These apprentices learnt their craft under their master's care and supervision.[15]

---

10. Ibid., p. 6.
11. EI, XXXI, pp. 81-86.
12. Ibid., XXXIX, pt. VI, pp. 189ff.
13. Ibid., V, pp. 122-26.
14. Ibid., IV, pp. 243-54.
15. Cf. B.P. Mazumdar, op. cit., pp. 209ff.

It appears from the *Kr̥tyakalpataru* of Lakṣmīdhara that this form extending ef knowledge of the craft in the guilds continued in the early medieval period. This text elaborately refers to the rules of apprenticeship that were observed.[16] The apprentice learned his craft from his master within a fixed period. Food was provided by the master in the workshop. The text explains the power of the master to order the *vadha* of the apprentice. According to it the *vadha* only meant the master's beating the probationer with a bamboo stick by way of some corporal punishment. *Śilpavijñāna* has been called *hemakūpyādi* in the text.[17]

The *rathakāra*s, *karmāra*s, *takṣa*s, *rūpakāra*s, and *citrakāra*s were of interrelated families, and later medieval inscriptions describe them at length with special reference to their knowledge of design, perfection in their art, and skill in using their tools. They are glorified as agents of creative art. A special mention is made of Viśvakarmā — the fountainhead of the learning of craftsmen and a master of textual knowledge in art. Such descriptions are found even in the comparatively modern inscriptions in the last two hundred years.[18]

Training by Individual Master Craftsmen

The artisans and craftsmen were generally engaged in their industry in their own cottages. Some of them had a number of apprentices under them. These apprentices got the training of the craft under the supervision of their masters. The masters provided them with food and lodging, but paid them no remuneration. The monetary recompense was made to them from their own output. Considering the importance of industrial products in everyday life, some of the Smr̥ti writers laid down certain rules for apprenticeship in the various crafts. According to *Nārada-Smr̥ti* (an earlier work of about fourth century CE), "if a young man wished to be initiated into a certain craft, he was to first obtain the sanction of his relations, and then proceed to live with a master (*ācāryasya vaset ante*)." The duration of his apprenticeship was fixed.[19] Hence, the house of a master craftsman was the learning centre where the pupils learnt their craft

---

16. *Vyavahārakāṇḍa*, pp. 382ff.
17. Ibid.
18. Cf. C. Sivaramamurti, op. cit., pp. 8-9.
19. *Nārada-Smr̥ti*, V, 16.

within a stipulated period. A rule enunciated in *Nārada-Smṛti* lays down that "the master must impart to his pupil his training at his own house, where he is to provide him boarding and lodging. He must not make the apprentice perform other works (*na ca anyat kāryet karma*), but must treat him like a son."[20] It adds that "if the apprentice deserts his master who duly instructs him and is not at fault in any way, the former should be compelled by forcible means to stay with his master and made liable to corporal punishment and confinement.[21] When the apprentice had mastered the art, he was to make gifts to his teacher, within his means, and return home after having taken leave of him.[22] The learner was expected to be always devoted and humble to his teacher. According to Nārada, learning is like a river, ever advancing to a humbler level, therefore, as one's knowledge grows broader and deeper, one should become ever more humble towards the source of one's knowledge.[23] *Bṛhatsaṁhitā* also mentions that he who learned crafts relating to gold, base metal and the like, worked at his teacher's house.[24]

This tradition of imparting technical education to probationers by a master craftsman at his own house was continued during the early medieval period. *Matsya Purāṇa*[25] mentions acceptance of a fee by the master from a pupil beforehand. This Purāṇa offers testimony to the effect that a master who did not teach a *vidyā* (science) or *śilpa* (craft) after taking a *mūlya* (fee) was to be fined the whole of this sum by a just king. Sometimes tuition fee was paid by a student to acquire proficiency in the different branches of a science.

Similar rules for apprentices are mentioned in *Smṛticandrikā*.[26] The text bears out that a *śilpa* (e.g. preparing ornaments of gold) was to be learnt by probationers in the house of the master. The period of apprenticeship was to be determined by

20. Radha Kumud Mookerji, op. cit., p. 349.
21. Ibid.
22. Ibid., p. 349. Cf. Raghu, V, 20-21.
23. *Narada-Smṛti*, V, p. 12.
24. *BS*, XV, p. 7.
25. Quoted by Aparārka from *Yājñ*, II, p. 198.
26. *Smṛticandrikā*, II, p. 195.

the master craftsman. Thus, the individual artisan or craftsman earned money by professing his art, and also by selling his goods. Skill in art was considered a precious treasure handed down from the master workman to the learner. The apprentice had to stipulate the period of his stay with the master, who was to appropriate the proceeds from the former's work, and provide him only boarding and lodging.[27]

The above-mentioned rules cited in the literature of the period indicate that industrial apprenticeship was treated as a contract based on several stipulations. There was the stipulation as to the limit of time within which the master was to complete the course of training for which he admitted the apprentice. *Vīramitrodaya* mentions the agreement executed commonly in this respect between the master craftsman and the apprentice.[28] The arrangement included the respective obligations of both the master and his pupil. The master was to treat his pupil as his son, and he was to teach him honestly and wholeheartedly, without keeping back from him any secrets of his craft. The master craftsman was expected not to exploit his pupil's skill and labour by employing him on work not related to his training. *Vīramitrodaya* takes into account cases of undutiful teachers who put off instruction of their pupils even after their admission, and condemns them severely, particularly for such neglect over a long time.[29] There were certain obligations on the pupil's side also. The pupil was expected not to leave his teacher before the expiry of the stipulated period of time, even if he had completed his training. For this unexpired period the pupil was to work for his master's benefit.

As pointed out by R.K. Mookerji, the system of this apprenticeship had many advantages. The apprentice lived and worked under the master's eye. Moreover, in this system the apprentice had opportunities of "observing the special points of his master's skill, his trade secrets, and imbibing his true inward method and genius."[30]

---

27. Vijñāneśvara on *Yājñ*, II, p. 184.
28. Radha Kumud Mookerji, op. cit., p. 350.
29. Ibid.
30. Ibid., p. 351.

An inscription of the tenth century CE describes the technical training that was provided by the proficient craftsmen to the apprentices.[31] This inscription mentions a family of architects, called the Dharkkaṭa family, from the glorious Pūrṇṇatallaka.

From generation to generation this family maintained their proficiency in the field of architecture (*vāstu-vidyā*). Then, the inscription talks of a renowned artist, Ārdraṭa, who was an expert in carving out sculptures in stone and was a votary of the Jain faith. Deddulaka, the son of Ārdraṭa, was also an expert in this field, and was widely respected for his attainments. His son, Sarvadeva, who had mastered all the fine arts in their entirety, was particularly held supreme among the architects of his time. It was he who built a beautiful and unique Jain temple at Siṁhapadra. The aforementioned inscription speaks of him in these terms:

> He, the blessed one, who was always skilful, attended upon by an assembly of persons who were his students, and who by his discources on sculpture replete with the knowledge of the science of architecture outshone the fame of (the divine architect) Viśvakarmā, which enveloped the three worlds, and got his name always appended with the epithet *sūtradhāra*.[32]

The second part of the same inscription refers to the wise and renowned leader of all architects, Varaṅga, son of Sarvadeva, was extremely proficient in architecture, and versatile in the art of speech. He is said to have been the very cloud for the *cātaka*s in the form of supplicants, and the very fire for the forest in the form of problems of architecture. The aforementioned inscription also describes four generations of architects, all of them highly reputed for imparting excellent training to apprentices.

Some of the sculptors mentioned were the pupils of the famous sculptor Indranīlamaṇi of the realm of the Pālas, such as Amṛta, who carved the fine image of Sūrya.[33] The typical attitude of the young sculptor to his master and to

---

31. Garh Stone Inscription of the time of Mahipāla, *EI*, XXXIX, Pt. VI, pp. 189-98.

32. *kurvāṇen-ātmano-dhas-tribhuvanavivara-vyāpinīṁ viśvakarmā-prakhyātim vāstuvidyā paricaya-caturaih śilpa-karmopadesaiḥ . . . . vidyārthinyā kṛtinya puruṣapariṣadā sevyamānena nityam nāma svaṁ sūtradhāropapadaviṣayataṁ yena dhanyena nitaṁ.*
— Ibid., verse 8.

33. *indranīlamaṇiśiṣyaḥ śilāya buddhiśālinā ghaṭitāya kṛtaynena amṛtena suśilpinā.*
— C. Sivaramamurti, op. cit., p. 6.

his artistic proficiency in the period under reference can be very clearly seen from the inscription, where the gratitude of the student to his master is highlighted. Someśvara, a sculptor from Magadha compares himself to a painter preparing a lovely painting of his young mistress with rapt attention. He is *śilpīn-māgadhaḥ*.[34]

In the bas-reliefs of the temples at Khajurāho, there is a sculpture which presents a sculptor at work with a number of apprentices around him.[35] It has always been a traditional belief in India that it is the grace of the master that gives the pupil deftness of hand, *hastoccaya* as it is known. The sculpture at Khajurāho which also depicts artists doing sketching, regularly underlines the glory of the craftsman.[36] The reference of a preliminary sketch is occasionally met with in Sanskrit literature. The preliminary sketch is known as the *hastalekha*.[37]

An important stage in preparing a large architectural edifice like a temple is a design prepared by the architect in the form of a small model known as the *varṇaka*. The *varṇaka* is also often referred to in Sanskrit literature, as in *Naiṣadhīyacarita* and *Kuṭṭanīmata*. Dāmodaragupta says in his *Kuṭṭanīmata* that the beautiful city of Banāras was made by Viśvakarmā so as to serve as a *varṇaka*, to impress Brahmā with his creative calibre.[38]

Training by Educational Institution

There were a number of famous centres of education in the early medieval period. Among these educational centres Nālandā, Vikramaśilā, Vaiśālī and Odantapur had gained great reputation. Al-Beruni refers to Varanasi as a renowned centre of learning. *Kuṭṭanīmata* and the *Kathāsaritsāgara* refer to Pāṭaliputra and Kashmira. Rajaśekhara mentions them as great centres for examinations in

34. Ibid., p. 6.
35. Ibid., p. 9, pl. I.
36. Ibid.
37. *purakṛtis strainam imam vidhātum abhūd vidhātuḥ kila hastalekhaḥ* in *Naiṣadhīyacarita*, where the entire feminine world created by Brahmā is represented as a preliminary attempt (*hastalekha*) for the final shaping of the beauty of Damayantī. An early example from our period of *hastalekhaḥ* is preserved at Nāgārjunakoṇḍa where the preliminary drawing on a slab, incised before the carving is made, represents the initial stage in preparing the sculpture. Ibid., pl. 2.
38. Ibid., pp. 9-10.

sciences.[39] Śrīmāla and Cittoṛ were two famous educational centres of Rajasthan. Śrīmāla was important for Brāhmaṇical studies, while Cittoṛ was known far and wide for Haribhadra Sūri and his desciples. Valabhī flourished as a great and renowned centre of learning in Kāṭhiāwāḍ, and students flocked there from all parts of western India. Ujjain had also developed as famous academic centre which attracted students even from far-off places. The city of Dhāra had a famous college founded by Paramāra king Bhoja. The presiding deity of this great educational institution was Vāgdevī Sarasvatī, the Goddess of learning, whose remarkable life-size standing image is now in the British Museum, London.[40] Whether in all these educational institutions technical training was provided, we are not certain. Though facilities for education in various branches of knowledge were available, the percentage of the literate class was not very high among artisans and craftsmen. In fact, technical education was only restrictedly available. As indicated earlier, greater stress was laid on religion, philosophy and grammar than on technical subjects.

The metal workers used iron crucibles for manufacturing objects of different shapes. The science of metallurgy is described in many contemporary works, such as *Rasārṇava, Rasendracūḍāmaṇi, Rasaratnasamuccaya, Rasaprakaśa-sudhākara* and *Śukranītisāra*. In the universities and famous educational centres technical experiments were carried out for the students. One of the monasteries excavated at Nālandā was seen equipped with huge ovens, which indicates that chemical experiments were performed for the students there.[41] It also appears probable that there were chemical laboratories at Nālandā, where chemical experiments were carried out by learned teachers for apprentices. It is almost certain that some training was provided here to the craftsmen who were interested in learning metallurgy and related branches of science.

Subjects of Study

The often talked-of sixty-four *kalā*s (arts) have been mentioned in a number of sources, such as *Kāmasūtra, Daśakumāracarita, Kādambarī* and in the works of

39. Kāv, p. 55.
40. B.N. Sharma, op. cit., p. 51.
41. B.P. Mazumdar, op. cit., p. 147.

Bhavabhūti. These arts are described in detail in *Śukranītisāra, Kalpāntaravācyāni,* Rāmacandra's commentary of the *Campūrāmāyaṇa* by Vidarbharāja, and Yaśodhara's commentary on the *Kāmasūtra* called *Jayamaṅgalā*.[42]

In ancient times there were written a number of books which deal with arts and crafts.[43] In the early medieval period there were some written works dealing with the *kalās*. These works elaborately discuss the method of preparing objects from various types of metals by the crucibles process and various other chemical means. Moreover, in some texts there are mentioned the technological subjects which were studied by artisans and craftsmen. Apparently these books must have been used by master craftsmen or learned teachers to provide technical education to the younger generation. Many preparations of gold, silver, copper, iron, tin and lead have been described in Vāgbhaṭa of the ninth century CE.[44]

In *Śukranītisāra*[45] there are described in detail ten *kalās* derived from Āyurveda, namely preparation of alchohol, surgical operations, cooking, gardening, metallurgy, confectionery, pharmacy, analysis and synthesis of metals, alloys and salts. It may be mentioned here that the learned author of *Mitākṣarā* regards Āyurveda as a *śilpa* meant to be learnt under the apprentice system. *Cikitsāsaṁgraha,* popularly known as *Cakradatta* and *Lohapaddhati* of Sureśvara deal with metallic preparations. The science of metallurgy is also expounded in contemporary works like *Rasaratnasamuccaya, Rasendracūḍāmaṇi* of Somadeva, *Rasaprakāśa-sudhākara* and *Rasārṇava*.[46] The writer of *Śukranītisāra* speaks of some technological subjects studied during the period under reference. Among them he enumerates construction of palaces and buildings, excavation of tanks and canals, manufacture of clocks, watches and musical instruments, dyeing, testing

42. Cf. Radha Kumud Mookerji, op. cit., p. 354.

43. *Arthaśastra, Caraka-Saṁhitā, Suśruta-Saṁhitā,* A.F.R. Hoernle, *The Bower Manuscript, ASI,* vol. XXII, Calcutta, 1893-1912. In these books most authentic information relating to knowledge of chemistry and metallurgy, making of spirituous liquors, etc. is given. For details see P.C. Ray, *The History of Chemistry in Ancient and Medieval, India,* pp. 59ff.

44. P.C. Ray, op. cit., pp.70-71.

45. *Śukra,* IV, 3.

46. P.C. Ray, op. cit., p.151ff.

of metals, preparation of artificial gems and metals, enamelling, extraction and preparation of oils from seeds, glass work, work in iron foundaries, testing of gems, ropemaking, thread-spinning, weaving, polishing of earthen, wooden, stone, and metallic vessels, and drawing.[47]

The *śilpī* digests like *Aparājitapṛcchā*, *Samarāṅgaṇasūtradhāra*, *Mānasāra* and *Mayamata* elaborately explain the general principles of architecture and sculpture which were applicable to any part of India. The knowledge of Vāstuśāstra which was the first qualification which an architect had to possess consisted of the knowledge of site planning and its layout, planning of buildings, laying out of gardens and parks, town and regional planning, and all that constitutes the traditional subject matter of architecture. All this falls under the discipline of *śilpa*. Apart from the knowledge of *ślipa*, the architect was supposed to possess the knowledge of carpentery, engineering, machine-making (*yantra-karma-vidhi*), etc.[48]

Viśvakarmā's works, consisting of a number of textbooks of the science of architecture, are records of the oral tradition and transmission going back to an undefined past. We have already mentioned several works going by the authorship of Viśvakarmā, such as *Viśvakarmā-Prakāśa* and *Viśvakarmā-Śilpa*, which together constitute complete treatise, on *śilpa* the former dealing mainly with architecture and the latter with sculpture.[49] The authentic date of these works cannot be warranted.

Viśvakarmā-Vāstuśāstra, comprising 87 chapters in about 1800 verses (more than 3500 lines), is a masterpiece of planning houses and habitations ranging from the smallest hamlets to the biggest metropolis, state buildings, especially palaces, comparable to modern secretariats, embassies and assembly-halls all taken together, residential houses, and religious buildings and temples.[50]

Aparājitapṛcchā of Bhuvanadeva a work of twelfth or thirteenth century CE is another manual on the science of architecture which may be regarded as one of

---

47. Radha Kumud Mookerji, op. cit., pp. 354-60.
48. D.N. Shukla, *Vāstuśāstra*, Hindu Science of Architecture (With Special Reference to Bhoja's *Samarāṅganasūtradhāra*, vol. I, p. 45.
49. Ibid., p. 90.
50. Ibid.

the most representative texts of Indian architecture, sculpture and painting. It fully covers the wide scope of Vāstuśāstra.[51] Its dissertations on practically all the branches of Vāstuśāstra are not only copious and full but also unique in some respects, and add to our knowledge on many other topics, such as prosody, astrology and music. It is based on the fundamental concepts of Indian art, rythm (prosody and music) and mystic ideas of the Hindus, which are full of immense significance and implication. The matter contained in the work is greatly compressed, and forms "succinct and scrappy indications" of structures of innumerable kinds.[52] The aphoristic method adopted by the author helps a good deal assist the memory in digesting the elements of the subject. The location and the influence of the deities involved are discussed in the work, as also a host of properties and phenomena for the benefit of the artisans and craftsmen.

The *Samarāṅgaṇasūtradhāra* of Bhoja is another famous treatise on the science of architecture. In the first forty eight of its eighty-three chapters there are discussed three principal subjects: town-planning, house-architecture, and construction of machines and articles of household furniture. The qualifications of a good architect are also described here. In the next 20 chapters, the text deals with the science of temple-architecture, and in the last 14 chapters with iconography, both sculptural and pictorial. According to this work, architecture, *vāstu-kalā*, is one of the basic arts, *mūla kalā*s. The term *vāstu* is taken to carry cosmological, metaphysical, geological-cum-geographical and astronomical implications. The philosophy of *Vāstu-Brahma* is fully illustrated in temple architecture. As mentioned in the work the artist of a temple was to be fully devoted to his profession.[53]

The qualifications of a *sthapati* (an architect) are given in great detail in *Samarāṅgaṇasūtradhāra* in two separate chapters entitled *sthapati-lakṣaṇa* and *aṣṭāṅga-lakṣaṇa*.[54] In the period under discussion, there were two kinds of architects: *sthapati*, the master architect, and *sthāpaka*, the architect priest, the *guru*, the *ācārya*. The latter had importance only in the planning and setting up of

51. Ibid., p. I44ff.
52. Mankad Popatbhai Ambashankar (ed.), *Aparājitapṛcchā*.
53. For details see D.N. Shukla, *Vāstuśāstra*, op. cit.
54. *Samarāṅgaṇasūtradhāra*, chaps. 44 and 45.

religious structures, namely the *prāsādas* (temples), while the former was the sole authority in any building activity, civil or royal. The architect (*sthapati*) was expected to possess knowledge of the Śāstras, and to be an adept builder, a skilled artist and craftsman (*karman*) with the faculty of personal insight (*prajñā*). Apart from these three qualifications, an architect had to be a man of righteous conduct and character (*śīla*). It is evident from the above description that in the period under review, the architect was expected to possess a thorough knowledge of all aspects of architecture, and to be very well conversent with Śilpaśāstra.

Mānasāra is a most popular and widely talked of text of Śilpaśāstra (architecture and sculpture).[55] There are 70 chapters in the text, of which the first 50 deal with architecture and the last 20 with sculpture. The qualifications of an architect are extensively described in Chapter 2. *Sthapati* was the highest in rank, being the master-builder. He was expected to be well-versed in all sciences (*śāstras*), and the Vedas. He was to play a leading part in different kinds of offerings (*bali*). The *sūtragrāhin* was to be an expert draftsman (*rekhājña*). He was to act as the *guru* of *vardhakī* and *takṣaka*. *Vardhakī* was to be expert in the field of painting *citra-karman*). He was to function as the instructor of *takṣaka*, while *takṣaka* was to be an expert in his own vocation, i.e. carpentry.

Several ways of making idols have been described in the same text.[56] Special instructions to sculptors are given for making the images of the triad (Brahmā, Viṣṇu, and Śiva — the *Trimūrti*). The characteristic attributes and poses, and ornaments, decorations, etc. of female deities are also described.[57] The process of casting images in wax (*madhūcchiṣṭa vidhāna*) by *sthapati* and *sthāpaka* are also discussed by the author of *Mānasāra*.[58]

Mayamata is another manual on the science of architecture in south India. Its treatment of sculpture represents the most ancient phase of the art, when the phallic emblem was the most popular object of worship. The iconographical details are rich but to *liṅga*-icons. There are 34 chapters in this text. Chapter V,

---

55. P.K. Acharya, *Architecture of Mānasāra.*
56. *Mānasāra*, chap. LI to LXX.
57. Ibid., chap. LIV.
58. Ibid., chap. LXVIII.

"Manopakaraṇam" offers the traditional system of measurements of *vāstu*, and deals with the fourfold orders of the architects — *sthapati, sūtragrāhin, takṣaka* and *vardhakī* and the qualifications and the relative position of each.[59]

Śilparatna of Śrīkumāra is a yet another architectural text of south India. It is an authoritative and comprehensive treatise of architecture. The first chapter of the text speaks of the qualifications, equipment and the relative positions of *ācārya, sthāpaka* and the fourfold guilds of architects — *sthapati* and *sūtragrāhin, takṣaka* and *vardhakī*.

Some inscriptions of the period under review mention technical subjects. References to the branch of Śilpavijñāna or Śilpaśāstra for sculptors are found in some of the inscriptions of this period.[60] The science of architecture is also referred to in Kaḷacuri inscriptions.[61] The science of testing "the three kinds of jewels" has been called *tri-ratna*.[62] Moreover, the Five Sciences, viz. draughtsmanship (*rekhā*) carving on wood, carving on stone, carving on gold, and the great science of machinery (*yantravidyā-mahāvidyā*)[63] are alluded to in these inscriptions.

The art of the period reflects the cultural effects of feudalism.[64] The feudal atmosphere encouraged traditionalism and conventionalism. The canons of *śilpa* and painting were laid down in textual form from the late Gupta period onwards. The artisans and craftsmen were expected to follow strict canonical dictates as regards the choice of the site, design and construction of the shrine, carving of the images, etc. from about the tenth century, art was mainly governed by the canons of various regional schools.[65] Significantly, in the period under review, temple architecture, based on contemporary writing, reached its perfection. These writings were meticulously followed by both the architects and their *gurus, sthapati*s and *sthāpaka*s.

---

59. Quoted in D.N. Shukla, op. cit., pp. 163ff.
60. CII, IV, Ins. no. 100, verse 43; Ins. no. 103-104, verse 1.
61. Ibid., Ins. no. 58, verse 17; Ins. no. 60, verse 36; Ins. no. 84, verse 22, etc.
62. Ibid., Ins. no. 42, verse 8.
63. Ibid., Ins. no. 103, verses 2-3.
64. Devangana Desai, "Art Under Feudalism in India (c. CE 500–1300)" *IHR*, vol. 1, no. 1, March 1974, pp. 10-17.
65. Stella Kramrisch, *Art of India*, p. 44.

7

Guilds

THE institution of guild came into existence in ancient India to protect the individual and collective interests of artisans and craftsmen. Probably the oppression of the artisans by the upper classes led to the formation of corporate bodies of workers. There are numerous terms referring to these bodies, which had various characters and functions, such as : *śreṇī, kula, pūga, jāti, vrāta, saṅgha, samudāya, samūha, gaṇa, sambhūya-samutthāna, pariṣat, varga, sārtha* and *naigama.*[1] These terms have been differently interpreted by scholars and commentators, but they all denote economic organizations of artisans and craftsmen, and indicate their corporate life. *Śreṇī* was a more general and popular term than the others to signify these corporate bodies. The *śreṇīs* were meant to protect the economic interests of their members and lend them social prestige and security.[2]

The term *śreṇī*[3] occurs in the *Ṛgveda,* where it is said that "Like *haṁsas* people work in groups."[4] It appears that artisans when at work used to sit in rows, and this gave the name to the corporate body.[5] However, whether guilds existed in the Vedic period cannot be said with certainty. According to Macdonell and Keith, "The Vedic evidence is inadequate to afford ground for positive assertion or denial of the existence of organization in Vedic times."[6] Pāṇini refers to *śreṇī*

1. See K.P. Jayaswal, *Hindu Polity,* p. 251 and Buddha Prakash, *Aspects of Indian History and Civilization,* p. 20.
2. K.P. Jayaswal, op. cit., p. 241.
3. Its literal meaning is "a row."
4. *ṚV,* I, 163, 19; I, 126, 4; V, 59, 7; IV, 38, 6; *Vedic Index,* 11, 403; p. V; Kane, *Kātyāyanasmṛti,* 1933, p. 258.
5. P.C. Jain, *Labour in Ancient India,* p. 233.
6. As quoted by P.C. Jain, op. cit., p. 242.

as an assembly of persons associated with a common commodity.[7] Kauṭilya uses the term *śreṇī* in the sense of "guild of workmen."[8] Manu, as explained by Medhātithi, takes the term to mean guilds of merchants, artisans, bankers, brāhmaṇas, etc.[9] Nārada defines *śreṇī* as "a corporation of industrialists."[10]

It is evident from the Buddhist literature that during the Kuṣāṇa period urban crafts and other occupations flourished extensively, and the number of professional guilds greatly increased. Jātakas mention 18 kinds of professional guilds.[11] *Mahāvastu* also gives a long list of guildmen.[12] The head of these guilds was called *pamukha* (*pramukha*) or *jeṭṭhaka* (*jyeṣṭhaka*).[13] Terms for industries like *gāma, śreṇī* and *vihī* have been used in the Jātakas.[14] In ancient India, each industrial organization had its own *jeṭṭhaka*, and consequently the nature of the work of every *jeṭṭhaka* was different from that of others. There were *kammakāra jeṭṭhaka, mālākāra jeṭṭhaka, vaḍḍhaki jeṭṭhaka,* etc.[15] Some early northern inscriptions refer to guilds of weavers, silk-cloth weavers, oilmen, oil-millers, potters, braziers, bamboo workers, ivory-workers and mechanics (fabricators of hydraulic engines,

---

7. A.W. Bose, *Social and Rural Economy in Northern India*, p. 282.
8. *Arthaśāstra*, 11. 4.
9. *Manu*, VIII, 41; Medhātithi as quoted by R.K. Mookerji in *Local Government in Ancient India*, p. 19.
10. *Nārada-Smṛti*, 1.7.
11. T.W. Davids Rhys, *Buddhist India*, pp. 90-96.
12. The guildmen referred to in this text are the musicians (*gandharvika*s), goldsmiths, bankers (*hairaṇyika*s), cloak-sellers (*pravarika*), workers in shell and ivory, jewellers, workers in stone (*prastarika*s), perfumers, sheath-makers or box-makers (*kośāvika*s or *kauśikāra*s), oil-dealers, hawkers of jars of *ghee* (*gṛtakuṇḍika*s), sugar factors (*gaulika*s), vendors of water (*varika*s), dealers in cotton, curds, cakes (*pūpika*s), dried treacle (*khaṇḍakāraka*), sweetmeats, *kandu* (a kind of eatable) wheat-flour and barley meal, hawkers of fruits, roots, perfumed oil from ground powder, *agrivaniya*s *aviddhaka*s, makers of confectionary from sugar and dried treacle, vendors of dried ginger (*sūṇṭhika*s), distillers (*sidhukāraka*) and factors of candid sugar. See J.J. Jones (tr.), *The Mahavastu*, SBE, XVI-XVIII; J.N. Banerjea, Calcutta, 1960, pp. 1-70; see Kameshwar Prasad, *Cities, Crafts and Commerce Under the Kushanas*, p. 26.
13. *Jātaka*, II, 12, 52.
14. As quoted by P.C. Jain, op. cit., p. 240.
15. *Jātaka*, III, 405.

odayantrikas connected with *vidyā yantras*).[16] During the second century CE some money (in silver *paṇas*) was deposited by the lay Buddhist devotees with guilds of the potters, the oil-millers, and weavers for the purpose of providing robes and other necessities to the monks.[17]

More interesting information of different kinds of guilds is furnished by the literary works of the Gupta period. *Raghuvaṁśa* mentions a guild of architects which worked for the development and benefit of the architects.[18] In *Mudrārākṣasa*, a well-known play of the period, Candanadāsa[19] is referred to as president of the guild of the jewellers. Guilds of weavers and oilmen are mentioned in the Mandasaur Inscription of the time of Kumāragupta[20] and the Indore Copper-Plate Inscription of the reign of Sakandagupta respectively.[21] A silk weavers' guild is mentioned as having built a Sun-temple at Daśapura (Mandasaur) in CE 437-38 and repaired the same in CE 473-74. A guild of oilmen donated two *palas* of oil daily.[22] The grant was perpetual. Moreover, from the Gupta texts we learn that the number of guilds had risen immensely.[23]

---

16. R.K. Mookerji, p. 122, op. cit., *Local Government in Ancient India.*
17. Luders' List nos. 1133 and 1137.
18. *Ragh*, XVI, 38.
19. *Mudrārākṣasa*, I, pp. 18- 20, 28.
20. *CII*, III, p. 70.
21. *CII*, p. 80ff.
22. Indore Copper Plate of Skandagupta, *CII*.
23. The scholars enumerate them as follows: architects (*śilpayatana*) (1) blacksmiths (*lohakārakas*), (2) braziers (*tāmrakūṭas*), (3) goldsmiths (*suvarṇakāras*), (4) makers of wooden bowls (*taddhukāras*), (5) blowers of pipes for blazing fire in factories (*pradhvāpakas* or *pradhmāpakas*), (6) testers of precious metals by rubbing them on touchstones (*rosinas* or *rosanyas*), (7) tinsmiths (*trapukārakas*), (8) makers of lead sheets (*śāsā-picatakāras*), (9) machine-workers (*jantrakārakas* or *vantrakārakas*), (10) garland-makers (*mālākāras*), (11) vegetable-growers (*parṇikas* which is a better reading for the obscure *purimakārakas*), (12) potters (*kumbhakāras*), (13) tanners (*carmakāras*), (14) oven-makers (*kandukāras*), (15) weavers of wool (*ūrṇsvayakas*), (16) makers of mail armour (*varūthatantravāyakas*), (17) makers of cloth for idols (*devatātantravāyas*), (18) dyers (*rakta-rajakas*), (19) laundrymen (*chailadhovakas*), (20) cleaners (*rajakas*), (21) embroiderers (*sūcikas*), (22) weavers (*tantravayas*), (23) cottonweavers (*tulavayas*), (24) painters (*citrakāras*), (25) carpenters and image-carvers (*vardhakirūpakārakas*), (26) carvers (*kālapatirikas*), (27) basketmaters (*pelalakas*), (28) modellers in clay →

The importance of guilds (*śreṇīs*)[24] is talked of in *Bṛhatsaṁhitā*. According to this work, different types of artisans and craftsmen organized themselves under their heads, who were known as *śreṇīśreṣṭhas*[25] or *śreṣṭhins*.[26] A progressive development of corporate organizations is indicated by the numerous laws and regulations laid down by Nārada and later discussed by Bṛhaspati. In the case of new guilds or corporations, before undertaking any work mutual confidence among the members was ensured by making a monetary deposit with all the stipulations in writing and with guarantee of umpires.[27] The guild constitution was considered a valid document and included the pact of guild laws. The members of the guild who did not abide by this pact while being able to do so, were to be banished from the town.[28]

Guilds in the Early Medieval Period

According to *Mitākṣarā* and the *Vīramitrodaya*, a *śreṇī* is an association of people differing in caste but maintaining themselves by the sale of the same kind of merchandize.[29] *Mitākṣarā* defines a *śreṇī* as a community of those who earn their livelihood by selling a particular vendible, or practising a particular craft.[30] Vijñāneśvara contrasts *pūga* and *śreṇī* on the basis of the former being domiciled

→ (*pustakārakas*), (29) plasterers (*pustakarmakārakas*), (30) barbers (*nāpitas*); (31) hairdressers or toiletmakers (*kalpikas*); (32) wood or grass-cutters (*cedakas*), (33) furnishers or decorators (*lepakas*), (34) architects and masons (*sthapatisūtradhāras*), (35) barn-makers (*uptakoṣṭhakārakas*), (36) miners or well-diggers (*kūpakhanakas*), (38) labourers who carry mud (*mṛttikāvāhakas*), (38) labourers who carry wood (*kāṣṭhavāhakas*), (39) merchants of straw (*tṛṇavaṇijas*), (41) merchants of barks (*valkalavaṇijas*), (42) merchants of grass and shrubs (*stambavṇijas*), (43) merchants of bamboos (*vaṁśavaṇijas*), (44) sailors (*nāvikas*), (45) raftsmen (*odumpikas*), (46) workers clearing gold dust (*suvarṇadhovakas*), (47) tricksters (*mauṣṭhikas*), etc. See Buddha Prakash, *Aspects of Indian History and Civilization*, pp. 15-17.

24. *BS.*, X, 13; XXXIV, 19.
25. Ibid., VIII, 10.
26. Ibid., XXIX, 10; XXXIII, 25.
27. Ibid., XVII.
28. Ibid., XVII, 13.
29. *Mitākṣarā* on *Yājñavalkya-Smṛti*, II, 192, II, 30; *Vīramitrodaya*, VII, p. 333.
30. Ibid., III, p. 48.

in the same locality irrespective of the castes and professions followed by the members, and the latter being a vocational organization consisting of a group of people belonging to different castes but following the occupation of one caste. He cites the examples of the *śreṇīs* of weavers, shoe-makers and betel-sellers.[31] According to R.K. Mookerji, "the *pūga* was a special kind of *saṁgha*, an association of men of various castes who, though having no fixed occupation or means of livelihood, united in the pursuit of wealth and pleasure as their main aim."[32] Medhātithi[33] distinguishes between the *śreṇīs* and the *gaṇas* by observing that though the members of the former followed the same profession, were free to have different ones, but the members of the *gaṇas* always acted collectively. He also brings out the distinction between the *śreṇīs* and the *saṁghas*. According to him the *śreṇīs* were associations of people following the same profession but the *saṁghas* were communities of people of different castes following the same kind of occupation.

In *Abhidhānacintāmaṇi*, the term *śreṇī* and *prakṛti* are taken to be synonymous.[34] This usage receives support from the fact that *pitāmaha*,[35] as quoted by the legal works of the period, gives the number of the *prakṛtis* is as eighteen, which we know is also the traditional number of the *śreṇīs* in the Buddhist and Jain texts. There are also references to eighteen *prakṛtis* in the inscriptions of the period.[36] *Triṣaṣṭiśalākāpuruṣacarita*[37] also refers to *śreṇīs* and *praśreṇīs*. Here *praśreṇīs* should not be taken to stand for the branches of a central guild in constituent districts. They were the sub-groups into which a particular guild or corporation was divided on the basis of division of labour.[38] Lakṣmīdhara,[39] Aparārka[40] and Devaṇa

31. Ibid., II, 30.
32. R.K. Mookerji, op. cit., p. 32.
33. On *Manu*, VIII, 2; VIII, 219.
34. *Ab Chin*, III, v. 174; *prakṛtayah pauraṇam śreṇayo pich*.
35. *Samṛticandrikā*, II, p. 29; *Parāśaramādhavīya*, III, p. 46; *Sarasvatīvilāsa*, p. 74.
36. *EI*, II, p. 220; *ASB*, 1877, p. 73; Vogel, *Antiquities of Chamba State*, pp. 162, 166 and 193.
37. I, p. 250.
38. L. Gopal, *The Economic Life of Northern India*, p. 84.
39. Devaṇṇabhaṭṭa, II, 223, This source mentions a variation of reading in *Kalpataru*.
40. *Aparārka*, pp. 792-93.

Bhaṭṭa,[41] all speaks of the *śreṇī*s and *gaṇa*s as just associations which made certain agreements binding all the members.

In some inscriptions we come across the term *deśī*. The meaning of this term is not certain, though some scholars opine that it should becounted synonymous with *śreṇī*. The same term appears in the Pehowā inscription, and scholars have taken it to mean "guild."[42] The expression *bhammaha deśya*[43] occurs in the Harṣa stone inscription of Vigraharāja (vs 1030). Kielhorn, suggests that it may be connected with the term *deśī*, which, according to him, means "guild," *bhammaha* being interpreted as denoting "a class of traders." In the Nāḍlai Inscription (vs 1020)[44] some *vañjārakas* (*vañjārī*s) are mentioned to have formed themselves into a *deśī*. Thus we can say that the term *deśī* denotes a *śreṇī*, and it has been used in the inscriptions of the early medieval period for association of artisans and craftsmen. It may be noted that now the word *deśī* in north India denotes "rural." Possibly during the period under study, the word *deśī* was used for "village craft organization." It appears that the rural or *deśī* craft was based on the vernacular forms of the artisan guild.[45] The term *goṣṭhī* has also been used in an inscription for the guild of stone-cutters (*śilpī goṣṭhī*).[46] It seems that the term *goṣṭhī* was not used during the earlier times in connection with the guilds but it rather just referred to assemblage or collection of people of a particular sort.[47]

Traditionally, the guilds were eighteen, but they were actually never limited to this number. Some epigraphical and literary sources of the early medieval period bear out the existence of the following guilds of artisans and craftsmen; the corporations or guilds of oil-millers (*tailikas*),[48] potters (*kumbhakāras*),[49]

41. *Samṛticandrikā*, II, pp. 222-23.
42. *EI*, I, p. I84ff.
43. Ibid., II, pp. 1l6ff; 130 n. 83.
44. Ibid., XI, p. 42ff.
45. Pupul Jayakar in *Craftsmen and the Creative Process: The Indian Experience*, p. 89.
46. Deopara Inscription of Vijayasena, *EI*, I, 307f; see *ASIR*, 1903-04, p. 101.
47. L. Gopal, op. cit., p. 85.
48. Sīyadoṇī Inscription, *EI*, I, 21, p. 177; XXIII, p. 138; I, 160.
49. Ibid., I, 21, p. 174; Introduction to *Kathākośaprakaraṇa*, I, p. 177.

architects (*sūtradhāras*),[50] stone-cutters (*śilākūṭas*),[51] goldsmiths (*sauvarṇikas*),[52] blacksmiths (*lohakāras*),[53] braziers (*kāṁsyakāras*),[54] perfumers (*gandhikas*),[55] distillers of liquor (*kallapālas*),[56] sugar-boilers (*kandujakas*),[57] gardners (*mālīs*),[58] weavers (*tantuvāyas*),[59] shoe-makers (*mocīs*),[60] shield makers,[61] basket-makers,[62] rope-makers,[63] barbers (*kāsavagas*), cloth-printers (*gañcias*), and tailors (*śīvagas*).[64] It may be noted here that passion about guilds during the period seems to have slackened.[65] Thus, there are no long lists of guilds in the texts of this period, as there are in those of the early period.

The details of the working of the guilds have been furnished by *Jambūdvīpaprajñapti*[66] and *Triṣaṣṭiśalākāpuruṣacarita*.[67] These texts speak more specifically and give the names of the guilds of *kumbhakāras*, *paṭṭaillas*[68] (weavers), *suvarṇakāras* (goldsmiths), *sūvakāras* (cooks), *gandharvas* (musicians), *kasavaggas*

50. Sīyaḍoṇī Inscription, I, p. 177.
51. Ibid., I, 20, 177; *Śilpī-goṣṭhī*, I, pp. 307ff.
52. Ibid., XIX, 58; *Kathākośaprakaraṇa*, Introduction, p. 1166.
53. Ibid., I, 179; *Kathākośaprakaraṇa*, Ibid.
54. Ibid., I, 175.
55. Ibid., XIX, 61.
56. Ibid., I, 175.
57. Ibid., I, 174.
58. Ibid., I, 160
59. On *Manu*, VIII, p. 41, E.C. Sachu, *Al-Beruni's India*, 1, p. 101.
60. On *Yāj*, 11, 30; *Samṛticandrikā*, II, p. 223.
61. E.C., Sachau, op. cit., p. 101.
62. Ibid.
63. *EI*, V.9-23.
64. *Jambudvīpaprajñapti*, 43, p. 193; *Kapuruṣacarita*, I, 258; III, 316; see . . . *Padmanandamahākāvya*, XVI, 193; A.K. Majumdar, *Chalukyas of Gujarat*, pp. 264ff.
65. L. Gopal, op. cit., p. 81.
66. 43, p. 193.
67. I, 258; III, 316,
68. A.K. Majumdar, *Chalukyas of Gujarat*, pp. 264ff. See Lallanji Gopal, *The Economic Life of Northern India*, pp. 88-89.

(barbers), *mālākāras* (garland-makers or gardeners), *kachakāras* (rope-makers), *tambolīs* (betel-sellers); *carmakāras* (leather-workers), *jantapilaga*[69] (oil-pressers), *gañcias*[70] (*cimpāyas*) (cloth printers), *kaṁsakāras* (braziers), *sīvagas* (tailors), *guaras* (*gopālas*, cow-herds), *bhillas*[71] and *dhīvaras* (fishermen).

Guilds (*śreṇīs*) of weavers, shoe-makers, betel-sellers, etc. are specifically mentioned by Vijñāneśvara.[72] Guilds of weavers are mentioned in the work of Devaṇa Bhaṭṭa.[73] Al-Beruni refers to eight classes of people namely the fullers, shoe-makers, jugglers, basket-makers, shield-makers, sailors, fishermen, hunters of wild animals and birds, and weavers, who formed guilds.[74]

The Organization of Guilds

The administrative machinery which helped the guilds to deal with various activities is clearly outlined by our sources. There was a chief or president, assisted by a number of executive officers. Only persons who were honest and acquainted with the Vedas and their duties, able, self-controlled, from good families, and skilled in every business were appointed heads of associations. The law books of Nārada and Bṛhaspati provide an account of the selection of the head of the guilds. The head of the guild was assigned various titles, such as *pamukha, jeṭṭhaka* and *seṭhi*.[75] The term *pamukha* is used for the head of the guild selected on the basis of his superiority of wealth or on the basis of his local influence. The title *jeṭṭhaka* was perhaps assigned to the oldest man of a guild whose selection as the head was made on the basis of his age and long experience. Person who were hostile, dissolute, bashful, indolent, timid, avaricious, or very young were excluded

69. A.K. Majumdar translates it as pressers of sugar cane, while for Lallanji Gopal they are oil-pressers.

70. *Deśīnāmamālā*, II, 84 takes the term to mean *varuḍas* (low-caste men).

71. Accorcling to Lallanji Gopal, the Bhillas were the aboriginals inhabiting forests and often robbing travellers and caravans and indulging in slave-trade. They had a close group life with a chief exercising the highest power, which probably explains their inclusion in this list.

72. On *Yājñavalkya*, II, 30.

73. *Smṛticandrikā*, II, p. 223.

74. E.C. Sachau, op. cit., I, p. 101.

75. *BS*, XVII, 9-10.

from the selection of the head of an organization. According to Aparārka,[76] the head of a guild had the power of reprimanding, condemning, and even excommunicating wrong-doers. The details of the working of the guilds in the legal works of the period do not register any improvement on the rules in the Smṛtis.[77]

It is significant that by this period the importance of the chief of the guild within his organization had increased. The inscriptions of our period refer to the head of a guild by various names. The term *mahattaka* is used in one inscription to denote the position of headship of *tailika*s or oil-millers.[78] There are likewise references to the chiefs of the distillers of liquor (*kallapāla-mahattaka*s),[79] the gardeners (*mālika-mahara*s),[80] and the betel-sellers (*tāmbolika-mahara*s).[81] The epithet *mahara* seems to be a local word carrying the same meaning as *mahattaka*. In the Jhālarapāṭan Inscription of CE 1086 the term *tailikapṭṭakila*[82] has been used for the head of a guild of oilmen. The head of the guild was also known as *māṇḍalika*,[83] *mahagaṇṭha*,[84] and *śreṣṭhī*.[85] Probably *śreṣṭhī*s and *māṇḍalika*s were heads of merchant guilds, and their economic position was sound.

Sometimes taxes were imposed on different types of guilds by its heads. A stone inscription of king Allaṭa at Udaipur (CE 963) describes certain taxes on horses and elephants and also on oil-mills.[86] Here we can make a guess about the economic condition of oil-mills. The legal writings of the period also refer to guilds framing rules to regulate their activities. We know from inscriptions that the

76. p. 794.
77. L. Gopal, op. cit., p. 87. The author deals here with the duties of *smūha*s, with special reference to *Smṛticandrikā*.
78. *EI*, I, p. 154ff.
79. Ibid., p. 175, I.26.
80. Ibid., I, 17.
81. Ibid., p. 174, II, 8-10.
82. *JASB*, 1914, pp. 241-43.
83. Arthuna Inscription, *EI*, XIV, p. 295ff.
84. *IB*, p. 57ff.
85. Lucknow Museum Copper Plate grant of Mahāsāmanta Balavarmadeva, *IA*, XX, p. 123.
86. *IA*, VIII, pp. 161-62.

guilds could also impose on their members periodical cesses, sometimes in consideration of an amount paid to or deposited with them. In this context the Kāman Inscription (CE 886-905)[87] refers to three different guilds, those of potters, artisans and gardeners, that levied a small cess on every individual member. The members of the last-named guild paid their contributions in kind, while those of the remaining two paid a small cess probably because the articles manufactured by them were not regularly required for the use of the temple, and the guild did not pay out of its common fund.

It appears from the charters of the Bhaumakara rulers of the eighth century CE[88] that collection of taxes was made for the purpose of maintenance of temples. Recovery of taxes, was made from weavers, cowherds and others. This gift was made to the god Vaidyanātha enshrined in the temple of Pulindeśvara, built by Pulindarāja, and the grant was made on the request of this same Pulindarāja, who was apparently a vassal chief of the Kara ruler Śubhakara II. The chief could accept any endowment, and in fulfilling this right could impose a cess on the members of the guild.[89] It appears that the rulers patronized skilled artisans and craftsmen and gave them pieces of land and even whole villages for their upkeep. Obviously, the heads of important guilds commanded great authority and respect. In the post-Gupta period grant of lands in lieu of services was becoming a mode of payment, and probably artisans were also paid in this manner. The Deopārā Inscription of Vijayasena of Bengal reveals that Śūlapāṇi, a head of the artisans of Vārendra (North Bengal) in the eleventh century held the title of Rāṇaka.[90] Generally when an officer was made a Sāmanta, he received landed property along with the title and some land in lieu of services rendered to the state as an artisan.

Smṛticandrikā[91] indicates the importance of the heads of guilds. The text elaborately refers to the situation where the *samūhas* find themselves incapable of stopping the insolence of their *mukhyas* (chiefs). In such, cases the king was

87. *EI*, XXIV, 333-36.
88. B. Misra, *Orissa Under the Bhauma Kings*, pp. 12-20.
89. *EI*, p. 174, II.8-10.
90. *EI*, 1.35, p. 311; *IB*, III, p. 49.
91. III, pp. 53ff.

required to interfere and to set the chief on the proper path. If the *mukhya* was still recalcitrant he was fined in proportion to the extent of his solvency, and sometimes even suffered the confiscation of all his property, and in extreme cases got banished from the kingdom by the king, who alone was competent to inflict such a punishment. The aforementioned text, however, adds that if *samūha* is at all competent to do so, it alone shall exercise the authority to punish the chief.[92]

EXECUTIVE COMMITTEE

According to *Smṛticandrikā*,[93] when *samūhas*, such as *śreṇīs* failed to decide cases unanimously, they appointed executive committees consisting of two, three or five *kārya-cintakas* or *hitavādins*. This shows that the guilds had a certain power to make laws relating to their business. In fact, the executive members of a particular craft were responsible for everything happening to their business, and their decision was final. The *samūhas* had the power to punish members who were hostile to the advisers and who denied a speaker his opportunity, made an unreasonable speech, betrayed secrets, created dissensions or were guilty of other similar offences.[94] Medhātithi observes that guilds were keen to protect themselves from frequent interference by the king's offences.[95] The inscription of the Vailabhaṭṭasvāmī Temple at Gwalior speaks of the executive officers of different guilds in detail.[96] It speaks of the chief of the guild of oil-millers (*tailika-mahattaka*), "and the other members of the three guilds of oil-millers." The chiefs of the three guilds of oil-millers were, according to this record, respectively four, two and five in number. Indeed it appears that these executives exercised considerable authority over their individual members. According to *Kathākośaprakaraṇa*,[97] the garland-makers, makers of scents, manufacturers of various scented oils, jewellers, sellers of oil and ghee and other traders had their own separate laws.

Medhātithi commenting on Manu tells us that *śreṇīs* or guilds were not only formed by artisans and craftsmen, but also by tradesmen, moneylenders, coach-

92. See L. Gopal, op. cit., p. 86.

93. II, p. 224

94. III, pp. 526ff.

95. On *Manu*, VII1.2.

96. *EI*, I, I54ff.

97. Jineśavara's *Kathākośaparakaraṇa*, p. 165.

drivers and so forth.[98] The same text also speaks of the architects, masons, carpenters and the like who jointly performed their respective shares of work according to the agreement of the group. One of the guiding principles for determining the recompense for the work put in was that one who performed the most laborious and difficult part of a work received the greatest reward.[99] Apparently, the quantum of work was laid down for masters, journeymen and apparentices. He who had more experience in his craft, e.g. a master craftsman, got more wages from the corporation or guild in which he worked.

Functions of Guilds

In the period under review guilds of artisans and craftsmen served as multipurpose organizations. The members of the guilds performed many functions which were over and above their professional work. These corporate bodies performed not only functions like carrying out joint contracts, plying trade and receiving money deposits, but also those of judicial and executive nature in the interest of their members. The guilds also acted as banks, so that people deposited money there, sometimes amounts large enough to enable them to make religious endowments out of their interest. Some outstanding functions of the guilds may be taken up in detail.

GUILDS AS BANKS

It appears that the guilds were so honest in their transactions with people that the latter willingly deposited money with them. Some inscriptions describe the banking functions of the guilds, of which people made full use, say in making permanent religious endowments. Sometimes the deposits were made with the guilds under proper deeds of agreements, which outlined the conditions under which they were made. The Kāman Stone Inscription refers to three guilds of potters (*kumbhakāraṇām śreṇyas*), gardners (*mālika-śreṇyas*), and artisans (*śreṇya sthapatinam*).[100] The guilds, in consideration of a sum of money, received by them in advance stipulated to pay a permanent cess in both cash and kind for the upkeep of a temple and worship of a deity. The guilds of potters paid this cess at

98. On *Manu*, VIII, 41.

99. Ibid., VIII, 211.

100. *EI*, XXIV, 45, p. 335ff.

the rate of one *paṇa* per wheel monthly for each of its members. The members of the other guilds, accordingly, agreed to pay one *drama* per month. It appears that the expenses were met out of the interest accumulated on the deposits. These guilds served to stimulate spiritual benefactions and pious gifts in the community, and their utility was appreciated and taken advantage of by the interested members. They functioned for a long time, and their acceptance of deposits was a regular feature of the period.[101] What is particularly worth noticing is that the chiefs of the guilds accepted the aforementioned obligations in ordinary course, and they also exercised their authority to bind their members requisitely.

We learn from some south Indian inscriptions that the related function were organized by the guilds as part of their duties. The Lakṣmeśavara Inscription[102] of Prince Vikramāditya, dated about CE 725 refers to the guild of braziers, and in the constitution drawn up therein for the town of Porigere it is distinctly laid down that the taxes of all classes of people were to be paid into the guild accounts in the month of kārttika. Thus it is clear that in the period under review the guilds served as local banks and treasury.

Members of guilds were sometimes entrusted with responsible state and public duties. Thus, they were sometimes appointed as witnesses. In the Anāvāḍā Stone Inscription of Śāraṅgadeva, VS 1348,[103] is recorded bestowal of a gift by five classes of people of a town, one of which was the class of *mahājanas*. Guild members, at times, acted as witnesses to a document which contained a solemn promise on their part to apprehend the wrong-doers. A list of those who could act as witnesses contained in the Nāḍol Stone Inscription of Rāyapāla (VS 1198),[104] includes the entire community of local bankers (*mahājanas*). It is worth noticing that the guilds of the artisan class served as local banks. It is clear from the inventories of the functions of the guilds available in the sources of the period that they were quite actively engaged in tasks of public welfare.

---

101. See B.N. Puri, *The History of the Gurjara–Pratihāras*, p. 130.

102. *EI*, XIV, p. 188ff.

103. *IA*, XLI, pp. 20ff.

104. *EI*, XI, p. 37.

GUILDS AS TRAINING CENTRES

Among other things, the guilds of artisans and craftsmen acted as training centres. The new members of a guild learned their craft and its trade from the elder members, to whom they served as apprentices. It is evident from *Kṛtyakalpataru* of Lakṣmīdhara[105] that this mode of passing on the knowledge of the craft and trade by the elders to the younger generation was common. The text refers to the rules of apprenticeship in vogue. The work mentions the power of the master to order the *vadha* of the apprentice (meaning only beating him with a bamboo-stick), which implies that the master had the power to empowers the master inflict some corporal punishment on the apprentice.

The craft guilds had three classes of members: masters, journeymen and apprentices.[106] The apprentices were the learners, Apprenticeship was used by new means of acquiring aspirants as a means of acquiring technical training. When the apprentice had completed the term of training, and was qualified in his craft, he could seek employment as a journeyman. When became highly proficient in his profession or art, he became a master-craftsman in his own right.[107] During the period under review, the guilds of artisans and craftsmen engaged in various industries generally carried on their activities in their own cottages. The apprentices learnt the craft under the master's direct care and supervision. The master was obliged to provide them food and lodging, but pay no remuneration for the output by the apprentices.[108] Thus the guilds served as tecnnical education centres in which the knowledge of superior workmanship was bequeathed from the master craftsman to the apprentices. People belonging to the same vocational caste used to reside together in the village or a specified quarter of the town.

GUILDS AS AGENCIES OF RELIGIOUS WORK

Sometimes, permanent religious endowments were made by the guilds of the poorer sections of the society. The members of a guild of gardeners including its chief (*mālika-mahara*) are mentioned among those who gave away fifty garlands

105. *Vyavahārakāṇḍa* of *Kṛtyakalpataru*, p. 384.
106. *Oxford Junior Encyclopaedia*, vol. VII, pp. 136-37.
107. Ibid. The word "mystery" denotes to mastery or craftsmanship.
108. B.P. Majumdar, *Socio-Economic History of Northern India*, pp. 209-10.

of such flowers as were available in a particular season.[109] It is stated in another inscription of CE 1161 that 300 people of the caste of toddy-drawers gave a handful of dried unripe fruit and a handful of ripe fruit on each basketful that they sold of ripe fruit and dried unripe fruit.[110] The inscription ends with a mandate to the people of the district of toddy-drawers to preserve this religious act. The basket-makers and mat-makers gave a flower-basket and resolved to perpetuate this ritual for ever.

The *śreṇīs* played a significant role in the erection and maintenance of temples of this period.[111] Apparently, the construction of temples on a massive scale in north India was not possible for a few architects, stone-cutters and craftsmen. In this process hundreds of workmen and their corporations were involved under the kind supervision of their heads. Guilds of stone-cutters[112] and architects[113] are mentioned in this connection in our sources. Some inscriptions refer to master-craftsmen and builders of higher rank by name. Thus, Rāṇaka Śūlpāṇi was the crest-jewel of the *goṣṭhī* (guild) of the *śilpī*s of Vārendra.[114] Similarly, Devagaṇa, who is described as a *rūpakāra śiromaṇi*, "the crest-jewel among the sculptors," is mentioned as having built an temple of Bilvapāṇi.[115] There were also craftsmen and apprentices to assist the master craftsman, including the *sūtradhāras*.[116] Thus the guilds of architects and of craftsmen played an important role in the construction of temples and royal palaces. According to Misra, although references to guilds are few, none the less, the scale of the construction activity required and the evidence of hereditary bequeathment by the *ācārya-śiṣya* system of the skills of arts and crafts constitute a strong ground for our hypothesizing the existence of guilds.[117]

---

109. *EI*, I, 154ff.
110. Ibid., V, 9-23.
111. Brajesh Krishna, *The Art Under the Gurjara–Pratihāras*, p. 24.
112. Sīyadoṇī Inscription, *EI*, I, 173f; Ibid., I, 307f.
113. *EI*, I, 177; *On Manu*, VIII, 211.
114. *CII*, IV, 249.
115. Ibid., 490, 515.
116. R.N. Misra, *Ancient Artists and Art Activity*, p. 34,
117. Ibid., p. 55.

Particularly oil-manufacturers paved a healthy economic position. Our contemporary inscriptions give abundant information in this regard. Their popularity is attested in these sources and possibly it was because oil was the main requisite for illuminating the temples, in day and at night. In every religious endowment, the need of oil for perpetual lamp was urgent and the guild of oilmen or manufacturers irrigated the lamps in the temples. An inscription at Gwalior in the year 933 records that the members of a guild of oil-millers decided to supply one *palikā* of oil each of the lamps of the temple.[118] These activities of the oilmen are also recorded in the inscriptions of Kaḷacuri king Bijjala (CE 1165),[119] which registers certain grants that were made to a temple of the god Viṣṇu in the form of Channa-Keśava, and for the perpetual lamp of the god, there was alloted one oil-mill, as a *sarvanāmasya* grant. Similar type of description is given in another inscription.[120] In which an oil-mill and a tax, for the maintenance of the perpetual lamp of the God, has been described.

It is called for here to briefly discuss the guilds of oilmen and weavers on the basis of an inscription at Managoli of the time of the Kaḷacuri king Bijjala (CE 1161),[121] who made religious endowments, probably in the form of tax. The guilds of oilmen were situated in one place, as did others too, and held their meetings regularly on account of the festival of the *Vyatipāta* in honour of god Siddhaliṅga-Kālīdeveśvara. For perpetuating the burning of a lamp before the image of the god and other rites dedicated to him the guilds of oilmen gave one image of the god and of oil per oil-mill. The guilds of weavers, headed by their *gauḍas* (the mention here of the *gauḍas* or the village headmen seems rather incongruous) gave five *viṣas*[122] per poll (i.e. a capitation tax of five *viṣas*) every year, for the *Nūlu* festival; and the *koṭṭalis* of the god gave five *viṣas* per poll every year for the same festival.

There is an interesting mention in an inscription of a joint donation made by the guilds of several different categories of artisans and craftsmen. The Sīyadoṇī

118. *EI*, I, 154ff.

119. *EI*, V, pp. 23-26.

120. Inscription of Perma-Jagadekamala II, CE, 1144, *EI*, V, pp. 232-34.

121. *EI*, V, pp. 9-23.

122. *Kittel's Dictionary* explains *vīsa* as one-sixteenth of a *paṇa; paṇa* being equivalent to four *ānnā*s and eight *kāsus, kāsu* being "the smallest copper coin."

Inscription of the latter half of the tenth century CE mentions the *kāṁsākārs* (braziers), *kaṇḍukas* (sellers of sweets), *tambolikas* (betel-sellers), *kallapālas* (wine merchants), *śilākūṭas* as having organized guilds and acted as corporate bodies in the grant of donations.[123]

Records also speak of the activities of temple committees (*goṣṭhīs*), where the community of goldsmiths (*sauvarṇika mahājanas*), was made the incharge of temple funds.[124] Purchase of house-sites on 99 years lease by the *sauvarṇika mahājanas* and the *goṣṭhīs* of a certain temples out of temple funds is mentioned in a number of documents bearing dates between CE 865 and 904 and belonging to the region of the Upper Gaṅgā basin.[125]

Transformation of Guilds into Castes

The guild in early medieval period were fossilized into occupational sub-castes, though they certainly retained some characteristics of corporate life and social control over their members.[126] Some literary sources of our period refer to *śreṇīs* in terms of castes. But the *Mitākṣarā*[127] clings to the occupational origin of *śreṇīs*, defining them as groups of people of different castes who subsisted by their occupation of one caste, e.g. the *hedābūkas* (horse-dealers), *tāmbulikas* (betel-sellers), *kuvindas* (weavers) and *carmakāras* (shoe-makers). *Smṛticandrikā*[128] and *Vīramitrodaya*[129] clearly admit the change and take *śreṇī* to mean the eighteen low castes. The transformation of guilds into sub-castes appears to have gone much ahead even by the time of Bhaṭṭotpala,[130] who, ignoring the professional basis of the guilds, represents them simply as corporations of many people belonging to the same caste. Generally profession was hereditary, passing from father to son. Sulaiman, an Arab writer, speaking in this context, notes that in all

123. *EI*, I, 173ff.
124. *The Age of Imperial Kanauj*, p. 384.
125. *EI*, XIX, 58.
126. L. Gopal, op. cit., p. 82.
127. On *Yāj*, II, 30.
128. III, pt. 1, p. 40.
129. L. Gopal, op. cit., pp. 82ff .
130. On *Bṛhatsaṁhitā*, XXXIV, 19. Quoted by L. Gopal, op. cit., pp. 82-83.

the kingdoms he had seen "the profession never went out of the caste."[131] Thus, it seems that the organization of *śreṇī*s or guilds was based on caste, and the artisans and craftsmen, though generally belonging to the lower fringe of the community that is the class of śūdras, had their own social and economic differentiations. In the Jain list,[132] some of the guilds are of aboriginal people, and some are associated with base occupations, especially from the point of view of the *ahiṁsā* ideal. The source divides the eighteen guilds into two groups, the *nāruā*s (*nārukāhs*), who were considered touchables and the *kāruā*s (*kārukāhs*), who were looked upon as untouchables.

Vaijayantī[133] takes the term *śreṇī* to mean a body of people belonging to the same caste and profession. Pitāmaha,[134] as quoted by the legal works of the period, distinguishes between the terms *prakṛti* and *śreṇī*.

According to this source *prakṛti*s fell outside the pale of the four *varṇa*s and *āśrama*s. In *Kānhaḍadeprabandha*[135] we find a reference to eighteen *varṇa*s, besides the four high castes. Both the aforementioned references clearly establish the transformation of guilds into sub-castes. We also find elsewhere that the members of *śreṇī*s like those of goldsmiths, potters, blacksmiths, washermen and craftsmen and artisans (*śilpa-karmakāra-samudāya*s) constituted the *adhama* (degraded) class of society.[136]

Decline of the Guilds

It appears that by this period the importance of the guilds or the industrial organizations had considerably dwindled.[137] The guilds seem in general not to have been in a position to wield complete control over their members. The growth of feudalism, with its emphasis on a rural and self-sufficient economy, may be

131. *HIED*, I, p. 6ff.
132. *Jambūdvīpa*, 43, p. 193.
133. p. 237, 1.179.
134. *Smṛticandrikā*, II, p. 29; *Parāśaramādhavīya*, III, p. 46.
135. I, 238, as quoted by D. Sharma, *Early Chauhan Dynasties*, p. 252; Cf. L. Gopal, op. cit., p. 83.
136. *Kathākośaprakaraṇa* of Jineśvara Sūri, Introduction, pp. 116f.
137. L. Gopal, op. cit., p. 81.

taken to have had an adverse impact on the fortunes of the guilds. The decline of trade and commerce on the international level affected the manufacture by industrial organizations. Because of the instability and chaos resulting from feudal wars and the local government, the artisans and craftsmen failed to form lasting groups. It may be supposed that among other factors a self-contained economy, and administrative shortcomings may have been responsible for the decline of the guilds.

The use of terms like *śreṇī* and *gaṇa* by Medhātithi clearly indicates weakening of guilds. The members of the *śreṇī*s followed the same profession and acted only singly, whereas the *gaṇa*s always acted collectively.[138] The same writer tells us elsewhere that the members of the guilds often referred their disputes to king.[139] The guilds did not like this because, as Medhātithi says, it gave the king's officers an opportunity to interfere in their working. It follows from Medhātithi that the hold of the guilds over their members was becoming loose, and they could not effectively carry out their decisions against members.

Concludingly, it may be reiterated that *śreṇī*s were that associations of persons who earned their livelihood by the same kind of labour, though they did not necessarily belong to the same caste. It was the unity of occupation which formed the basis of the corporations working for the benefit of the artisans and craftsmen. Justice was provided to the workers by the heads or executive officers of the guilds. Guilds or corporations of such persons made their existence felt in the society, insofar as they were also members of the state administration. Guilds worked as technical institution where new young men learned their craft and prepared themselves for a trade for lifetime.

---

138. On *Manu*, VIII.2.

139. Ibid.

8

Social Status

It is generally believed that artisans and craftsmen in ancient India mostly belonged to the śūdra class, but divergent opinions are held as regards their social position in ancient India. Some scholars think that they were originally part and parcel of the vaiśya class but that they gradually lost their social position and importance, and came to be ranked with the śūdras.[1] Some others are, however, of the view that they were śūdras, or of a low mixed caste, right from the beginning of the social stratification.[2] Still others contend, on the basis of numerous references in the texts, that they were different from the śūdras,[3] and that they were given the right of following arts and crafts only later on.[4] The social structure in India from BCE sixth century to the fifth century CE is often called "vaiśya-śūdra based," it being believed that the "vaiśyas were peasants and the śūdras were artisans, slaves and hired labourers."[5] It is also possible that artisans and craftsmen were originally not śūdras but above their rank and were kept apart from them, and that it was only later that they became vaiśyas, and as such followed all sorts of economic persuits including even artisanry.[6] Considering that the law-givers of the early period refer to them as śūdras or low-caste people, it may be supposed

1. *The Vedic Age*, pp. 389, 400, 455 and 466.
2. P.C. Jain, *Labour in Ancient India*, p. 2.
3. *Mahābhārata*, Śānti Parva, 294.4; *Manu-Smṛti*, X, 99-100, 120; *Yājñavalkya-Smṛti*, 120; *Viṣṇu-Smṛti*, 11, 4; *Vāyu Purāṇa*, 6, 163; *Mārkaṇḍeya Purāṇa*, 28, 3-8; *Viṣṇu Purāṇa*, 3, 8-32; Medhātithi, On *Manu*, X, 99-100; Kullūka on *Manu*, X, 99-100; Hemacandra's *Śabdānuśaśana*, VI, 1-2.
4. P.C. Jain, op. cit., pp. 16, 18; M.P. Singh, *Life in Ancient India*, pp. 64-65; R. Panthri, *Prācīna Bhārata mein Sāmājika Parivartana*, pp. 49, 54.
5. R.S. Sharma (ed.), *Survey of Research in Economic and Social History of India*, p. 52.
6. Mahesh Vikram Singh, *Social Status of Artisans in Early Period of Indian History, PIHC, 51st Session* (Calcutta 1990), pp. 127-34.

that they were drawn to artisanry in the later period.[7] It is not that in any of these instances śūdras were given the right to practise arts and crafts but rather that the community pursuing these vocations came to be treated as vaiśyas.

Historically we find that artisanry, as is evident from the Haṛappan culture as well as from the post Haṛappan Chalcolithic cultures,[8] was more developed in the non-Aryan communities. The *Atharvaveda* clearly refers to the *āsuras* being efficient in the art of metal or iron smelting.[9] The art and skill of artisans was also rated very highly during the early Vedic times.[10] The skill of *tvaṣṭa* or *rathakāra* (chariot-making) was greatly appreciated and was given much importance in the society of the period under review.[11] It was included among the *ratnins*. There was, of course, no social stigma attached to the artisans and craftsmen.[12] However, the situation changed when artisanry and craftsmanship were adopted by the Aryans from the non-Aryans. This indicates that the professional communities joining the ranks of Vishahor vaiśyas as artisans and craftsmen must have been non-Aryans. This was the reason why they were not given higher status in the social set-up by the theorists of the Vedic Aryans. In the later Vedic age the caste system originated with the division of the society into four *varṇas*, and the *varṇa*-divided Brāhmanical society came to develop a more complex *jāti* system under the influence of certain material factors. The process led to significant modifications in the norms of conduct and the status of the interrelated elements of this system.[13] For instance, it was because of the progeny of different *varṇas* and castes adopting arts and crafts as their profession that they sank to a lower level of social recognition.

The system of establishing villages on the basis of a particular caste or community was well-known in ancient India, and is frequently found mentioned

7. R.C. Hazra, *Studies in Purāṇic Records of Hindu Rites and Customs*, p. 209.
8. D. Kosambi, *An Outline of History and Culture of Ancient India*, p. 72; see Mahesh Vikeram Singh, *PIHC*, 49th Session.
9. *AV*, 7.56.
10. P.C. Jain, op. cit., p. 3.
11. *Ṛ̥V*, 1, 61, 4; 1, 161, 5; X, 86, 5.
12. P.C. Jain, op. cit., p. 3.
13. Suvira Jaiswal, "Changes in the Status and Concept of the Śūdra Varṇa in Early Middle Ages", *PIHC, 41st Session* (Bombay, 1980), pp. 112-21.

in the Buddhist-Pāli literature. The texts refer to smith villages of 1000 families,[14] villages of wood wrights numbering 500,[15] and villages famous for potters.[16] More over, the Jātakas also have numerous references showing how different professions were assigned different localities. The ivory-workers' bazaar in the city of Varanasi,[17] localities of dyers, perfumers and florists,[18] and streets of washerman[19] clearly point to there having been systematic settlements of artisans and craftsmen.

Though Patañjali enumerates the economic divisions of the artisan class, he does not refer to their status in the society in Ancient India. According to him, the low professions included those of mat-makers, who fastened together with strings wooden pegs and straw;[20] weavers (*tantuvāyas*), who made cloth from threads,[21] and hair-weavers.[22]

It is a noticeable, however, that crafts were not always determined by caste. Nārada states that the consideration of caste did not affect the admission of apprentices into a craft.[23] An important consideration that mattered was the consent of the apprentice's parents or guardians, and when that was obtained, the youth was free to learn the craft which he desired to. Obviously the barriers between occupations were not so fixed and rigid as those between castes. There was, however, a great pride attaching to descent, and sons, especially among artisans, tended to follow the paternal industry.

Artisans and craftsmen were subjected to social disapproval on account of their profession in the Hindu law books. The term low-traders mentioned in the Smr̥tis covered wide cross-section of artisans and craftsmen, for it took its reference from the stricter ideals and the more orthodox standpoint of the brāhmaṇas.

14. *Jātaka*, III, 281-6.
15. Ibid., II, 18, 405; IV, 208.
16. Ibid., III, 376, 508.
17. Ibid., I, 320, II, 197.
18. Ibid., IV, 81-82.
19. Ibid., IV, 81.
20. *Mahābhāṣya*, III, 17, p. 14.
21. Ibid., I, 1, 45, p. 112.
22. Ibid., IV, 3, 84, p. 313.
23. See R.K. Mookerji, *Local Government in Ancient India*, p. 60.

Among the professionals of the arts and crafts on which there rested a social stigma were makers of bows, blacksmiths, goldsmiths, dealers in weapons, carpenters, weavers, dyers, oil-manufacturers, architects, tailors, basket-makers, and workers in cane.[24]

Social Status in the Early Medieval Period: Position in the Varṇa System

During the period under survey, the rules laid down by the law-givers were not strictly observed. The artisans and craftsmen changed their profession according to their personal interests. śūdras sometimes worked as agriculturists. Occasionally kṣatriyas took to agriculture. At times brāhmaṇas worked as *śilpīs* (sculptors),[25] though as a rule sculptor was assigned by the Dharmśāstras to the śūdras. Sometimes Kṣatriyas worked on metal.[26] In exceptional cases vaiśyas adopted the occupations of the śūdras. Notwithstanding these exceptions, however, the artisans and craftsmen generally belonged to the social class of the śūdras.

The Śūdras

Devala, in *Mitākṣarā* on *Yājñavalkya-Smṛti*, provides for the śūdras earning their livelihood by practising arts and crafts. According to him the śūdras were to serve the twice-born, and adopt the occupation of agriculture, rearing cattle, carrying loads, selling of commodities, drawing and painting, dancing, singing, and playing on musical instruments like the flute, the lute, the drum and the tabor.[27] However, Medhātithi also allows for the śūdra to live without serving the higher *varṇa*s as if they were economically sound.[28]

Some arts and crafts were so profitable that the śūdras who adopted them

---

24. *Manu*, III, 150-63; IV, 84.210-16; VIII, 65-66; II, 64; 12, 45-46; *Āpastamba*, 1, 6, 14; *Gautama*, XVII, 17; *Vasiṣṭha*, III, 3; 14, 2-3; *Baudhāyana*, 1.5, 10, 24, 11.1-2, 13; *Nārada*, 1.178, 181, 183-85; *BS*, XXII, 3; *Viṣṇu*, 37, 22, 23, 32; 48, 10, 13, 14-15; LXXXII., For details see, Radha Kumud Mookerji, op. cit., pp. 68ff.
25. *Vaikhānasa-Smārtta-sūtra*.
26. *EI*, XXXIV, pp. 31-32; Ibid., XXVIII, pp. 1-11.
27. Devala in *Mitākṣarā* on *Yājñavalkya-Smṛti*, I, 120.
28. On *Manu*, III, 156, 415; R.C. Majurndar (ed.), *Struggle for Empire*, p. 475.

not only made their economic position sound but also elevated their social status in the society. They often took to arts and crafts despite the Smr̥tis not favouring accumulation of wealth in the hands of the śūdras.

Al-Idrisi (b. towards the end of the eleventh century CE)[29] in his *Nuzbatu-i-Muṣtāk* and Marvazi in his *Sharāf-Al-aman-Tahir* (CE 1120)[30] refer to the seven classifications of the Hindu society. Ibn Khurdādbeh also mentions the seven classes of the Hindus.[31] He speaks of the divisions of the society of the period under study on occupational basis, and refers to the status of the people of different castes and their interrelations. The śūdras were both agriculturists and practisers of arts and crafts. Al-Idrisi calls them craftsmen and tradesmen in one place and artisans and mechanics in another. The observations of these travellers indicate that both śūdras and vaiśyas were sometimes artisans and craftsmen and sometimes agriculturists and merchants.

The Antyajas

Al-Beruni mentions the *antyajas*, the low-caste people, who were treated as untouchables.[32] They were regarded only as members of certain crafts and professions. There were eight classes among them who freely intermarried between them, except the washermen, the show-makers and the weavers, with whom none would have anything to do. They lived near but outside the villages and towns of the four castes were divided into two groups on the basis of their profession and cultural and social status.[33] As we are told by Al-Beruni, one group was nearer to the main four castes than the other, which had a lower status than the first. Nevertheless, the occupations pursued by both the groups were held in contempt. The group of the *antyajas* held higher in status performed such jobs as washing, shoe-making, boating, fishing, basket- and shield-making,

29. *HIED*, I, pp. 74-93.
30. B.N. Puri, *The History of the Gurjara-Pratihāra*, p. 118.
31. *HIED*, I, pp. I6-17.
32. E.C. Sachau, *Al-Beruni's India*, p. 101. See Mahendra Pratap Singh, *Life in Ancient India* (*CE 800-1200*), pp. 72ff.
33. Mahendra Pratap Singh, ibid., p. 75.

hunting and weaving. The *antyajas* of the second group were occupied with dirty chores, such as cleaning the villages and rendering other similarly low-services. Among them the *cāṇḍālas* and the *ḍomas*, however, also customarily played on musical instruments.

Adhama and Adhamādhama

Jineśvara classifies the low caste people as the *adhamas* and the *adhamādhama*. In the *adhama* class he puts the makers of mats, washermen and actors.[34] The leather-workers were held untouchables. The makers of baskets and tents were *ḍomas*, and were also considered untouchable.[35] In the works of the Jainas, certain arts and crafts are divided into the categories of touchables and untouchables. The first category included weavers, gardeners, potters, oil-millers and barbers, and the second comprised washer- men, carpenters, smiths, blacksmiths and goldsmiths.[36] Thus, the Jainas speak of the śūdras as being of two kinds: artisans (*kāru*) and non-artisans (*akāru*).

Untouchability of Artisans and Craftsmen

In the period under study the term *antyaja* denoted all the low castes.[37] The position of the *antyajas* was very pitiable, and they were regarded as untouchables in the community. However, their status improved in course of time. According to *Bṛhaddharma Purāṇa*, some of the *antyajas* like weavers came to be included in the *uttamasaṅkaras*, while boatmen and leather-workers remained in the *adhamasaṅkara* category. On the contrary, Kane, interpreting the information given in Manu, Hārīta and Aṅgīras,[38] observes that the seven well-known *antyajas* were not untouchables in the time of Medhātithi and Kullūkabhaṭṭa,[39] meaning thereby that their touch was not so polluting as to require an actual bath. An illuminating study by Vivekanand Jha has distinguished four major stages in the origin and

34. *Kathākośaprakaraṇa*, p. 115.
35. *RT*, VI, 192.
36. Pannalal Jain (ed.), *Ādipurāṇa*, pp. 19-22. See also Winternitz, *History of Indian Literature*, 2, p. 481.
37. *Atri Saṁhitā*, 199; *Yama*, 33 and *Vedavyāsa*, 1, 12-B mention 12 *antyajas* in all.
38. *HDS*, II, pt. 1, p. 173.
39. Ibid,

proliferation of the untouchables in India up to CE 1200.[40] In the fourth phase, extending from CE 600 to 1200, a number of occupational groups such as the *carmakāras* and the *rajakas* were degraded to the category of untouchables, and several new ethnic groups were added to the list. This means that during the early medieval period the number of untouchable groups increased.[41] The stagnant village economy allowed little mobility to artisans and craftsmen, and the resistance to the process of Hinduization by the aboriginal people and their consequent degradation to the position of untouchables presents only one side of the picture. We should also note that the greater integration with the Brāhmanical society meant greater economic dependence and exploitation of these people.[42]

Settlement Patterns of Artisans and Craftsmen

The works on architecture (Vāstuśastras) of the period under study make provision for residences of potters, barbers, weavers, tailors, carpenters, oilmen, fishermen, washermen, physician, hunters, dancers, drummers, basket-makers, leathers-workers, meat-sellers (butchers), *cāṇḍālas* and sometimes even prostitutes in the villages.[43] Mayamata gives a rather complicated plan. The location of the weavers is fixed in the south and the wheelwrights or carters (*cakrināḥ*) are located in the outermost parts. These texts not only describe the location of artisans and craftsmen but also mention the separate blocks of dealers which were reserved for special purposes. Some of the blocks and their respective selling goods are (a) fish, meat, dry food and vegetables, (b) staple food, (c) pottery, (d) brass and bronze, (e) cloth shops, (f) rice or paddy, (g) tailoring and salt and oils, (h) perfumeries and flowers, etc. All these establishments were arranged in the above serial order in respect of residential sites. There were also the business centres or industries where artisans and craftsmen worked for their livelihood. Moreover, along the roads within the boulevard were located shops of jewels and precious stones, gold, clothes and condiments like *mañjiṣṭha*, pepper, *pīpal*, ginger, and of honey, ghee,

---

40. Vivekanand Jha, *Early History of Untouchables in India,* unpublished thesis, Patna University, 1972.
41. B.N.S. Yadava in *The Indian Historical Review,* II, no. 2 (January 1976), 514-15.
42. Ibid.
43. *Maya,* 9.88-96; *Mānasāra,* 9.72-78, 116-27.

oil, medicines, etc. Thus the plan shows that stalls and residential quarters were placed side by side in the interior of the towns. Evidently groups or families of artisans and craftsmen were provided special places in the towns and cities, which shows the economic importance and the social status of artisans and craftsmen.

An alternative order of planning was to place artisans and manual workers in the outer zone of the city, so that, having common interests, they could work more efficiently.[44] The potters, barbers and other craftsmen were assigned the site to the east or north; fishermen to the north-west; butchers to the west; oil-men to the north; architects to the south-east or the north-west; further off washermen; and the sweepers' quarters at a distance of about a *krośa*. It can easily be seen that the location of the artisans and craftsmen was according to their social value. However, collective residence of people belonging to the same occupation must have been an important factor contributing towards the development of industrial and other corporations.

The inscriptions of the period show that sometimes whole villages were inhabited by a particular class of artisans and craftsmen. This indicates the lucrativeness of their professions. In this context the Nāgarī plate of Anaṅgabhīma III (Śaka 1151-52) speaks of a village which was inhabited by artisans and craftsmen practising particular crafts, such as merchants, perfumers, workers in conch-shells, goldsmiths, braziers, sellers of betel, florists and weavers, etc. The *śilpīs* (craftsmen) find a separate mention in the list.[45] The village in which these artisans and craftsmen lived is described as having several buildings of different types.[46] In such villages administrative activities or by guilds and corporations, the social status of which was equal and which worked together with co-operation between them. Localization is also evidenced by the Kahla Plate of the Kaḷacuri Soḍhadeva,[47] in which the different localities inhabited by different classes of people are specified. There may have grown a tendency for the subdivisions of

44. *Maya*, 9.88-96.

45. *EI*, XXVIII, lines 127ff; XXII, p. 259.

46. Ibid. Apparently, the resident *śilpīs* must have been the builders who were settled in the locality and may also have helped in the building of tihe local Jagannāth temple which finds mention in the verse 27 of the inscription; See R.N. Misra, *Ancient Artists and Art Activity*, pp. 33-34.

47. *EI*, VII, pp. 85ff.

the same community to sometimes occupy separate portions of the village, in order to protect and augment their respective interests.

The village potters (*kumbhakāras*) are referred to in the Nidhanpur Copper Plate of Bhāskaravarman[48] and the copper-plate grant of Vaidyadeva, king of Kāmarūpa.[49] If the expression *kumbhakārabhogyavahiḥ* of the latter[50] is taken to mean land or field belonging to the *kumbhakāras*, it follows that the potters in Assam, like the fishermen (*kaivarttas*), were connected with agriculture as well. We may then conclude that professional potters, besides carrying out their own business, also cultivated land. Similarly weavers are referred to in the Śubhaṅkarapātaka grant of Dharmapāla where the land belonging to 24 weavers, and to the weavers of the Oraṅgī class[51] is mentioned.

Information regarding engravers of a village is also available. Several Pāla Copper Plate grants were engraved by *śilpīs* (artisans) hailing from the village Poshāli.[52] N.N. Vasu[53] identifies this village with the modern Posela situated at a distance of five miles from Maṅgalkoṭ towards the south-east in the Burdwan district of West Bengal. The Bhatera Plate of Govindakeśavadeva refers to the barbers (*nāpitas*), washermen (*rajakas*) and bell metal workers (*kāṁsyakāras*) of the village Bhatapada and the ivory workers of the village Siṁhaura.[54] This type of localization of artisans and craftsmen points to the well-established characteristic of economic corporations and their flourishing occupations.

Right of Saṁskāras

Medhātithi tells us that in course of time the condition of śūdras greatly improved. They freed themselves from certain disabilities. Though they were engaged in arts and crafts, they could become teachers of grammar and other sciences, perform rites allowed to all classes in the Smṛtis, utter the names of deities according to

---

48. *EI*, XII, No.13, last plate, 1.46.
49. *EI*, 11, No. 28, 1.60.
50. Ibid.
51. *Kāmarūpa Śāsanāvalī*, pp. 146ff; 11.49 and 54-55, 62.
52. *EI*, XXIX, no. IA, 11, 57-58; Ibid., XXIX, no. 7, 1, 48.
53. *Brāhmaṇa-kāṇḍa*, vol. 1, p. 122 referred to in *EI*, XXIX, no. 1, p. 6.
54. *EI*, XIX, no. 49, 11.45-46, 48-49, and 51,

the views of revered teachers, and observe the *nāmakaraṇa* and other sacraments without uttering the *mantras*.[55] Medhātithi and Viśvarūpa also tell us that śūdras in the period under study could not be enslaved or made dependent on a brāhmaṇa. Lakṣmīdhara in his *Gṛhasthakāṇḍa* denies all these rights to the śūdras. However, he emphasizes that the śūdra committed no sin if he gave rice to a brāhmaṇa for getting it cooked at the latter's house.[56] Further, he approves of the rules of Yājñavalkya, Devala and Aṅgiras, according to whom brāhmaṇa could take the meals offered by artisans and craftsmen. This gives us an idea of the social status in the society of the time. Lakṣmīdhara includes in the śūdra class barbers, potters, dancers, actors, carpenters, cobblers, musicians, blacksmiths, weavers, washermen, garland-makers, painters, cart-drivers, oil-millers, and cow herds and peasants.[57]

On the contrary, Aparārka[58] (twelfth century CE) mentions segregation of people following professions which were held unclean and socially low. In this context, "the ancient Hindus," observes Kane, "had a horror of uncleanliness and they desired to segregate those who followed unclean professions like those of sweepers, workers in hide, tanners, guardians of cemeteries, etc. This segregation cannot be said to have been quite unjustifiable."[59] In those times the caste was chiefly a matter of race, and the caste status had a simple correlation with the Nasal Index of its members.[60] Hence, the social status of artisans and craftsmen was not purely dependent on their professions. Aparārka[61] quotes *Brahma Purāṇa* to show that the food which came from the hands of or which was owned by the following was forbidden: a singer, an actor, a physician, a surgeon, a goldsmith, a distiller or seller of liquors, a vendor of weapons, a tailor, a washerman, a bard, a carpenter, one who made his living by astrology, one

55. "Medhātithi on Manu," III, 67, 121, 156; X, 127; *Viśvarūpa on Yājñavalkya-Smṛti*, 1, 13.
56. *Niyatakālakāṇḍa*, p. 356; *Gṛhastharatnākara*, p. 336.
57. *Niyatakālakāṇḍa*, pp. 262-63.
58. *Aparārka*, pp. 1177-79.
59. P.V. Kane, *HDS*, II, Chap. IV, p. 170.
60. H.H. Risely, *Tribes and Castes of Bengal Anthropometic Data;* Idem, *The People of India*, see Survira Jaiswal, "Studies in Early Indian Social History: Trends and Possibilities," in R.S. Sharma (ed.), *Survey of Research in Economic and Social History of India*, p. 40.
61. Aparārka, pp. 1177-79.

whose duty was to ring bells, a village officer, a worker in hides, a potter, a wrestler, a worker in bamboo, an indigenous banker, and one who served as a priest to the whole village. One wonders how in the age in question a nation could effectively defend itself against foreign invasions when it segregated all those who were engaged in manufacturing and selling arms, armours, or chariots.[62]

Religious Endowments by Artisans

Birth no doubt fixed one's place in the caste system, but equally important were the socio-religious ceremonies called the *saṁskāra*s, which were supposed either to remove some taint or to give some new capacity to the individual. Some professional classes of artisans and craftsmen had a fairly good position in society and were also religious-minded. During the period, certain artisans and craftsmen individually and collectively made endowments for religious purposes. The Kumbhakārai, according to Uśanas, was the offspring of a brāhmaṇa from a vaiśya.[63] Sometimes the members of the *kumbhakāra* caste could rise to high and responsible positions, just as *sajjana* was appointed the Governor of Cittoṛ.[64]

Kaḷacuri inscriptions are an important source of information about the socio-economic history of the period under study. The professionals *sūtradhāra*,[65] *lohakāra*[66] and *mocī*[67] are mentioned in these inscriptions. They were treated as low caste people. It is curious to note that sometimes low castes like these were involved in religious ceremonies and made endowments. The shoe-maker (*mocī*) named Devapāla, referred to in the Khalāri Stone Inscription of Haribrahmadeva, was a religious-minded man, and was rich enough to have a temple of Nārāyaṇa constructed at Khalvatika.[68]

62. B.P. Mazumdar, *Socio-Economic History of Northern India*, p. 78.
63. B.N. Sharrna, op. cit., p. 29.
64. Dasharatha Sharma, *Early Chauhan Dynasties*, p. 248.
65. *CII*, IV, Ins. nos. 64 (line 26) and 105 (line 20).
66. Ibid., Ins. no. 65, line 19.
67. Ibid., Ins. no. 108, line 10.
68. R.K. Sharma, *The Kaḷacuris and Their Times*, 295.

Social Status of Artisans and Craftsmen

According to *Brahmavaivartta* and *Bṛhaddharma Purāṇas*, the *gandhavaṇika, śaṅkhika, kāṁsyakāra*, and *svarṇakāra*, were all *śūdras*,[69] but their status rose in Bengal in the seventh century CE.

SVARṆAKĀRA

Vallālacarita of Ānandabhaṭṭa tells us that Vallālasena had particular animosity against the *svarṇavaṇika*, that is, traders in bullion for certain reasons. He is said to have avenged an insult to him by degrading the *svarṇavaṇikas* (the goldsmith caste) to such an extent that even drinking of water touched by them was prohibited by him for the higher castes. Vallabhānanda, the rich merchant of Saṅkakoṭa, agreed to lend a crore and a half of gold coins to Vallālasena on condition of receiving the revenues of Harikeli. In addition, goldsmiths had alliance with the Pāla kings and the Sena rulers and acted as credit and banking agents on a large scale.[70] The law books[71] of ancient times, Śaṅkha and Sumantu quoted by Aparārka[72] and Bhavadeva and Hemādri place the *svarṇakāras* and *svarṇakāras* on a level with *karmakāras*, *niṣādas*, washermen, actors, kaivarttas, tailors, medas and bhillas.[73] According to Kṣemendra the goldsmiths were expert in the 64 arts, including twelve of movements, six of hissing, eleven of new ways of deception and five of reducing weight.[74] Sometimes the *suvarṇakāras* made donations of images.[75] They knew the art of writing, and several inscriptions were engraved by them.[76] However, according to Mazumdar, the main reason for assigning them to a low class was habitual theft of gold by them.[77] But it

---

69. B.P. Mazumdar, op. cit., p. 108.
70. R.C. Mazumdar, *History of Bengal*. vol. 1, pp. 240-41; *Indian Historical Quarterly*, Calcutta, XVI, 702, 705.
71. *Manu*, IV, 215; *Yājñavalkya*, I, 163.
72. pp. 1175-76.
73. *HDS*, II, pt. 1m p. 98.
74. For more description see *Kalāvilāsa* of Kṣemendra, VIII.
75. *JBORS*, XXVI. 245 on gift of Keśava in the 31st year of Mahipāla.
76. See chapter two, engravers of this books.
77. B.P. Mazumdar, op. cit., p. 109.

appears that stealing gold by professional *suvarṇakāra*s was not the only reason for the social stigma attaching to them; another, and an important, reason was their profession.

Even as it is the social status of goldsmiths was considered higher than that of many other categories of artisans and craftsmen. Possibly this was due to their prosperity during the period. Sometimes a few proficient goldsmiths were also patronized by the royal court, particularly those who prepared ornaments for the royal family. Moreover, production of luxury gift articles also required skilled labour by craftsmen. These articles were not meant for ordinary consumption but for the use of kings, princes, and chiefs. Since there were many rulers and a large number of feudatories in early medieval period, the need for such articles was great. These articles were not produced everywhere. Areas which were famous for the manufacture of such goods supplied them to the consumers all over the country and even abroad.[78]

SŪTRADHĀRA

Among the craftsmen, *sūtradhāra*s played a very significant role in the building activity, and as stated by Misra,[79] "their status was, without doubt, respectable, and such respect arose out of their skill and its recognition by people." Expert craftsmen were often close to the elite, particularly the ruling princes and others who had the resources to commission temples, etc. This may have helped them in achieving greater recognition. It has been noted that the kings had their own *sūtradhāra*s[80] or *sūtradhārapitāmaha*s, "chief among the *sūtradhāra*s,"[81] or *ācārya*s,[82] who evidently enjoyed a respectable position in society. Some *sūtradhāra*s also came from higher *varṇa*s, though this must not have been a general rule.[83] As far as the social status of architects is concerned, their position is not quite clear. But from the functions assigned to each of the four classes of architects (as in the texts), it would appear that the first three, namely *sthapati*, *sūtragrāhin*, and

78. Anjali Bagai, *Merchandise and Merchantile Community in Post Gupta Times in Northern India* (unpublished thesis, Delhi University, 1985), p. 87.

79. R.N. Misra, op. cit., p. 57.

80. *Epigraphia Carnatica*, I, no. 123, p. 168.

81. *IA.*, XIX; R.N. Misra, op. cit., p. 57.

82. P.K. Acharya, *An Encyclopaedia of Hindu Architecture*, p. 586.

83. R.N. Misra, op. cit., p. 57.

vardhakī, belonged to the higher level.[84] This statement may be true in the case of *sūtradhāras*, also for they are often mentioned as having been proficient in Śāstras and *vidyās* which included Śilpaśāstra, astronomy, and the science of numbers.

ARCHITECTS

Architects and sculptors most probably belonged to the lower caste clans, and as a caste they were treated with contempt, even though their hand-made products, such as icon sculptures, had great value in the ancient Indian society. These craftsmen were sometimes duly honoured by the king. A graphic instance of the honour shown to them is mentioned in *Harṣacarita*, where Prabhākaravardhana receives decorators on the eve of the marriage of princess Rājyaśrī. There is a great eclat. Wonderful terracotta work and other kinds of decoration are entrusted to the sculptors after due honour is shown to them. Rājaśekhara in his *Kāvyamīmāṁsā* mentions the special place given to sculptors, painters, dancers, actors and others in the royal assembly of poets (*kavisamāja*). The Apabhraṁśa *kavi*s (vernacular poets) were honoured with the next place, and craftsmen were given their due rank in a particular order.[85] Thus, architects and sculptors were generally held in good esteem, and the art of which they were exponents was also well regarded. Hence, we may assume that efficient architects, sculptors and other craftsmen who were patronized by rulers possessed a high place in the ancient Indian society.

Though artisans and craftsmen were at liberty to change their craft, as Coomaraswamy says,[86] "it is very important to realize that the artisan or artist possessed an assured status in the form of a life contract or rather a hereditary office. He was trained from childhood as his father's disciple, and followed his father's calling as a matter of course." He calls it "guild socialism in a non-competitive society."

It has already been said that the status of all artisans and craftsmen was not equal. The *rathakāras*, *karmāras*, *takṣakas*, *rūpakāras* and *citrakāras* were of corrlated

84. P.K. Acharya, op. cit., pp. 591-92.

85. C. Sivaramamurti, *Indian Sculpture*, p. 7.

86. Quoted in Brajesh Krishna, *The Art Under The Gurjara Pratiharas*, p. 29.

families.[87] The practice of the same craft in a family for two generations or more is inferred from the epigraphical sources of our period. This indicates a trend towards specialization.

The position or social status of *mālākāras* (florists), *kumbhakāra* (potters) and weavers improved during the period, particularly during the Sena regime in Bengal.[88] The *Vallālacarita* refers to them as being raised to the status of sat-śūdras, and Vallālsena conferred the feudatory title of *mahāmāṇḍalika* to Maheśa, the headman of the kaivarttas. It seems that Dhoyī, who belonged to the community of weavers, rose to the position of a court-poet of king Lakṣmanasena.[89]

Organizations of Artisans and Craftsmen and their Social Status

We have noted that artisans and craftsmen organised themselves into guilds.[90] These guilds were assigned a social status equal to that of the low castes and sometimes even to that of the outcastes. In *Kathākośaprakaraṇa*[91] Jineśvara Sūri makes of members of *śreṇīs* like goldsmiths, potters, blacksmiths, washermen and other craftsmen and artisans (*śilpa-karmakāra-samudāya*) forming the *adhama* (degraded) class of society. We observe that it was the low castes and groups that brought down the general standing of the guilds to a low rung. It should be noticed that in the Jaina list[92] some of the guilds of the low order are those of aboriginal people, and some others are those of base occupations, especially from the point of view of the *ahiṁsā* ideal. The text itself indicates this when it divides the eighteen into two groups, the *nāruās* (the *nārukāh*), the touchables, and the *kāruās* (the *kārukāh*), the untouchables. But the fact of the guilds being bracketed with the low sub-castes or groups could not by itself have been sufficient to bring

87 C. Sivaramamurti, *Indian Sculpture*, p. 8.

88. B.P. Mazumdar, op. cit., p. 111.

89. Sukumar Sen, *Prācīna Baṅgāla*, p. 19; Niharranjan Ray, *Vāṅgālir Itihāsa*, p. 319.

90. For detail see chapter on Guilds of Artisans and Craftsmen of this book; Vikram Mahesh Singh, "Social Status of Artisans in Early Period" in *PIHC*, 51st session, pp. 127-34.

91. Introduction, pp. 116f.

92. *Jambūdvīpa*, 43, p. 193.

them down in social ranking; it is obvious that there had already appeared a corresponding decline in their economic position.

Artisans and Craftsmen Aided

It is worth noting that during the period under review some artisans and craftsmen were very poor. Sometimes the state government or the rulers provided them some aids.

Some inscriptions of our period inform us that sometimes artisans and craftsmen were at the mercy of kings. For instance King Govindakeśava gave away houses belonging to washermen, ivory-workers and boatmen to a Śaiva temple.[93] It is also noted that Raṭṭarāja, the Śilāhāra chieftain, assigned one family each of washermen, potters, gardeners and oilmen to the service of the Karkaroni branch of the Mattamayūra Śaiva Ācāryas.[94] In some cases kings assigned the whole-time service of artisans and craftsmen to a temple or a Śaiva monastery.

Impact of the Arab Invasions

The last centuries of our period witnessed the frequent Arab invasions which had created a stir in the Hindu society. The conquest and occupation of some of the frontier districts gave the Musalmans an impetus to push their arms further into the interior, and satisfy their missionary zeal by converting Indians to Islam, and this tide threatened the social structure.[95] The rigidity of the caste system on the one hand, and reclaiming of those lost to Islam on the other hand went on side by side as both the phenomena were important for preserving the existing social order. Social mobility in Indian society did not necessarily mean a change in the actual status of a caste but perhaps more often an attempt to improve its ritual status or else to deny its importance.[96] Hence, the division of society into four or more classes, and the workers practising arts and crafts not only maintained their socio-economic structure but also improved it. Artisans and craftsmen became more conscious about their perpetual professions so that Muslim artisan

93. *EI*, XIX, 277ff.

94. Ibid., III. 296.

95. B.N. Puri, *The History of Gurjara Pratihāras*, p. 116.

96. Romila Thapar, *Ancient Indian Social History*, p. 129.

class would not displace them in their hereditary skill. North Indian artisans and craftsmen were quite conscious of their professions. Thus it seems that *varṇa* system became rigid due to "Muslim" invasions, for Hinduism tried to protect its culture from the onslaught of Islam by laying stress on the purity of birth, blood, etc.[97] The contracting economy with its emphasis on agrarian and local character, was reflected in the growing rigidity of caste.[98] Again it is stated that the growing power of Muslims was a "contributory factor" to the growth of the rigidity of caste rules.

It appears that during the period under review, the social status of artisans and craftsmen was better than it had been in earlier periods. They improved their social status by dint of their mastery of the skill of their trades and their creative activities. Some artisans and craftsmen were patronized by the rulers and by noble families. Some of them were also members of the administrative councils. They performed religious endowments, made donations and exercised the right of *saṁskāra*s.

It is interesting to note that some artisans and craftsmen were very rich, and their sound economic position also made them respectable in the eyes of the higher classes. Sources reveal that during the ancient period in Indian history, artisans and craftsmen sometimes adopted the professions of vaiśyas, kṣatriyas and brāhmaṇas, which lent them high social status and prestige. We can say that profession or occupation of the artisan class did not always invariably prove their social status in the society, frequently some other factors were also responsible for their social status.

---

97. Dashrath Sharma, *Rajasthan Through The Ages*, 1; pp. 444, 535; B.N. Sharma, op. cit., p. 9; R.C. Mazumdar, *The Struggle for Empire*, p. 498; Kailash Chand Jain, *Malwa Through The Ages. From the Earliest Times to 1305* CE, p. 482.

98. B.N.S. Yadav, *Society and Culture in Northern India in the Twelfth Century*; pp. 6-7, 61.

9

Economic Condition

THE economic condition of a nation or people generally depends on the agricultural products and natural wealth of the land. India has always primarily been an agricultural country, the fertile Indo-Gangetic Plain providing her ample scope for commercial enterprise in the form of agriculture. Haṛappans knew a number of arts, e.g. that of smelting metals to produce alloys. The artisans and craftsmen manufactured articles of copper and bronze on a large scale. In urban parts they had a greater scope of earning, and so there they were in a sounder economic position. Some artisans and craftsmen, such as goldsmiths, architects, sculptors, potters, weavers and leather workers, fulfilled the daily needs of the community and played an important part in its economy. Specialization in arts and crafts is also known in the Vedic period, and subsequently crafts such as those of the carpenter, goldsmith, ivory-worker and stone-cutter reached a high state of development. Clearly, the artisans and craftsmen greatly gave rise to urban development.[1]

The Mauryan times witnessed an unprecedented expansion of arts and crafts. Artisans and craftsmen possessed a thorough knowledge of the technological aspects of their occupations, including metallurgy. Superintendents[2] of crafts supervised the work of the industrial workers, and were responsible for their production. The rights and wages of the artisan class were secure, and their earnings were enough to serve their purpose. The various professions of the artisans and craftsmen flourished on a large scale during the Kuṣāṇa period, as is attested

1. P.C. Jain, *Labour in Ancient India*, pp. iv-v.
2. Kauṭilya mentions *sūtrādhyakṣa*, *lohādhyakṣa*, and *ākarādhyakṣas*, etc. See R.S. Sharma, *Perspectives in Social and Economic History of Early India*, pp. 130-31.

by archaeological and literary sources.[3] The *Milandapañho* enumerates as many as 75 occupations in contemporary society, about 60 of them being connected with various kinds of crafts.[4] The artisans and craftsmen formed guilds for preserving their economic interests, and amassed money.[5] This shows their sound economic position in the society of the period.

In the Gupta period the economic conditions of the artisans and craftsmen seems to have improved. It seems that the general peace and security in the Gupta period created conditions conducive for unfettered development of various arts and crafts. It is curious to note that 64 arts (*kalās*) have been listed in the *Kāmasūtra*[6] and other texts. Metal workers, jewellers, weavers, stone-cutters, wood-workers, garland-makers, potters, tailors, painters, leather-dressers and shell-cutters, etc. have been mentioned in the literary and archaeological sources of this period.[7] This shows that these crafts were considered important in society. They are also frequently referred to in the epigraphs of the period as creditable.[8] The expansion of these arts and crafts not only brought beneficial results to the society at large, but also improved the economic position of the artisans and craftsmen. Moreover, an important aspect of the economic life of the artisans and craftsmen was formation of guilds and corporations. The artisan class thus had ample scope for developing their skills and ingenuity. The guilds' laws and regulations also safeguarded the interest of the artisans and craftsmen against internal or external on slaughts on them.[9]

Early Medieval Period

The economic condition of the artisans and craftsmen has always depended on the nature of their craft. The artisans and craftsmen of the early medieval period

3. For details, see Kameshwar Prasad, *Cities, Crafts and Commerce under the Kushanas*, pp. 95ff.
4. *Milindapañho*, p. 331.
5. Luder's Lists, nos. 1133, 1137.
6. *Kāmasūtra*, III, p. 23.
7. For details see S.K. Maity, *Economic Life of Northern India*, pp. 99ff.
8. J. Fleet, pp. 118, 122, 127, 131; see S.K. Maity, op. cit., p. 119.
9. See S.K. Maity, op. cit., pp. 155ff.

used the tools and implements to which they had been accustomed for generations. We do not know for certain the utility of these tools for large-scale production. The choice of an industry was almost always based not on its nature and scope for development, but on heredity.[10] During the early medieval period professions were hereditary, because the child could avail of better facilities of learning his craft under the care and supervision of the members of his family. In this connection, Sulaiman writes that in all the kingdoms he had seen, "the profession never went out of the caste."[11] Thus it was quite natural that the artisans and craftsmen working under the apprenticeship system produced bright results and sound earnings.

Organization of Guilds for Economic Benefit

The various guilds of artisans and craftsmen played a significant role in their economic development. The available sources refer to existence of guilds of stone-cutters, architects, potters, wood-workers, basket-makers, shield-makers, etc. in the early medieval period. *Kṛtyakalpataru* of Lakṣmīdhara lays down elaborate rules regarding the privileges of guilds (*śreṇī*s), and shows their importance in the economic set-up.[12] Such organizations preserved the economic rights and privileges of the artisans and craftsmen. Guilds appointed executive committees[13] and their heads commanded great authority and respect.[14] Some of the guilds were so rich that they made religious endowments, and carried out elaborate works of public welfare.

Changing of Profession for Economic Benefits

Artisans and craftsmen could change their profession to suit their economic interests and their skills. It appears that the traditional theory regarding the professions to be followed by the four *varṇa*s was not scrupulously adhered to during the period.[15] The sources of the period indicate that sometimes the pressure

10. A.L. Basham, *The Wonder That Was India*, p. 216.
11. *HIED*, p. 5.
12. Quoted by B.N. Sharma, *Social and Cultural History of Northern India*, p. 152.
13. See *Smṛticandrikā*, II, p. 224.
14. Ibid., II, p. 49; *EI*, I, p. 154ff.
15. B.P. Majumdar, *Socio-Econoniic History of Northern India*, p. 77.

of economic circumstances compelled many brāhmaṇa families to encroach upon the preserves of the three other *varṇas*.[16] Vijñāneśvara, in explaining *Yājñavalkya*,[17] quotes Devala to show that it was the duty of a śūdra to practise agriculture, rearing of cattle, selling of commodities, and drawing, painting, dancing, singing, and playing on musical instruments like the flute, lute, drums and tabors. It is clear that adoption of occupation by the different classes of society depended on the personal interests of the artisans and craftsmen, who mainly belonged to the śūdra class of community, and had many options in choosing their profession. The sacerdotal class in the period under review came to regard not only the fine arts but also the professions which had been held peculiar to the vaiśyas in olden times as fit for persons of the lowest stratum.[18]

It is also evident from the literature of the period that the artisan class were free to change their profession. Sometimes they adopted a new profession for a short time. Inscriptions and copper-plates were engraved by the *pītalakāras* (braziers),[19] the *lohāras* or *lohakāras*,[20] the *suvarṇakāras*,[21] the *rūpakāras*,[22] the *sthapatis*,[23] the *śilpins*,[24] or the *sūtradhāras*.[25] It seems that engraving of inscriptions was a side-business of some artisans and craftsmen. We also find a mention of people of the upper classes of the society doing engraving. There are clear references to brāhmaṇas,[26] kṣatriyas[27] and kāyasthas,[28] doing engraving.

---

16. Ibid.
17. *Yājñ*, p. 120.
18. See B.P. Majumdar, op. cit., pp. 78-79.
19. *EI*, XXXII, pp. 123-25; ibid., IV, pp. 153-70.
20. Ibid., IV, pp. 97-129.
21. Ibid., XX, pp. 143-52; XXX, pp. 237-42.
22. Ibid., XXXII, pp. 139-56.
23. Ibid., IV, pp. 221-25.
24. Ibid., XXXVIII, pp. 312ff.
25. Ibid., XXXIII, pp. 31-36; 11, pp. 40ff.
26. Ibid., XIX, pp. 69-75; *JAOS*, VII, p. 24.
27. Ibid., XXXIV, pp. 31-32; XXVIII, pp. 1-11.
28. Ibid., XXI, pp. 41-50.

Richer Section of Artisans and Craftsmen

Some artisans and craftsmen formed a prosperous class during the period. Contemporary literature and inscriptions of the period under survey reveal that the goldsmiths, oil millers, metal workers, textile workers and architects were rich, and some of them achieved international fame in their crafts. In this period the goldsmiths (*suvarṇikas*) constituted a very prosperous community.[29] They were also rich bankers and supplied loans to people.[30] In some inscriptions they have been called *śeramānlokapperundattans*. which means "the great goldsmiths of the world."[31] Apparently, economically they had earned a sound position in the society of the period.

Among the metal workers the *kāṁsyakāras* and the *śaṅkhikas* workers in brass and shells respectively, were not always poor.[32] The Bhaṭera Copper-plate of Govindakeśava mentions that the *kāṁsyakāras* were donors of houses.[33] Similar references are available about *śaṅkhikas* elsewhere.[34] Oil was used in domestic life for numerous purposes, and oil-pressing from several sources was a regular business of oilmen and they were in great demand in the society. They made donations to the temples during the period.[35] Textile workers had achieved international fame. The contemporary epigraphs and literature refer to the weavers,[36] clothing fabric markets[37] and great centres of textile products.[38] All these had great value and demand in the society, and apparently, economically their position of the professions concerned was more advanced than that of other artisans and craftsmen.

---

29. As stated in Pushpa Niyogi, *Contributions to the Economic History of Northern India*, p. 258.
30. Ballala Kirti, *Uttarachanda*, Chapter 11; p. 44; See P. Niyogi, op. cit.; p. 258.
31. *EI*, IV, pp. 290-97.
32. B.P. Majumdar, op. cit., p. 108.
33. *EI*, XIX, pp. 277ff.
34. Ibid., XXIII, p. 141.
35. For details, see "Oil-Manufacturers" in the present book.
36. *EI*, XXIX, pp. 878; *Naiṣadh,* of Śrīharṣa, I, 12; *Ab Chin,* III, 577.
37. *EI*, XIX, p. 205; *HIED*, I, p. 92.
38. Arbian writers mention a number of textile centres. A few of them were Rahmi (Bengal), Malwa (Gujarat) and Banāras, etc. Our literary and epigraphical sources also speak of famous centres of textile industry. For details, see "Weavers."

During the period a number of "sky touching" buildings and temples[39] were erected by architects. Many terms like *śilpin,*[40] *śilākūṭa,*[41] *rūpakāra,*[42] *sūtradhāra,*[43] etc. were used for builders and workmen. In some inscriptions their names are accompanied by due mention of the nature of their mastery over their craft.[44] Thus, it may also be assumed that they got handsome recompense for raising huge architectural structures.

There are definite indications that some artisans and craftsmen kept deposits of customers with them, and that their corporations or guilds accepted deposits on promise to pay interest. The guilds of potters and stone-cutters in our sources are found encouraging persons to deposit their surplus money with them by promising interest on the capital in advance.[45] Sīyadoṇī inscription mentions Nāgāka, a merchant, as having given to a deity the capital of 1350 *śrīmadādivarāhadramma*s which had been invested with distillers of spirituous liquor.[46] This implies that some guilds in the society were so rich that they indulged in banking.

Paying of Taxes by Artisans and Craftsmen

Some artisans and craftsmen paid taxes, which indicates their sound economic position. The terms *pravaṇī*s[47] and *pravaṇīkara*[48] are used in two epigraphs. *Pravaṇīkara* was the source of the income collected from village crafts. The artisans of villages were the manufacturers of individual localities. The term *pravaṇī* stands

39. *RT,* VII, 608; See *HIED,* II, pp. 144-45.
40. *EI,* VIII, pp. 96ff.
41. Ibid., I, p. 177; *IA,* XV, p. 40.
42. *EI,* VIII, pp. 96ff.
43. Ibid., XXXI, pp. 165-66; *ASIR,* XXI, pp. 34-35; IX, p. 12; *JBBRAS,* XXIII, p. 80; *EI,* XI, pp. 44-46; XXVII, p. 27.
44. For details, see the chapter on "Stone Workers".
45. Sīyaḍonī and Kāman Inscriptions: *EI,* I, p. 175; II, pp. 19-20; XXIV, pp. 328ff.
46. *EI,* I, pp. 162-79.
47. *EI,* III, pp. 263ff.
48. Ibid., XI, pp. 147ff.

for *niṣparvaṇī* of the lexicons,[49] meaning "recently from the loom."[50] Thus, most probably by *pravaṇīkara* is meant a tax on the cloth newly woven on the looms.[51] Orissa, Gujarat and Bengal were the main centres of cloth industry, and inscriptions from these regions mention this term pertaining to tax.[52] Textile workers, as already mentioned above, were economically well off, and they were in a fair position to pay the taxes imposed by the state.

There appear in the sources of the period different terms for the various taxes that were in promulgation. *Kṛtyakalpataru* describes *kara* as the receipt of the fixed money from artisans and cultivators.[53] The land-grants of the Kaḷacuris refers to the term *rasavatī*, which is annotated as "the tax on liquor."[54] *Tailapalikā* (small measures of oil)[55] mentioned in the inscriptions of *Paramāra*s is a term which means "a tax paid by the oil-millers." Similarly, the term *suvarṇṇadaṇḍa* denotes a tax which was imposed either on goldsmiths or on gold-washing.[56] The Basahi grant of Govindacandra mentions *ākara*, which refers to "a tax on the output of mines" allowed to be worked by private individuals.[57] The salt manufacturers also paid a tax called *lavaṇākara*.[58]

A number of our sources speak of the taxes on the following items, which were classed under what we know as excise duty: bamboo, leather, earthen ware glass and stone products, minerals like gold, silver, copper, zinc, iron, and gems and lead.[59] Lakṣmīdhara endorses a levy of 20 per cent on gold mentioned in

---

49. *Ab Chin*, III, 335.
50. Monier-Williams, *A Sanskrit–English Dictionary*, p. 436.
51. *Ab Chin*, III, 335.
52. Ibid.
53. *Gṛhastha*, p. 255.
54. *CII*, IV, 645-52.
55. *EI*, XXXII, 148-56; see L. Gopal, op. cit., p. 64.
56. *EI*, XXXIII, 264ff; XXVIII, 324ff; see L. Gopal, op. cit., p. 61.
57. *IA*, XIV, 101-04.
58. *EI*, X, 95.
59. *Agni Purāṇa*, Ch. 223, 24ff; *Mānasollāsa*, *Viṁśati*, 11, 165-66; *Śukra*, IV, 2, 118-19; *RT*, pp. 88-89.

Manu and *Viṣṇu*.[60] Some inscriptions also mentioned taxes on wood and mines.[61] Sometimes taxes were also paid in the form of religious donations.

Several manufacturers and craftsmen were poor, but they had to pay the taxes levied by the state. Law givers and lexicons mention many taxes imposed by the King on the artisan class. *Viṣṭi* was a tax which was mainly paid in the form of physical labour.[62] (*uśanas*, quoted by Maskarin in his commentary on Gautama, holds the view that the artisans were either to perform one days' work every month without any remuneration or pay one *kārṣāpaṇa* as tax.[63] This type of tax is also recommended by Medhātithi.[64] Śukra, instead of one day's free service prescribes two day's work from the artists and artisans.[65] Medhātithi defines variations in the king's share owing to the cost of labour involved in the production. As the plantation of trees and the production of perfumes, of skins and canes, of earthenwares, vessels and stone articles probably cost little labour, only 1/6th share was prescribed as being due to the king.[66]

The *Agni Purāṇa* definitely lays down that the king must provide food to those from whom forced labour was to be taken.[67] Lakṣmīdhara quotes the view of Gautama who prescribes supply of food to the workers. He cites the blacksmiths, porters, boatmen, owners of carriages, and actors as the categories of persons who are liable to pay labour tax once a month.[68] These references favour the suggestion that forced labour was often commuted in the form of cash or kind payment.

Thus literary and epigraphical records of the period under review reveal a high social and economic condition of some of the artisans and craftsmen. The

60. *RT*, pp. 88-89; quoting *Manu* VII, 130 and *Viṣṇu* III, 408.
61. *IA*, VI, 56; XVIII, 17.
62. Manu clearly declares that this tax was accruable mainly from artisans, craftsmen and the śūdra caste. See VII, 138.
63. On *Gautama*, X, 31; See, Sushil Malti Devi, *Economic Condition of Ancient India*, p. 265.
64. On *Manu*, VII, 138.
65. *Śurkra*, IV, ii, 148.
66. Ibid., pp. 131-32.
67. *Agni Purāṇa*, chap. 223.
68. As quoted by B.P. Mazumdar, op. cit., pp. 188-89.

localization of various arts and crafts and their development in cities and villages were based on industrial products, their market values, and the skill of the workers. The artisans and craftsmen living in an area had knowledge of superior workmanship bequeathed from father to son for generations as a result of the training given by master-craftsmen. The Guilds served as training centres, and apprentices learned their craft from highly technical texts. The level of high efficiency in industries of the artisans and craftsmen and their superior economic position were purely based on these aspects. During the period there certainly had been a marked development in various arts and crafts, and numerous professions and occupations based on them had come to exist. The artisans and craftsmen had achieved international fame in their crafts. They made, collectively or individually, donations; their guilds functioned as banks; some of them were members of the state government, were very rich, and paid taxes to the state, and their sound economic position also lent to them a high social status in the society of the time.

To have a look at the impact which the industrialization have left upon the profession of the artisans of the period i.e. 700 to 1200 CE, and now most of the artisans like potter have been greatly affected by the impact of industrialization. The trade of pottery and earthen lamp has replaced by king size refrigerators, candles and electric bulbs. Similarly, the carpenter and iron iron-smith who used to thrive on the part of wheel, plough, yoke on bullock, bullock-cart, Persian-wheel, cot, chisel, spade, oil and sugar presser and agricultural implements etc., which have been replaced by tractor, trolley, cultivator, harrow, combine harvesting machine and tube-well, sugar-mill and factories etc.

fig. 1: General view of Stepped Tank (*vāpī*), eleventh century, Sandstone, Tewar, Jabalpur Distt., MP. (Represents the workmanship of architect and construction of well.)

fig. 2: Vimal Vasahi, Southern Bay, Nabhimandaraka Ceiling, *c.* CE 1150, Mount Abu, Sirohī Distt., Rajasthan. (Wheel, the symbolof change, development anddestruction, the attractive creation of the *śilpī*.)

fig. 3: Paṭṭaśālā, South Ceiling, Sarasvati vs 1288-96/CE 1232-40, Mount Abu, Luna Vasahi, Sirohī Distt. Rajasthan. (A view of different musical instruments made by artisans.)

fig. 4: Pillar, *c.* tenth century, Sandstone, Shahdol Distt., Singhpur, MP. (Picture shows the workmanship of architect and the use of metal bell in the temples.)

fig. 5: Śiva Temple, Sanctum doorway, *c*. thirteenth century, Sandstone, Dharar, Distt. Ratlam, MP. (The skill of architect and the use of metal bell in the temples.)

fig. 6: Miniature Temple, no. 2, front view, *c*. ninth century, Stone, Gwalior Fort, Distt. Gwalior, MP. (The perfection of the architects and sculptors.)

fig. 7: Sāsabahū (smaller), central view of Saṁvaraṇa from west *c.* CE 1093, Buffsandstone, Gwalior Fort, Distt. Gwalior, MP. (The creation of sky touching temple of the period.)

fig. 8: Fort view showing sculptures embedded in fort wall, *c.* ninth-tenth century, Sandstone, Hiṅglājgaṛh, Distt. Mandsore, MP. (Picture showing the necessity of architects and construction of forts by the rulers.)

fig. 9: Ādināth temple, view from south, *c*. fourteenth century, Stone, Cittoṛgarh, Distt. Cittoṛ, Rajasthan. (Skilled workmanship of architects.)

fig. 10: Tṛtīyadeva temple, view from south, *c*. twelfth century, stone, Suvarnapur, Distt. Cuttak, Orissa. (Highness of artisan class of the period.)

fig. 11: Sun Temple from South-East, mid-thirteenth century, Distt. Koṇārk Purī, Orissa. (Skilled workmanship of *śilpī*s.)

fig. 12: Samidheśvara Temple *c.* third quarter of twelfth century, quartzite, Cittoṛ, Distt. Cittoṛ, Rajasthan (Famous for its impressive tiers.)

fig. 13: Lakṣmaṇa Temple, General view from the east, *c*. CE 954, Jejākabhubti style, Khajurāho, Distt. Chhatarpur, MP. (Main attraction for the foreign tourists.)

fig. 14: First frontal wheel on the Southern wall, Sūrya Temple, Koṇārka, Orissa. (The wheel represents the importance of time, development and destruction.)

fig. 15: Sun Temple, Naṭamandir Jagatī, showing drummer and dancer, mid-thirteenth century CE, Sandstone, Koṇārk, Distt. Purī, Orissa. (Depiction of performing artists was also important on temple walls.)

fig. 16: Sun Temple, Naṭamandir showing female musicians, mid-thirteenth century CE, Sandstone, Koṇārk, Distt. Purī, Orissa. (Music performers are shown aesthetically.)

fig. 17: Scene of Dance and Music, tenth century, Buff sandstone, 298 x .442 m, Khajurāho, Distt. Chhatarpur, MP. (Use of musical instruments in a ceremony.)

fig. 18: Dancing Gaṇeśa, *c.* tenth-eleventh century, Purple sandstone, .820 x .490 m, Doni, Distt. Damoh, MP. (Picture represents worship of Gaṇeśa, importance of weapons and jewellery.)

fig. 19: Pārśvanātha temple (no. 11), showing *apsaras*es applying, Collyrium, *c*. later half of tenth century, Sandstone, Khajurāho, Distt. Chhatarpur, MP.
(Picture highlights the requirement of the cosmetic-makers.)

fig. 20: Lady with mirror, *c*. tenth century, Sandstone .920 x .290 m, Calcutta Indian Museum, Khajurāho, Distt. Chhatarpur, MP.
(The scene represents the skilled-workmanship of *śilpī* and the importance of cosmetic, mirror and ornament makers.)

fig. 21: Lady at toilet, standing *c*. tenth century, Buff sandstone, .450 x .240 m, Indore Central Museum, Hiṅglājgaṛh, Distt. Mandsore, MP. (The picture represents the demand of cosmetic and ornament maker.)

fig. 22: Ādināth Temple (no. 9), *c*. late eleventh century, Sandstone, Excellency of the (Beauty & Artisan), Khajurāho, Distt. Chhatarpur, MP. (Represents the use of mirror, cosmetics and jewellery. The demand of skilled *śilpīs* was very high.)

fig. 23: Lakṣmaṇa Temple, *c*. CE 953-54, Sandstone, Khajurāho, Distt. Chhatarpur, MP. (Represents the artistic hand of sculptor as well as of the beautiful woman, Jewellery and make-up.)

fig. 24: Pārśvanātha Temple, showing *apsaras*es painting foot, *c*. later half of tenth century, Sandstone, Khajurāho, Distt. Chhatarpur, MP. (Shows the highly talented workmanship of the sculptors and the passion for beauty in Indian culture.)

fig. 25: Architectural fragment with Brahmā, *c*. tenth-eleventh century, Sandstone, Ramban Tulsi Sangrahalaya, .325 x .400 m, Khajurāho, Distt. Chhatarpur, MP. (Shows the proper knowledge of *śilpavidyā* gained by the *śilpī* as per the directions of *Manasāra*.)

fig. 26: Lakṣmaṇa Temple, *c*. CE 953-54, Teacher educating the new apprenties, Sandstone, Khajurāho, Distt. Chhatarpur, MP. (Represents how artisan class got professional knowledge from their *guru*.)

fig. 27: Viśvanātha Temple, Highness of the Sculptors, *c.* CE 1002, Khajurāho, Distt. Chhatarpur, MP. (Represents the keen interest and dedication of sculptors towards their profession with long and wide experience from generation to generation.)

fig. 28: Scene showing sculptors at work, *c*. eleventh century,
Sandstone, Khajurāho, Distt. Chhatarpur, MP.
(Scene represents how the sculptors and workmen in guilds worked for the society.)

fig. 29: Īśāna Dikpāla, standing, *c*. tenth century, Greyish pale sandstone, .370 x .290 m,
Indore Central Museum, Hinglājgaṛh, Distt. Mandsore, MP. (Note the perfect
measurements of the figure and its placement inside the niche.)

fig. 30: Surasundarī Playing flute, *c*. eleventh-twelfth century, Red specked sandstone, Jabalpur, .950 x .340 m, Rani Durgavati Museum, Tewar, Distt. Jabalpur, MP. (Represents the use of musical instrument and passion for jewellery.)

fig. 31: Male with moustaches, bust profile, *c*. eleventh century, showing skillness of barber, stone .330 x .190 m, Allahabad Museum, MP. (The artisan created the skillness of barber and the taste of men in the society.)

fig. 32: Jina Pārśvanātha, brass, Western India, Gujarat, eighth century AD, 22 x 17.5 cm. (Represents the skilled workmanship of the metal workers.)

fig. 33: Mañjuśrī, seated, *c*. eighth-ninth century, Bronze ht. .170 m, Raipur, MGM Museum no. 371, Sirpur, Distt. Raipur, MP. (Highness of the metal workers.)

fig. 34: Lady in Languor (*Alasākanyā*), Sandstone, eleventh century CE, Khajurāho. (Highly appreciable creation of the sculptor representing the passion for Jewellery, make-up and the fondness of beauty.)

fig. 35: Kubera with water pot on neck/*c*. tenth century, Gwalior State Museum No. 228, Sandstone .85 x .44 m, Pathaoli, Distt. Morena, MP. (Represents the use of water pot in different forms and thus creating demand of the potters in the society.)

fig. 36: Artistic hand of Sculptor/engraver with date, *c*. later half of tenth century, Sandstone, Pārśvanātha Temple (no. 11), Khjurāho, Distt. Chhatarpur, MP. (Shows the creation of engravers, as a prefessional class of artisan.)

fig. 37: Inscription of King Dhaṅga, Viśanātha Temple (engraver did not mention his own name), dated CE 1002, Sandstone, Khajurāho, Distt. Chhatarpur, MP. (Represents the perfect art and skill of the engraver.)

fig. 38: Expertness of engraver like printing press of modern time, Virūpākṣa Temple, *c*. twelfth century, Bilpank, Distt. Ratlam, MP. (The high quality of engraving can be seen.)

fig. 39: Lakṣmaṇa Temple, showing scene of musicians dated CE 953-54, Sandstone, Khajurāho, Distt. Chhatarpur, MP. (Shows the different musical instruments used in that period.)

fig. 40: Lakṣmaṇa Temple, Showing teachings to artisans, Sandstone, Khajurāho, Distt. Chhatarpur, MP. (Scene represents the method of learning by the artisan class from their *guru*.)

fig. 41: Śakti Kuṇḍa, Niche, Viśvakarmā, *c*. third quarter of twelfth century, Stone, Akhaj, Mehsana Distt. Gujarat. (Scene represents the knowledge of *śilpvidyā* from the scriptures and the use of tools by the Viśvakarmā and the *śilpīs*.)

Bibliography

Original Sources: Literary Texts and Translations

Abhidhānacintāmaṇi, Hemachandra, ed. Hargovindadas Bechardas and Muni Jinavijaya, Bhavanagar, 1914, 1919.

Abhidhānaratnamālā, Halāyudha, ed. J.S. Joshi, Lucknow.

Agni Purāṇa, Eng. tr. M.N. Dutta, Calcutta, 1901.

Amarakośa, ed. G.P. Shastri, Banāras, 1950.

Aparājitapṛcchā, Bhuvanadeva, ed. P.A. Mankad, Baroda, 1950.

Apastamba Dharmasūtra, ed. G. Buhler, Bombay, 1863-1872.

Arthaśāstra, Kauṭilya, ed. R. Shamasastri, Mysore, 1924.

Āryamañjuśrīmūlakalpa, ed. T. Ganapati Shastri, Trivandrum, 1920.

Āryasaptaśatī, Nirnaya-Sagara Press, Bombay, 1895.

Aṣṭādhyāyī, Nirnaya-Sagara, Press, Bombay.

Atharvaveda, tr. Damodar Satvalekar, 3 vols., Sitara, 1929.

Aucityavicāracarcā, Kṣemendra, ed. Dhuṇḍhirājaśāstrin, Banāras, 1933.

Bhāgavata Purāṇa, Gita Press, Gorakhpur, vs 2010.

Bhaviṣya Purāṇa, Bombay, 1910.

Bodhisattvāvadānakalpalatā, 2 vols., Calcutta, 1888.

Bṛhaddharma Purāṇa, Bibliotheca Indica, Calcutta: Asiatic Society of Bengal, 1897.

Bṛhaspati-Smṛti, tr. Jolly, Sacred Books of East, Oxford, 1889.

Bṛhatkathākośa, Hariṣena, ed. A.N. Upadhye, Bombay, 1943.

Bṛhatkathāmañjarī, Kṣemendra, ed. Shivadatta and K.P. Parab, Nirnaya-Sagar Press, Bombay, 1931.

Bṛhatsaṁhitā, Varāhamihira tr. S. Shastri and M. Ramakrishna Bhatt, Bangalore, 1947.

Bṛhatsaṁhitā of Varāhamihira with Bhaṭṭotpala's Commentary, ed. Sudhakara Dwivedi, Banāras, 1895, 1897.

Budhacarita Aśvaghoṣa, tr. E.H. Johnson, rpt., Delhi, 1972.

Caturvargacintāmaṇi, Hemādri, ed. Bharatachandra Siromani, Bibliotheca Indica, Calcutta, 1873-1911.

Daśakumāracarita, Daṇḍin, ed. M.R. Kale, Bombay, 1917; Eng. tr. W. Ryder, Chicago, 1927.

Daśāvatāracarita, Kṣemendra, ed. Durgaprasad and K.P. Parab, K.M. 26.

Deśināmamālā, Hemacandra, ed. R. Pischel, P.V. Ramanujaswami (2nd edn.), BORI, Poona, 1938.

Deśopadeśa, Kṣemendra, ed. M. Kaul, Poona, 1923.

Devala-Smṛti, Anandasharma Sanskrit Series, Poona; tr. M.N. Ray in JBORI, 1927.

Divyavadāna, ed. E.B. Cowell and R.A. Neil, Cambridge, 1886.

Dohākośa, Sarahapada, ed. R. Shamkrityayana, Patna, 1958.

Dravyāśrayakāvya, Hemacandra, ed. A.V. Kathvate, 2 vols; Pub. Bombay Sanskrit Series, Bombay, 1915, 1921.

Garuḍa Purāṇa, tr. M.N. Dutta, Calcutta, 1908.

Gauḍavaho, Vākpati, ed. N.B. Utgikar, Poona, 1927.

Gautamdharmasūtra with Haradatta's Commentary, ed. Anandasrama Sanskrit Series, Poona, 1910.

Gṛhasthakāṇḍa, Lakṣmīdhara, vol. II, Gaekwad's Oriental Series, Baroda (No. Cl), 1944,

Gṛhastharatnākara, Caṇḍeśvara, Pub. Bibliotheca Indica, Calcutta, 1931.

Harṣacarita, Bāṇabhatta, Eng. tr. E.B. Cowel and F.W. Thomas, London, 1897.

Jambūdvīpaprajñapti, Devachand Lālbhāi Jaina Pustakoddhara Series (Nos. 52 and 54), Bombay, 1920.

Jātakas, E.B. Cowell, Cambridge, 1895-1913.

Kādambarī, Bāṇabhatta, ed. K.P. Parab, Bombay, 1932; Eng. tr. C.M. Riddling, London, 1896.

Kalāvilāsa, Kṣemendra, Nirnaya Sagar Press, Bombay, 1886.

Kālikā Purāṇa, Venkatesvara Press, Bombay, Sam. 1829.

Kāmasūtra, Vātsyāyana, ed. G.D. Shastri, Banāras, 1929,

Karpūramañjarī, Rājaśekhara, ed. Sten Know, Eng. tr. C.R. Lanman, Cambridge, 1901.

Kathākośaprakaraṇa, Jineśvara Sūri, tr. C.H. Tawney for San. Manuscript, London, 1895.

Kathāsaritsāgara, Somadeva, Eng. tr. C.H. Tawney, ed. Durga Prasad and Parab, Nirnaya Sagar Press, Bombay, 1930.

Kātyāyana-Smṛti, tr. P.V. Kane, Bombay, 1933.

Kāvyamīmāṁsā, Rājaśekhara, ed. C.D. Dalal and R.A. Shastri, Gaekwad's Oriental Series, 3rd edn., Baroda, 1934.

Kṛṣiparāśara, ed. and tr. G.P. Majumdar and S.C. Banerji, Bibliotheca Indica, 1960.

Kṛtyakalpataru, Lakṣmīdhara, ed. K.V. Rangaswami Aiyanger, Gaekwad Oriental Series, Baroda, 1941 to 1953.

Kumārapālacarita, Hemacandra, ed. P.L. Vaidya, Poona, 1936 (also in *IA*, vol. IV, pp. 72ff).

Kumārasambhavam, ed. Gangadhar Bhardwaj, Benaras: Sastri Vidya Vilas Press.

Kuṭṭanīmatam, Dāmodaragupta, ed. Tansukharam Manisukharam Tripathi, Banāras, 1924.

Lekhapaddhati, ed. C.D. Dalal and G.K. Shrigondekar, Baroda, 1925.

Līlāvatī, Bhāskarācārya, ed. H.C. Banerji, Calcutta, 1893.

Mahābhārata, ed. P.C. Roy, Calcutta, 1882.

Mahābhāṣya, P.C. Chakravarty, *Indian Historical Quarterly*, vols. 1 & 2.

Mahāvastu, AL Imprimere National, Paris, 1882.

Mahāvīracaritam, Bhavabhūti, ed. Kāśī Nath, Bombay, 1901.

Maitrayāṇī Saṁhitā, ed. L.V. Sehroder, Leipzig, 1881-86.

Mālvikāgnimitra, ed. M.R. Kale, Bombay, 1918.

Mānasollāsa, Someśvara, ed. G.K. Shrigondekar, Gaekwad's Oriental Series, 2 vols., 1925, 1939.

Manu-Smṛti, tr. Sir William Jones, Calcutta, 1794.

Manu-Smṛti with the Manubhāṣya of Medhātithi, ed. G. Jha, Calcutta, 1932-39. tr. G. Gha, Calcutta 1922-29. ed. with the Commentary of Kulluka, ed. N.R. Acharya, Bombay, 1946.

Matsya Purāṇa, Pub. Anandasarma Sanskrit Series, Poona, 1907.

Mayamatam, ed. by T.G. Ganpati Sastri, Trivandrum: Government Press, 1919.

Meghadutam, Kasi Sanskrit Series, Banaras, 1946.

Milindapañha, V. Trenckner, London: The Royal Asiatic Society, 1928.

Mudrārākṣasa, tr. K.H. Dhura, Poona: Oriental Book Agency, 1930.

Mṛcchakaṭikā, Śūdraka, ed. and tr. R.D. Karmarkar, 2nd edn., Poona, 1950.

Naiṣadhacarita, Śrī Harṣa, Eng. tr. K.K. Handiqui, Motilal Banarsidass, Lahore, 1934.

Nārada-Smṛti, ed. J. Jolly, Sacred Books of the East, XXXIII, part I.

Narmamālā, Kṣemendra, ed. M. Kaul, Poona, 1923.

Nītikalpataru, Kṣemendra, ed. V.P. Mahajan, Poona, 1936.

Nītisāra, Kāmandaka, ed. R. Mitra, Bibliotheca Indica, Calcutta, 1884.

Pañcatantra Viṣṇuśarmā, tr. F. Edgerton, American Oriental Series, 1924.

Prabandhacintāmaṇi, Merutuṅgācārya, Eng. tr. C.H. Tawney, Bibliotheca Indica, Calcutta.

Prabodhacandrodaya, Kṛṣṇamiśra, Nirnaya-Sagara, Press, Bombay, 1904.

Prāyaścittaprakaraṇa, Bhavadevabhaṭṭa, ed. Girisa Chandra Vedantatirtha, Vārendra Research Society, Rajshahi, 1927.

Pṛthvīrājavijaya, Jayānaka with Commentary by Janaraja, ed. S.K. Belvalkar; Bibliotheca Indica; Extracts in *JRAS*, 1913, pp. 259ff.

Priyadarśikā, Harṣa, ed. V.D. Gadre, Bombay, 1884.

Raghuvaṁśam, ed. C.D. Varma, Lahore, 1924.

Rājanītiratnākara, Caṇḍeśvara, ed. K.P. Jayaswal, Bihar and Orissa Research Society, Patna, 1936.

Rājataraṅgiṇī, Kalhaṇa, Eng. tr. M.A. Stein, Westminster, 1900; Eng. tr. R.S. Pandit, Allahabad, 1935.

Rāmacarita, Sandhyākaranandī, ed. R.C. Majumdar, R.G. Basak and N.G. Banerji, Rajshahi, 1939.

Rāmāyaṇa of Valmiki, ed. by Hemchandra Bhattacharya, Calcutta, 1869-84, and ed. P.C. Roy, Calcutta, 1881-82.

Ṛgveda, tr. by Indian Press Prayag, 1954.

Ṣaḍdarśana Samuccaya, Haribhadra Sūri, ed. K.S. Murti, Tenali, 1954.

Samarāiccakahā, Haribhadra Sūri, ed. H. Jacobi, Calcutta, 1932.

Samarāṅgaṇasūtradhāra, Bhoja, ed. T. Ganapatisastri, Baroda, 1925.

Samayamātṛkā, Kṣemendra, ed. Durga Prasad and K.P. Parab, Bombay, 1925.

Saundarānanda Kāvya Aśvaghoṣa, ed. Hari Parsad Sastri, Calcutta, 1939.

Śāraṅgadharapaddhati, ed. P. Peterson, vol. I, Bombay, 1888.

Smṛticandrikā, Devaṇṇabhaṭṭa, ed. L. Srinivasacharya, Government of Mysore, Mysore and ed. J.R. Gharpure, Bombay, 1918.

Subhāṣitaratnakoṣa, Vidyākara, ed. D.D. Kosambi and V.V. Gokhale, Harvard, 1957.

Śukranītisāra, Śukra, ed. Jivananda Vidyasagara, Eng. tr. B.K. Sarkar, Pāṇini Office Allahabad, 1914.

Sūktimuktāvali, Jalhaṇa, ed. E. Krishnamacharya, Baroda, 1938.

Taittirīya Brāhmaṇa, Anandashrama Sanskrit Series, Poona, 1899.

Tilakamañjarīkathā, Dhanapāla, ed. Bhavadatta Shastri and K.P. Parab, Bombay, 1903.

Tṛṣaṣṭiśalākāpuruṣacarita, Hemacandra, Prasaraka Sabha, Bhavnagar, 6 vols., 1905-09. Eng. tr. H.M. Thonson, 4 vols, Baroda, 1931, 1937, 1949 and 1954.

Udayasundarīkathā, Soḍḍhala, ed. C.D. Dalal and E. Krishnamacharya, Baroda, 1920.

Vajasaneyī Saṁhitā, ed. by A. Webber, London, 1852.

Vaiyākarṇasiddhāntakaumudī, ed. Pandit Shiva Datta Shastri, Venkateshwar Steam Press, Bombay, 1914.

Varṇaratnākara, Jyotīrīśvara, ed. Suniti Kumar Chatterji and Babua Misra, Royal Asiastic Society of Bengal, Calcutta, 1940.

Vastu Śāstra, 2 vols. Bhartiya Vastu Sastra Series.

Viddhaśālabhañjikā, Rājaśekhara, ed. J.B. Chaudhary, Calcutta, 1943.

Vikramāṅkadevacarita, Bilhaṇa, ed. G. Buhler, Bombay Sanskrit Series, Bombay, 1875.

Vīramitrodaya (*Rājanītiprakāśa*), Mitra Misra, ed. Viṣṇu Prasad, Banāras, 1916.

Vyākaraṇa Mahābhāṣya, Patañjali, ed. F. Kielhorn, Bombay, 1892.

Yājñavalkya-Smṛti, ed. T. Ganapati Shastri, Trivandrum, 1922-24.

Yājñavalkya-Smṛti with Aparārka's Commentary, ed. Anandasrama Sanskrit Series, 2 vols. Poona, 1903, 1904.

Yājñavalkya-Smṛti of Mitākṣarā with Vijñaneśvara's Commentary, ed. Babu Ram, Calcutta, 1812; S.S. Setlur, Madras, 1912; and J.R. Gharpure, Bombay, 1914.

Yuktikalpataru, Bhoja, ed. Ishwarchandra Shastri, Calcutta Oriental, Series, Calcutta, 1917.

Foreign Accounts

Beal, S., *Life of Hiuen Tsang*, London, 1911.

Beal, S., *Si-yu-ki: Buddhist Records of the Western World*, 2 vols, London, 1884.

De, D., *Tabaqāt-i-Nasīrī* of Minhāj-ud-dīn b. Sirāju-ud-din, Bibliotheca Indica, Calcutta, 1913-1940.

Elliot, H.M. and Dowson, J., *History of India as Told by its Own Historians*, vols. I, II and III, London, 1866-77.

Gibb, H.A.R., *Ibn Battutā: Travels in Asia and Africa*, London, 1929.

Hirth, F. and Rockhill, W.W. *Chau-Ju-Kua*, his work on the Chinese and Arab Trade in the twelfth and thirteenth centuries entitled Chu-fan-Chi, Petersburg, 1912.

Hodivala, S.H., *Studies in Indo-Muslim History*, Bombay, 1939.

Hudud-ul-Alam, *India as described by an unknown Geographer of the 10th Century*, published in PIHC, Calcutta, Session 1939.

Renaudot, E., *Ancient Accounts of India and China by two Mohammedan Travellers* (Sulaimān and Ābu Zaid), London, 1733.

Sachau, E.C., *Kitāb-ul-Hind of Al-Birūnī* (*Al beruni's India*), 2 vols. in one, Trubner Oriental Series, London, 1914.

Tāranātha, Eng. (tr.), "History of Buddhism in India" by U.M. Ghosal and N. Dutt, in *IHQ*, vols. III, IV, V, VIII, X, XXVII and XXVIII; Extracts tr. into English W.L. Heeley in *IA*, IV, 101ff.

Watters T., *On Yuan Chwang's Travel in India*, 2 vols., London, 1904, 1905.

Yule, H., *The Book of Ser Marco Polo*, 2 vols., London, 1933; tr. A. Ricci, ed. D. Ross, 1931.

Inscriptions and Coins

Bhattacharya, P.N., *Kāmarūpa Śāsanāvalī*, Rangpur Sahitya Parisad, 1838 Śaka (= CE 1931).

Bhandarkar, D.R., *List of Inscriptions of Northern India*, Appendix to *EI*, XIX-XXIII,

Bidyabinod, B.B., *Supplementary Catalogue of the Coins in the Indian Museum*, Calcutta, Non-Muhammadan Series, vol. 1, Calcutta, 1923.

Choudhary, R.K., *Select Inscriptions of Bihar*.

Cunningham, A., *Coins of Medieval India*, London, 1894.

Fleet, J.F., *Gupta Inscriptions* (or *Corpus Inscriptionum Indicarum*, vol. III), Calcutta, 1888.

Maitreya, A.K., *Gauḍalekhamālā*, Rajashahi, BS 1819.

Majumdar, N.G., *Inscriptions of Bengal*, vol. III.

Mirashi, V.V., *Inscriptions of the Kaḷacuri-Chedi Era*, vol. IV, Ootacamund, 1955.

Mukherji, R.R. and Maity, S.K., *Corpus of Bengal Inscriptions*, Calcutta, 1967.

Phogat, S.R., *Inscriptions of Haryana*, Kurukshetra, 1978.

Sircar, D.C., *Select Inscriptions*, vol. I, Calcutta University, 1942.

Vogel, J.Ph., *Antiquities of the Chamba State*, Calcutta, 1911.

Modern Works

Acharya, G.V., *Historical Inscriptions of Gujarat*, part 2, Bombay, 1935.

Acharya, P.K., *Architecture of Mānāsara*, Oxford Press, 1933.

Acharya, P.K., *An Encyclopaedia of Hindu Architecture*, reprint, Bhopal, 1978.

Agarwal, Urmila, *Khajurāho Sculptures and Their Significance*, S. Chand and Co., New Delhi, 1964.

Agarwal, V.S., *Harṣacarita — Eka Sāṁskṛtika Adhyayana*, Bihar Rastrabhasa Parisad, Patna, 1953.

Allchin, Bridget and Raymond Allchin, *The Rise of Civilization in India, and Pakistan*, Selectbook Service Syndicate, New Delhi, 1983.

Altekar, A.S., *Rastrakutas and Their Times*, Poona, 1962.

———, *Education in Ancient India*, Banāras, 1951.

Asher, Frederick M., and G.S. Gai, *Indian Epigraphy, Its Bearing on the History of Art*, New Delhi, 1985.

Asher, Frederick M., *Art of India, Pre-history to Present, Encyclopaedia*, Britanica, 2003.

Bagai, Anjali, *Merchandise and Merchantile Community in Post-Gupta Times in Northern India*, CE *600 – 1200* CE, Thesis presented to the University of Delhi for the Degree of Doctor of Philosophy, 1985.

Baijnath Sharma, *Harṣa and His Times*, Sushma Prakasan, Varanasi, 1970.

Bamzai, P.N.K. A *History of Kashmir*, Metropolitan Book Co. Pvt. Ltd., Delhi, 1962.

Bandyopadhyaya, N.C., *Economic Life and Progress in Ancient India*, 2nd edn., Calcutta, 1945.

Bandyopadhyay, Bimal, *Metal Sculptures of Eastern India*, Sundeep Prakasan, Delhi, 1981.

Banerjea, J.N., *Development of Hindu Iconography*, Calcutta, 1956.

Barrett, Ken and Suresh Sharma (ed.), *The Indian Experience*, Transasia Thailand Ltd.,1982.

Basham, A.L., *The Wonder that was India*, London, 1954.

Bhargava, P.L., *India in the Vedic Age*, Lucknow, 1971.

Bhattacharyya, D.C. and Devendra Handa (eds.), *Prācī Prabhā, Perspectives in Indology*, New Delhi, 1989.

Bhattacharyya, T., *The Canons of Indian Art*, Calcutta, 2nd edn., 1963.

Bose, N.S., *History of the Candellas*, Calcutta, 1956.

Brown, P., *Indian Architecture (Buddhist and Hindu)*, Bombay, 1956.

Buhler, G., The Laws of Manu (Sacred Books of the East), Oxford, 1886.

Chakravarti, P.C., *The Art of War in Ancient india*, Oriental Publishers, 1972.

Choudhary, A.K., *Early Medieval Village in North-Eastern India* (CE *600-1200*), Punthi Pustak, Calcutta, 1971.

Choudhury, P.C., *The History of Civilization of the People of Assam to the Twelfth Century* CE, Gauhati, 1959.

Codrington, K. De B., *An Introduction to the Study of Medieval Indian Sculpture*, London, 1929.

Coomaraswamy, A.K., *History of Indian and Indonesian Art*, Dover Publications, Inc., New York, 1965 (reprint).

Dar, S.N., *Costumes of India and Pakistan, A Historical and Cultural Study*, Bombay, 1969.

Das, S.K., *Economic History of Ancient India*, Calcutta, 1925.

David E. Hunter, *Readings in Physical Anthropology and Archaeology*, Harper and Row Publishers, New York, 1978.

David, L. Sills, *International Encyclopaedia of the Social Sciences*, vols. 1 and 3, The Macmillan Company and the Free Press, 1968.

Dehejia, Vidya, *Early Stone Temples of Orissa*, New Delhi, 1979.

Desmukh, C.D., *Amarakośa* (*Gems from the treasure house of Sanskrit words*), New Delhi, 1981.

Dey, N.E., *The Geographical Dictionary of Ancient and Medieval India*, London, 1927.

Dodwell, H.H., The Cambridge History of India, 5 vols., Cambridge, 1922ff.

Donaldson, T.E., Hindu Temple Art of Orissa, 3 vols., Leiden, 1985-87.

Ganguly, A.B., *Sixty-four Arts in Ancient India*, New Delhi, 1962.

Ganguly, D.C., *The Art of the Candellas*, Calcutta, 1957.

Ghurye, G.S., *Caste and Class in India*, Bombay, 1957.

———, *Indian Costume*, Bombay, 1966.

Goetz, H., *The Early Wooden Temples of Chamba*, Leiden, 1955.

Gopal, L., *The Ecomomic Life of Northern India, c. 700-1200* CE, Varanasi, 1955.

Gopinatha Rao, T.A., *Elements of Hindu Iconography*, 2 vols., Madras, 1914-16.

Gupta, Dharmendra Kumar, *Society and Culture in the Time of Dandin*, Delhi, 1972.

Hazra, R.C., *Studies in the Puranic Records in Hindu Rites and Customs*, University. Dacca, 1940.

Hourani, G.F., *Arab Sea Faring in Indian Ocean in Ancient and Early Medieval Times*, Princeton, 1951.

Hutton, J.H., *Caste In India*, Oxford University Press, 1961.

Jain, K.C., *Ancient Cities and Towns of Rajasthan*, Delhi, 1972.

Jain, P.C., *Labour in Ancient India* (*from the Vedic up to the Gupta Period*), Thesis submitted for the Degree of Philosophy in the Department of Sanskrit, Kurukshetra University, Kurukshetra, 1965.

Jolly, J., *Hindu Law and Custom*, tr. B.K. Ghosh, Calcutta, 1928.

John, L. Stouterburgh, *Dictionary of Arts and Crafts*, Petur Owen Ltd., London.

Joseph, M. Dye III, *The Arts of India*, Virginia Museum of Fine Arts, New Delhi, 2001.

Kane, P.V., *History of Dharmaśāstra Literature*, 4 vols., Poona, 1930-53.

Keith, A.B., *History of Sanskrit Literature*, Oxford, 1928.

Kramrisch, S., *The Hindu Temples*, 2 vols., Calcutta, 1946.

———, *Pāla and Sena Sculptures*, Calucutta, 1929.

Krishna, Brajesh, *The Art Under the Gurjara-Pratihāras*, Delhi, 1989.

Madan, A.P., *The History of the Rastrakutas*, Delhi, 1990.

Maity, S.K., *Economic Life of Northern India in the Gupta Period (Circa,* CE *300-500)*, Calcutta, 1957.

Majumdar, A.K., *Early Hindu India, A Dynastic Study*, vol. III, Delhi, 3rd edn., 1981.

Majumdar, R.C., *Corporate Life in Ancient India*, 2nd edn., Calcutta, 1922.

Majumdar, R.C. (ed.), *The History of Bengal*, vol. 1, University of Dacca, 1st edn., 1943.

Majumdar, R.C., *History and Culture of Indian People*, Vol. 3: The Classical Age.

Majumdar, R.C. and A.D. Pusalker (ed.), *History and Culture of Indian People*, Vol. 2: The Age of Imperial Kanauj; The Struggle for Empire, Bombay, 1957.

Majumdar, R.C., *History and Culture of Indian People*, Vol. 1: Vedic Age, Bombay: Bharatiya Vidya Bhawan, 1951.

Marshall, J., Mohenjo-Daro and Indus Valley Civilization, London, 1931.

Mazumdar, B.P., *Socio-Economic History of Northern India (c.* CE *1030-1194)*, Calcutta, 1960.

Michell, Geogre, *Hindu Art and Architecture*, London, 2000.

Minorsky, V., Hudud-e-Alam, London, 1937.

Misra, R.N., *Ancient Artists and Art Activity*, Simla, 1975.

Misra, S.N., *Gupta Art and Architecture*, Delhi, 1992.

Misra, S.S., *Fine Arts and Technical Sciences in Ancient India with Special Reference to Someśvara's Mānasollasa*, Varanasi, 1982.

Misra, V.B., *The Gurjara Pratiharas and Their Times*, Delhi, 1966.

Mitra, S.K., *The Early Rulers of Khajurāho*, Calcutta, 1958.

Mookerji, R.K., *Local Government in Ancient India*, rpt., Delhi, 1989.

———, *Ancient Indian Education*, Delhi, 1969.

———, *A History of Indian Shipping and Maritime Activity*, London, 1912.

Motichandra, *Sārthavāha*, Patna, 1953.

———, *Trade and Trade Routes in Ancient India*, Delhi, 1977.

Munshi, K.M., *The Glory that was Gurjaradeśa*, Bombay, 1955.

Murari, Krishna, *The Calukyas of Kalyāni (from cir.* CE *973 to 1200* CE), Delhi, 1976.

Nagaraja Rao, M.S. (ed.), *Madhu: Recent Researches in Indian Archaeology and Art History*, Delhi, 1981.

Niyogi, Pushpa, *Contributions to the Economic History of Northern India, from the tenth to the twelfth century* CE, Calcutta, 1962.

Niyogi, R., *The History of the Gahadavala Dynasty*, Calcutta, 1959.

Pal, Pratapaditya,*The Arts in India*, Marg Publications, 2000.

Prakash, Vidya, *Khajurāho*, Bombay, 1967.

Pran Nath, *A Study of Economic Condition of Northern India*, London, 1929.

Prasad, Kameshwar, *Cities Crafts and Commerce Under the Kushanas*, Delhi, 1984.

Puri, B.N., *India in the time of Patanjali*, Bombay, 1957.

———, *The History of the Gurjara-Pratiharas*, Bombay, 1957.

Randhawa, M.S. and D.S. Randhawa, *Indian Sculpture: The Scene, Themes and Legends*, Bombay, 1989.

Rao, S.R., Dawn and Devolution of the Indus Valley Civilization, Delhi, 1991.

Ray, H.C., *Dynastic History of Northern India*, 2 vols., Calcutta, 1931-1936.

Ray, P.C., *History of Hindu Chemistry from the Earliest Times to the Middle of the 16th Century* CE, Calcutta, 1905.

Raychaudhuri, H.C., *Political History of Ancient India*, 6th edn., University of Calcutta.

Saraswati, S.K., *A Survey of Indian Sculpture*, Calcutta, 1957.

Sastri, K.A.N., *The Cholas*, 2 vols., Madras, 1935, 1937.

Sen, B.C., *Some Historical Aspects of the Inscriptions of Bengal*, Calcutta, 1942.

Sharma, B.N., *Social and Cultural History of Northern India* (*cir.* CE *1000-1200*), Delhi, 1972.

Sharma, D., *Early Chauhan Dynasties*, Delhi, 1959.

Sharma, R.K., *The Kaḷacuris and Their Times*, Delhi, 1980.

Sharma, R.S., *Śūdras in Ancient India*, Patna, 1958.

———, *Perspectives in Social and Economic History of Early India*, Delhi, 1983.

Sharma, R.S. (ed.), *Survey of Research in Economic and Social History of India*, Ajanta Publications, 1986.

Sinha, B.P., *Bhārtīya Kala ko Bihar kī Den*, Patna, 1958.

Sircar, D.C., *Indian Epigraphy*, Delhi, 1965.

———, *Studies in the Geography of Ancient and Medieval India*, Delhi, 1960.

Sivaramamurti, C., *Indian Sculpture*, New Delhi, 1961.

———, Indian Bronzes, Bombay, 1962.

Thaplyal, K.K., *Inscriptions of the Maukharīs, Later Guptas; Puspabhutis and Yaśovarman of Kanauj*, Delhi, 1985.

Tripathi, R.S., *History of Kanauj*, Banāras, 1937.

Vaidya, C.V., *History of Medieval Hindu India*, vols. I-III, Poona, 1921, 1924 and 1920.

Vasudeva Sastri, K. and N.B. Gadre, *Viśwakarmā Vāstuśāstram*, Tanjore Saraswati Mahal Series, no. 85, 1958.

Vats, M.S., *Excavation at Harappa*, New Delhi, 1940.

Vogel, J.Ph., *Antiquities of Chamba State*, pt. 1, ASI, NSI, Calcutta, 1911.

William, M., *A Sanskrit-English Dictionary*, London, 1956.

Yadav, B.N.S., *Some Aspects of Society in Northern India in the 12th Century* CE, Allahabad, 1973.

Yule, H. and H. Cordier, *The Travels of Marcopolo*, London, 1921.

Journals and Periodicals

Ancient India

Annals of the Bhandarkar Oriental Research Institute

Annual Report of the Archaeological Survey of India

Arts Asiatic

Asiatic Researches

Bhāratīya Vidyā

East and West

Epigraphia Carnatica

Epigraphia Indica

Indian Antiquary

Indian Culture

Indian Historical Quarterly

Journal of the Asiatic Society of Bengal

Journal of Asiatic Society of Orient Art

Journal of Bihar Research Society
Journal of the Bihar and Orissa Research Society
Journal of the Bombay Branch of the Royal Asiatic Society
Journal of the Department of Letters, Calcutta
Journal of the Economic and Social History of the Orient, Leiden
Journal of the Gujarat Research Society
Journal of the Royal Asiatic Society of Great Britain and Greenland
Journal of the U.P. Historical Scoiety
Lalit Kalā
Mārg
Memoirs of Archaeological Survey of India
Memoirs of the Asiatic Society of Bengal
Numismatic Chronicle
Panjab University Research Bulletin (Arts)
Patna University Journal
Prācī Jyoti
Proceedings of Indian History Congress
Rajasthan Lalit Kalā
Roopa-Lekhā
Rupam

Index